John Garrard

Leadership and power in Victorian industrial towns 1830–80

Manchester University Press

First published
by Manchester University Press
Oxford Road, Manchester M13 9PL, UK
and
51 Washington Street, Dover, N.H. 03820, USA

British Library cataloguing in publication data

Garrard, John
    Leadership and power in Victorian industrial
    towns 1830–80.
    1. Municipal government — Lancashire (England)
    — History
    I. Title
    352.0422'57   JS3115

    ISBN 0-7190-0897-2

Library of Congress catalog card number
82-62260

Library of Congress cataloging in publication data
applied for

Printed in Great Britain by
Butler & Tanner Ltd,
Frome and London

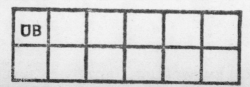

Contents

List of tables

Acknowledgements

For a stimulating and uniquely focussed interdisciplinary environment, my colleagues and friends in the Department of Politics and Contemporary History at the University of Salford; for limitless help, encouragement and comment, Michael Goldsmith of the same department; for endless assistance of a cheerful kind, the staffs of the Local History Libraries at Bolton, Rochdale and Salford; for varied sorts of help, sometimes unwitting but always generous, George Jones, Peter Hennock, Derek Fraser, Maurice Garretts and many others; for excellent typing, Pat Bellotti, Joan Cooper and Ruth Fingerhut; for comment, proof reading, endless patience and support, general suffering duties and much else besides, my wife Eve. The mistakes I managed without assistance.

J.G.
Salford, 1982

Abbreviations

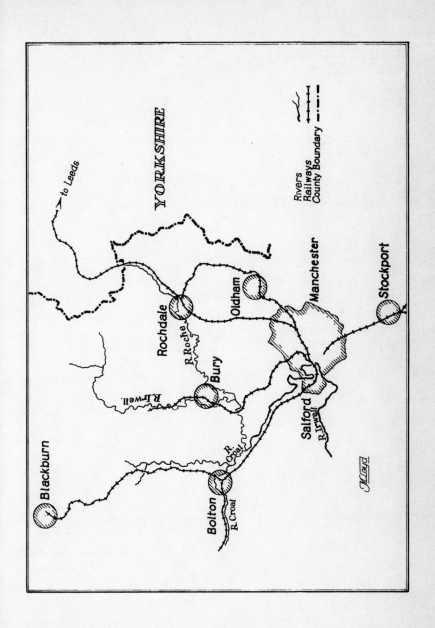

YORKSHIRE

to Leeds

Rivers
Railways
County Boundary

Blackburn

Bolton

R. Croal

R.
Croal

R. Irwell

Bury

R.Roche

Rochdale

Oldham

Salford

R. Irwell

Manchester

Stockport

Mᶜᶜᶜ Lloyd

1
Introduction

This is a community power study: its concern is with who had power and how much. It is interdisciplinary, and attempts to apply some of the concepts and methods of the political scientist to the politics of three nineteenth-century industrial towns — Rochdale, Salford and Bolton. It falls into a tradition of studies begun in the 1950s whose aim was to study power at the local level — partly for its own sake, partly in the hope of revealing something about how power operates in a wider national, and even general, context.[1] The aim here is cautiously twofold: I want (1) to say something precise about nineteenth-century urban politics and power; (2) to offer some thoughts about the configuration of power when a social and economic elite is 'in office'.

Such concerns make this study decidedly unusual in historiographical terms. Rightly or wrongly, historians write about power and powerful people without properly taking into account the agonised debates among political scientists about meaning and measurement. Meanwhile the expanding literature on urban political history has been largely concerned not with power but with what might loosely be called political processes and recruitment.[2] Derek Fraser,[3] in his recent valuable study of nineteenth-century urban politics, argues that local governmental institutions were 'politicised' — in the sense (significantly left implicit) that they were the subjects of intense political division. Yet he too fails to consider the implications of this for the distribution of power. Two recent urban historical studies (those of John Foster and Patrick Joyce[4]) have taken power as a central concern. Yet here, too, there has been little worry about definition and measurement. Partly as a result, these studies, from a political scientist's viewpoint, have been rather restricted in scope and lacking in rigour.

The study is also unique in terms of political science. While community power analysts have examined present-day configurations with increasing conceptual care, their generalisations about the past have been less rigorous.

Dahl, for example, argues that nineteenth-century Newhaven politics were distinguished by 'cumulative inequalities of political resources' and therefore elitist. This he contrasts with, and uses to highlight, the 'dispersed inequalities' characterising the town's altogether more pluralist politics by the 1950s. Yet, whereas his twentieth-century generalisations are tested by case studies, Dahl's arguments about the nineteenth-century are based solely upon the occupational analysis of local office-holders. He merely assumes that men who combined economic, social and political leadership must have held untroubled political sway.[5]

The study is also comparative, and thus concerned with similarities and differences in the configuration of power in the three towns. Moreover, since our period runs from 1830 to 1880, we are interested in *changes* in that configuration. This partly explains why our concern is not just with power but also with identifying some of the factors governing who had it, and who did not, at any given time.

The focus is primarily municipal, and centres on the relationship between municipal leaders and those at the receiving end of municipal policies. Our main interest is in the multi-purpose councils of the three towns, and their predecessors. The treatment of Poor Law politics has necessarily been more cursory, and of those surrounding the education board and the constituencies even more so (the last two being analysed primarily in terms of their effect on the municipal sphere). Since the various levels of nineteenth-century politics were interconnected,[6] this means that our assessment of power is based upon an incomplete survey of the evidence available. However, given limited space, it seemed better to ensure that at least one sector of activity could be analysed in depth rather than covering all in a more cursory way. Similar reasoning has dictated the shallower treatment of Salford, compared with Rochdale and Bolton. In fact, even had the focus been more general, my impression is that the picture would not have been very different.

It is impossible here to include a detailed discussion of the concept of power and its measurement. However, particularly given the foregoing strictures on fellow historians, a few points about these matters, and about the assumptions underlying this study, are appropriate. I make no distinction between 'power' and 'influence': the words are used interchangeably and are understood simply to mean the ability to achieve intended effects. The exercise of power may be either active and explicit or passive and implicit. Let us examine each in turn.

Our attempts to measure the first will centre upon issues, conflict, and political *activity* of all kinds.[7] To assess power properly in this sense we need ideally to examine both the real intentions of those trying to exercise it and the motives of those apparently complying. Obviously, if a nineteenth-century pressure group really wanted something other than what it demanded and ultimately got from a council, or if municipal leaders acted for reasons unconnected with the pressure on them, then no successful exercise of power can be said to have taken place. Equally, if compliance cost councillors little, the group successfully demanding it may well be deemed less influential than if compliance had been costly.[8] Again, if, say, a council's initial response to pressure turns out simply to have been a bargaining position, any movement in directions desired by those applying the pressure is a less impressive tribute to their influence than if that initial response had been dictated by unwavering principle. Any measurement of power must also take into account the range and importance of the issues upon which it is exercised, and the number of a given group's wishes that are fulfilled.

Finally, the estimation of power may depend upon whether its results were positive (the achievement of policy advantages) or negative (the successful application of vetoes). In the twentieth-century at least, a group only able to prevent governmental action may well be deemed less influential than one also able to gain policy advantages. Given the all-pervasive influence of *laissez-faire*, such assumptions may be less valid for the nineteenth-century: many groups desired simply to be left alone by government, free to emit smoke or build houses how and where they chose. On the other hand, few local leaders can have wanted the municipal paralysis so often produced by their conflicts in all three towns.

As far as possible, the foregoing *caveats* have been taken into account when considering active politics in chapters 5-11. Often, however, they can do no more than induce caution about conclusions. The motivations of those influencing, or being influenced, are always hard to assess even where it is possible to interview. For the historian, with less control over his material, and at the mercy of what time and decay have left behind, it is doubly difficult. For the urban historian these problems are compounded by his reliance on public sources and by the relative lack of diaries, letters, etc., wherein contemporaries confided their private intentions and discreet political activities. Victorian local newspapers — the main source for this study — can compensate for the deficiency, but only partially.

Meanwhile, no assessment of power can now be confined to political activity and issues. Recent work[9] has drawn attention to whole areas of politics where there are no issues, no conflict and no visible movement of any kind, yet where exercises of power are nevertheless taking place. Indeed, political calm may itself result from persons or groups so controlling the political agenda as to ensure that problems are not discussed and do not become issues. They may do this by occupying strategic positions in the political system (committee chairmanships, for example). They may do it simply by possessing 'a reputation for power' — by being assumed to be hostile to a policy that otherwise might be adopted, and to have the ability effectively to veto it if it were. Finally, they may do it by so controlling social reflexes as to ensure that certain problems are not seen as fit matters for governmental remedy. This 'non-decisional' form of politics (like the whole question of social control, to which it is related) clearly involves major problems of conception and measurement.[10] Such problems may even be irresolvable. Yet, as we shall argue in chapter 3, any discussion of power in the nineteenth-century town is incomplete without some analysis of private and inactive politics, and without some consideration of those whose 'interests' are served by a political system whether they consciously will it or not. Moreover, the idea of non-decisions sensitises us to the possibility that many apparently 'non-political' areas of nineteenth-century urban life may have strong implications for any consideration of the location of power.

In one sense, our analysis of power in these towns should be easy. As we shall see in chapter 2, Rochdale, Bolton and Salford were each municipally presided over by men who substantially combined political, economic and social leadership. By far the largest group among the improvement commissioners, guardians, trustees, councillors, etc., of these towns were manufacturers and merchants. Indeed, large proprietors probably represented a majority of all these bodies (except perhaps the guardians) for most of the period. Even taking other occupational groups into account, there was a substantial economic gap between representatives and represented. Finally, most municipal representatives were also social leaders. This overall situation, as we shall see, reflected strong hierarchical pressures on political recruitment, as well as more general trends towards hierarchy and dependency in local urban society.

With access to such an impressive array of 'political resources',[11] one might expect such a leadership to experience little difficulty in achieving intended effects. One might also expect power, more generally, to centre upon the class from which municipal leaders were most generally drawn. As we shall see in chapters 3 and 4, and periodically later, there is much to support this view. In the right circumstances municipal leadership was impressively powerful, and able to proceed with little interference from outside — and this ability stemmed partly from its massive endowment of political resources. Even its difficulties often stemmed from groups on a comparable economic level. Particularly when, as in chapter 4, we take the area of discreet politics into account, we cannot deny the permanent existence of a substantial gradient of political influence coinciding with the socio-economic hierarchy. Certainly at no point in any of these towns do we find the sort of lower-class 'control' claimed by Foster to exist in Oldham in the 1830s and 1840s.[12]

However, the description of nineteenth-century urban politics as elitist hides as much as it reveals. Several arguments will run through these pages. First, though justly characterised as a form of squirearchy, urban leadership was different from its rural counterpart. Social prominence, though sometimes inherited, was equally likely to be earned by economic and/or political effort. Political leadership itself might thus be the means of achieving social leadership, as well as vice versa. This meant that the municipal elite was less oligarchic than its rural counterpart — a characteristic heavily reinforced (as we shall see in chapter 4) by the limits set upon political activity by the need for continued economic activity.

Second, though highly important, economic factors were not the only ones determining the configuration of power. As will become evident in chapter 4, expertise was a more important determinant of power in municipal bodies than was the relative economic substance of the participants — and increasingly so. Meanwhile, municipal leaders' power in the world beyond the legislative walls was determined by four other closely intertwined factors: the level of conflict within the elite; the nature of the local institutional system; municipal leaders' attitudes towards outside pressure, and the level of mass political mobilisation. Chapters 6, 7, 9 and 11 analyse the varying character of these factors in each town and over time. Chapters 8, 10 and 11 assess their impact on the configuration of power.

Third, the disproportionate possession of political resources by municipal elites did not guarantee them an easy life politically. Indeed, nineteenth-century municipal leadership was a thoroughly hazardous business. Chapter 4 shows that local leaders' occupational circumstances plus the complexity of municipal business increasingly meant that they had to share power with paid officials. Chapter 5 argues that they were also subject to major constraints stemming from beyond the municipal boundaries — from interests in adjacent areas and from Parliament. Finally, from chapter 7 onwards, we argue that municipal elites were constrained by forces within town boundaries. These included, most importantly, minority sections of the elite itself and groups on a comparable economic level who were formidable to the point of being able to induce long-term paralysis. They also included more humble groups — sometimes a long way down the social scale. In the right circumstances these could exert vetoes; on occasion, most frequently in Rochdale, they could obtain more positive advantages.

Before looking at our three towns one final point must be made. Central to many of our generalisations about nineteenth-century politics and power is local autonomy — both its strength and its limits. As we shall see in chapter

2, the role and influence of economic and social leaders in urban and municipal life can be understood only in terms of economic and social operations that were substantially confined to the locality; local government that was highly independent of central control, and a local arena that absorbed the attention of people at many levels in local society. The constraints upon local leadership must be seen in the same context. The relative autonomy of local decision-making, and the fact that municipal activity had to be paid for almost exclusively out of the rates, meant that local government was, for many people, a primary focus of political activity. Furthermore, as will become evident in chapter 4, the increasing role of paid officials can be understood partly in terms of a local arena wherein they could rival elected councillors as celebrities. Finally, the restricted role of central government meant that there were only limited and unsatisfactory means of arbitrating local conflicts.

As all this suggests, the idea of 'community power' is more appropriate to the nineteenth-century than to the late twentieth-century town. Nevertheless there were limits on local autonomy, and these too had political implications. As we shall see in chapter 5, local authorities and their elites were seriously constrained by their immediate hinterland and by Parliament itself.

The towns chosen for study are comparable in important respects: they were all factory towns, and they were all textile towns in the sense that textiles formed by far their largest single industry. In 1851 textile spinning, manufacturing and processing employed 338 in every 1,000 persons over twenty in the Rochdale Union; 187 in every 1,000 in the Salford Union, and 284 in every 1,000 in Bolton municipal borough.[13] The top six occupational categories among males over twenty were as shown in table 1.

At the same time we should note that these were not single-industry, or company, towns in the same sense as, say, Crewe or Darlington or the South Wales mining communities. This is most clearly the case in Salford. In 1851, apart from machine-making and coal mining (important sources of employment in all three towns), there were at least twenty other occupational groups among males over twenty numbering 200 or more.[14] Even in Rochdale — the most textile-dominated of the three — there were twelve such groups.[15] Furthermore, in all three towns, many women were employed in various sorts of domestic service.

Most of these other trades were heavily dependent on textiles in the sense that any change in that industry's economic fortunes affected them strongly. Moreover, as we shall suggest in chapter 3, many non-textile occupational groups were part of the network of dependency surrounding the industry — in the sense that their social and political perceptions were influenced by the

Table 1. The six main occupational categories, 1851

Rochdale Union		Salford Union		Bolton M.B.	
Textiles	7,648	Textiles	4,779	Textiles	5,550
Farming	1,253	General labouring	874	Iron manufacturing	1,364
Coal mining	950	Machine manufacturing	763	General labouring	582
General labouring	842	Military	712	Machine manufacturing	581
Machine manufacturing	712	Shoemaking	662	Shoemaking	392
Cabmen, etc.	456	Carpenting/joining	612	Agricultural labourer	391
Total males over twenty	19,094		22,558		15,753

Source. 1851 census.

awe in which the great employers were held. At the same time they were not as intimately attached to that network, in either psychological or economic terms, as were textile workers and their families. Thus, even if one accepts the central importance of deference in determining all forms of political behaviour among textile workers, it was likely to be less significant for the rest. The point is important if we are to understand the responses of those on the receiving end of municipal policies.

In common with other industrial towns, Rochdale, Bolton and Salford all rose steadily in population throughout our period. As is evident from table 2, the area of Rochdale that became the parliamentary borough in 1832, and comprised the municipal borough after its expansion in 1872, rose by an average of around 22 per cent every ten years, from 21,127 in 1821 to 66,886 in 1881. The area that became Bolton municipal borough upon incorporation in 1838 rose from 32,045 in 1821 to 105,414 in 1881 — with average decennial rises of about 22 per cent. The townships of Salford, Pendleton and Broughton, which constituted the municipal borough after amalgamation in 1853, rose from 32,600 to 176,235 in the period 1821-81. Here the decennial jumps were much larger (around 33 per cent) — probably owing to Salford's close proximity to Manchester.

Ratable value generally more than kept pace with these population increases. Rochdale's rose from £118,516 in 1859 (£3.26 per head of population) to £312,505 in 1877 (£4.68 per head); Bolton's ratable value was £119,333 in 1838 (2·46 per head), £203,625 in 1861 (£2·90 per head) and £314,368 in 1876 (£3·30 per head); Salford's rose from £314,841 in 1853 (£3·70 per head) to £801,192 in 1881 (£4·55 per head).

Table 2. Population, 1831-81

Rochdale	1831	1841	1851	1861	1871	1881
Municipal borough	-	24,423[a]	29,195	38,114	44,556	68,886
Parliamentary borough	27,899[a]	34,004	41,513	53,308	63,485	68,886
Parish	58,441	67,874	80,214	100,900	119,191	121,911
Union	52,387[a]	60,577	72,522	91,758	109,858	121,911

% Population rise, parliamentary borough	1831	1841	1851	1861	1871	1881
	32·05	21·9	22·0	28·4	19·1	8·5

Bolton	1831	1841	1851	1861	1871	1881
Municipal borough	42,245[a]	51,029	61,171	70,395	82,853	105,414
Parliamentary borough	-	51,029	61,171	70,395	92,655	105,965
Parish	63,034	73,898	87,280	97,215	112,503	
Union	-	97,519	114,688	130,270	158,408	192,405

% Population rise, municipal borough	1831	1841	1851	1861	1871	1881
	31·8	20·8	19·9	15·1	17·1	27·2

Salford	1831	1841	1851	1861	1871	1881
Municipal borough	40,786[b]	53,200[b]	63,850[b]	102,449	124,801	176,235
	50,810[c]	68,386[c]	85,108[d]			
Parliamentary borough	50,810[a]	68,386	85,108	102,449	124,801	176,235
Parish[d]	NA	NA	NA	NA	NA	NA
Union	-	70,224	87,523	105,335	128,890	181,526

% Population rise, parliamentary borough	1831	1841	1851	1861	1871	1881
	55·9	34·6	24·45	20·4	21·8	41·2

[a] Estimated.
[b] Area incorporated under 1830 Police Act, and 1844 Incorporation (Salford township).
[c] Area incorporated in 1853 (Salford, Pendleton and Broughton townships).
[d] Not applicable: the relevant parish is Manchester.

The increase in ratable value was just as well, since it provided the resources, if not the will, to alleviate some of the burgeoning social and environmental problems evident in all three towns. Salford's were the worst: rather frequently in the 1870s, for example, the town sported the highest death rate (around thirty-three per thousand) among the English towns for which the Registrar General was recording quarterly figures.[16] Bolton, though improving by this time, had a similarly unenviable record in the 1840s and 1850s. Rochdale's position was better — partly owing (it was thought at the time) to its higher, more exposed and thus healthier geographical position. Nevertheless it too suffered the problems of high mortality, disease, poverty, overcrowding and insanitation typical of growing industrial towns in the period.

These problems had implications for the exercise of power, since they produced demands both for and against collective remedy — demands to which philanthropic organisations and the institutions of local government had to respond in some way. For municipal governments, sooner or later, this meant parliamentary applications for local improvement powers — over building, pollution, overcrowding, water and gas supply, etc. Such moves automatically put the municipal elites in a vulnerable and unpredictable position — as regards local interests and as regards Parliament itself. Meanwhile, once gained, the powers had to be administered, and were again likely to arouse the interested attention of some of those affected. Moreover the steady expansion of municipal functions also raised other problems for businessmen-turned-councillors — problems of time, knowledge, control and the power of paid officials.

Though there were important similarities, the three towns also differed from one another — and did so in ways likely to have political significance. They differed in size. By 1881 Rochdale's population was around two-thirds that of Bolton, which in turn was approximately two-thirds that of Salford. Rochdale's smaller size may help to explain why its politics were more popular than those of the other two.

There were also differences in geographical location. Whilst Bolton and Rochdale were relatively separate entities until well beyond 1880, Salford was always indistinguishable from Manchester — the two being separated only by the convoluted waters of the Irwell. As we shall see, proximity to a city that constituted the social and economic focus of south-east Lancashire had very significant effects on Salford's politics, and on the power of the municipal elite.

There were economic differences. Salford, like Manchester, was less directly dominated by textiles and its industrial base more diversified than Bolton or Salford. Meanwhile Rochdale, well to the east of Salford and

Bolton, and only five miles from the Yorkshire border, was not just a cotton town. Although cotton represented the largest source of employment, the woollen industry was also important and increasingly so. In 1851 there were 5,504 persons over twenty engaged in woollen (particularly woollen cloth) manufacture, compared with 7,701 adult cotton workers.

This last fact is important, since it helps explain another difference — that Rochdale's factories were generally smaller than those of Bolton and Salford. In 1841 the woollen mills in Rochdale parish employed an average of 52·9 workers each, whilst the cotton mills employed 119. By 1862 the borough's woollen mills contained 147 on average, whilst its cotton factories employed 170. The cotton mills of Bolton parish employed an average of 201 in 1841, whilst the borough's contained 184 in 1863. There are no comparable figures for Salford in 1841, since the town was part of Manchester parish. Nevertheless it seems probable that Salford's cotton factories were larger still at that time, and were certainly so by the early 1860s. Average factory size for Manchester parish in 1841 was 285, whilst in 1863 the cotton factories of Salford municipal borough were employing an average of 243 workers.[17]

As this suggests, the differences between the three towns were narrowing significantly. Nevertheless they may throw light on the contrasts in political style and content. If, as Patrick Joyce[18] suggests, relations between employers and workforce were more egalitarian in small than in large factories, this may partly explain why Rochdale's working class were more frequent, more autonomous and more welcome participants in the political process than Bolton or Salford's. Several factors besides factory size were also important, as we shall see — and probably more immediately so. Nevertheless this factor is clearly likely to be influential.

Another politically important difference was religion. Here the contrasts are very noticeable. Rochdale had a much higher proportion of Nonconformists and a much lower proportion of Anglicans among its population than Salford or Bolton. According to the 1851 census, of 13,077 sittings in Rochdale only 21 per cent (3,050) were Anglican, whilst 71·5 per cent (9,352) were variously Nonconformists, with 675 (7·2 per cent) Roman Catholics accounting for the rest. This contrasts with Bolton, where 41·7 per cent (9,373) of the 22,487 sittings were Anglican, 44·3 per cent (9,961) Nonconformist and 13·1 per cent (2,953) Catholic. It also contrasts with Salford. Here, out of 23,359 sittings, 42·3 per cent (9,893) were Anglican, 40·8 per cent (9,531) Nonconformist and 15·4 per cent (2,500) Roman Catholic.[19]

There were also important differences among the Nonconformists of the three towns. The two largest groups in Rochdale were the Methodist Association (28·8 per cent of Nonconformist sittings in 1851) and the Baptists (20·5 per cent). Of these, the former was much the most influential, commanding the allegiance of most of the liberal municipal elite. It was uncompromisingly anti-Anglican, and militantly expressed the social as well as the religious aspirations of Rochdale's new industrial middle class. Its influence partly accounts for the sharper edge to religious and political controversy that, as we shall see, was evident in Rochdale. This becomes clearer when Rochdale is compared with Bolton and Salford. Here Wesleyan Methodism was much more important (35·5 per cent of Nonconformists in Bolton and 30 per cent in Salford in 1851). Together with the Independents, it commanded the bulk of Nonconformist adherents. It was more hierarchically inclined than the Methodist Association (which had broken away in 1834 because of disagreements about internal government), and its attitudes towards both Anglicanism and Conservatism were much more ambivalent.[20] Not surprisingly, as we shall see, religious and party controversy were more muted in Bolton and Salford.

We can now turn to the location of power, and begin by examining political recruitment.

Notes

1 As examples, see F. Hunter, *Community Power Structure* (Chapel Hill NC., 1953); A. H. Birch, *Small Town Politics* (London, 1959); R. H. Dahl, *Who Governs* (New Haven Conn., 1961); J. M. Lee, *Social Leaders and Public Persons* (Oxford, 1963); W. F. Hawley and F. Hirt, *The Search for Community Power* (Englewood Cliffs, N. J., 1968); N. Polsby *Community Power and Political Theory* (2nd ed., New Haven, Conn., 1980). For critical review of community power studies and of more recent trends in urban political analysis see M. Goldsmith, *Politics, Planning and the City* (London, 1980); P. Dunleavy, *Urban Political Analysis* (London, 1980); P. Saunders, *Urban Politics: a Sociological Interpretation* (Harmondsworth, 1980).

2 See respectively D. Fraser, *Urban Politics in Victorian England* (Leicester, 1978), and E. P. Hennock, *Fit and Proper Persons* (London, 1973).

3 *Op. cit.*

4 J. Foster, *Class Struggle and the Industrial Revolution* (London, 1974); P. Joyce, *Work, Society and Politics: the Culture of the Factory in Late Victorian England* (Brighton, 1980).

5 Dahl, *op. cit.* For expanded discussion see J. A. Garrard, 'The history of local political power', *Political Studies*, vol. XXV, No. 2, June 1977.

6 See Fraser, *op. cit.*

7 The best short discussion of power in this sense is R. H. Dahl, *Modern Political Analysis* (New Jersey, 1963).

8 This is not invariably the case. Any group able to get most of its interests fulfilled must be deemed highly influential irrespective of how little it costs governmental authorities to comply.

9 See particularly P. Bachrach and M. S. Baratz, 'Decisions and non-decisions: an analytical framework', *American Political Science Review*, vol. 57, No. 3,

1963; P. Bachrach and M. S. Baratz, *Power and Poverty* (New York, 1970); articles by R. Wolfinger and F. Frey in *American Political Science Review*, vol. 65, No. 4, December 1971; G. Parry and P. Morris, 'When is a decision not a decision?', in I. Crewe (ed.), *British Political Sociology Yearbook*, vol. I (London, 1974); S. Lukes, *Power: a Radical View* (London, 1975); M. A. Crenson, *The Unpolitics of Air Pollution* (Baltimore Md., and London, 1971); articles by N. Polsby and K. Newton in *Political Studies*, vol. 27, No. 4, December 1979.

10 See pp. 41f.

11 Here I am using the term in R. H. Dahl's sense of 'anything that can be used to sway the specific choices or the strategies of another individual' (*Who Governs*, *op. cit.*, p. 226).

12 Foster, *op. cit.*

13 No figures are available for Salford or Rochdale's municipal areas. Rochdale Union was much larger than the improvement commissioners' area; Salford Union was only a little larger than what was to comprise the municipal borough in 1853.

14 Soldiers, tailors, shoemakers, clerks, railway workers, warehousemen, agricultural labourers, shopkeepers, bricklayers, masons, brewery workers, ironworkers, blacksmiths, general labourers, cabmen, etc.

15 Tailors, shoemakers, cabmen, etc, farmers, agricultural labourers, carpenters, masons, publicans, shopkeepers, quarrymen, blacksmiths, labourers.

16 See, for example, *SWN*, 13 November 1875, p. 2.

17 These figures are mainly drawn from the *Annual Reports of the Chief Factory Inspector, 1833 ff*. Some figures are also available from police superintendents' reports during the cotton famine, e.g. *RO*, 31 May 1862, p. 5; *SWN*, 22 March 1862, p. 2; *BC*, 30 May 1863, p. 5.

18 Joyce, *op. cit.*

19 In addition there were 200 Presbyterian sittings in Bolton and 195 Church of Scotland sittings in Salford.

20 For a survey of Methodist controversies in the area see D. A. Gowland, *Methodist Successions: the Origins of Free Methodism in Manchester, Rochdale and Liverpool*, Chetham Society XXVI (Manchester, 1979).

2

The nature of municipal leadership

This chapter surveys the socio-economic background of local political leaders. We shall see that political, economic and social leadership overlapped very considerably and that, within the context of the nineteenth-century industrial town, men of substance and station constituted a group possessing major advantages in the process of political recruitment, and in terms of being accepted as legitimate once recruited. We shall suggest that the best way of understanding this leadership — particularly its style and bases of power — is to see it as an urban squirearchy. However, we shall also argue that such a picture — though accurate as far as it goes — is oversimplified, and that urban political recruitment, at least in these towns, was more open than the equivalent process in the countryside.

'Men of property . . .'

The occupational background of those serving on the main governing bodies in Salford, Bolton and Rochdale shows that they constituted an economic elite — whether compared with any given town's population as a whole, or with its voting population. The property qualification prescribed by the various Acts establishing these bodies was alone sufficient to ensure this — ranging, as it did, from the possession of property to the minimum annual ratable value of £15 for Rochdale councillors; to £20 for Little Bolton Trustees; £30 for Great Bolton trustees, and Bolton and Salford councillors; and £35 for Rochdale improvement commissioners. As an example of the effect of such restrictions, we can note that, in 1856, during Rochdale's incorporation battle, it was estimated that a £30 qualification would limit the pool of political recruitment to a maximum of 550 persons,[1] while even the £15 qualification eventually adopted would produce only 958 potential councillors.[2] These figures may be set against a total population, at that time, of around 34,000, and an electoral roll, as it emerged for the first council elections, of 3,115. Thus, in Rochdale at least, the higher qualification would have restricted eligibility to under one burgess in six, whilst the £15 minimum limited it to fewer than one in three.[3]

In any case, members of the legislature seem normally to have come from the higher end of those qualified. Thus the 120 police commissioners ruling Salford between 1830 and 1844 regularly included between 35 and 45 per cent proprietorially engaged in manufacturing, or large-scale merchandising — that is to say, their occupation is given as 'manufacturer', 'merchant', 'cotton spinner', 'bleacher' and so on. As table 3 shows, larger proprietors also constituted a very significant proportion of the membership of Salford's council up to, and beyond, 1880. Manufacturers comprised between 35 and 53 per cent up to the end of our period, and indeed remained the largest single occupational group on the council until the mid-1890s. If those designated as 'merchants' are added, the combined proportions of those who might reasonably be considered to be large proprietors rises as high as 60·4

Table 3. Quinquennial occupational analysis of Salford Council, 1845-80

	1845 -50	1851 -55	1856 -60	1861 -65	1866 -70	1871 -75	1876 -80	
Manufacturers	53·45	39·3	35·2	36·5	37·45	44·2	39·5	%
	85	86	113	112	109	129	122	N
Merchants	6·9	5·9	4·4	6·5	9·6	11·3	10·4	%
	11	13	14	20	28	33	32	N
Total large	60·4	45·2	39·6	43·0	47·1	55·5	48·4	%
proprietors	96	99	127	132	137	162	154	N
Shopkeepers,	8·2	10·95	10·9	14·65	14·4	12·3	12·9	%
dealers, etc	13	24	35	45	42	36	40	N
Building trades	3·1	5·0	5·6	6·2	5·5	6·85	8·1	%
	5	11	18	19	16	20	25	N
Total small	11·3	16·0	16·5	20·8	19·9	19·2	21·0	%
proprietors	18	35	53	64	58	56	65	N
Named merchants	1·9	2·7	3·7	4·6	5·15	5·1	2·3	%
	3	6	12	14	15	15	7	N
Agents	-	1·4	0·9	-	4·1	1·7	1·6	%
		3	3		12	5	5	N
Other businessmen	1·9	4·1	6·5	6·2	4·5	3·1	1·6	%
	3	9	21	19	13	9	5	N
Total all	75·5	69·4	67·3	74·6	80·8	84·6	76·4	%
proprietors	120	152	216	229	235	247	236	N

Table 3. (cont'd)

	1845 -50	1851 -55	1856 -60	1861 -65	1866 -70	1871 -75	1876 -80	
'Gentlemen'	18·2	12·8	13·4	10·4	6·2	6·2	11·65	%
	29	28	43	32	18	18	36	N
Professionals	6·3	17·8	19·3	15·0	13·05	9·25	12·0	%
	10	39	62	46	38	27	37	N
Others	-	-	-	-	-	-	-	
Total all	6·3	17·8	19·3	15·0	13·05	9·25	12·0	%
non-proprietors	10	39	62	46	38	27	37	N
N =	159	219	321	307	291	292	309	

Notes

Manufacturers include those designated as manufacturers, cotton spinners, sizers, dyers, ironfounders, machine makers, brewers, brickmakers, quarry masters, colliery proprietors, mill furnishers, manufacturing chemists.

Merchants: only those specifically designated as 'merchants', plus bankers.

Shopkeepers/dealers, etc., include shopkeepers, dealers, tea dealers, drapers, grocers, corn merchants, pawnbrokers, stationers, butchers, bakers, chandler, chemist, druggist, cordwainer, licensed victuallers, beer-sellers.

Building includes builders, joiners, carpenters and plumbers.

Named merchants include those designated as iron, timber, wine and spirit, coal, tea.

Professionals include solicitors, barristers, doctors, surgeons, veterinary surgeons, surveyors, sheriff's officers, engineers, journalists, editors.

per cent, with an average over the whole period 1846-80 of 47·8 per cent — and both these latter figures, as we shall argue shortly, represent a conservative estimate of the large proprietorial position.

Given only minimal evidence from rate returns — for Salford, as for Bolton and Rochdale — it is difficult to estimate how wealthy most of these men really were.[4] Judging, however, by their frequent reputations as 'the proprietor(s) of extensive manufactur(ies)', by the size of their numerous charitable contributions, by the magnificence of the houses, and the select-ness of the areas in which they often resided, both police commissioners and councillors seem to have included, at one time or another, many of the town's economic leaders.

One example may give a sense of the economic flavour of at least the council in these years. In 1860 its members included E. R. Langworthy, a

Table 4. Quinquennial occupational analysis of Bolton Council, 1843-80

	1843-5	1846-50	1851-5	1856-60	1861-5	1866-70	1871-5	1876-80	
Manufacturers	50·8	53·0	44·4	42·4	44·0	42·6	42·0	36·55	%
	66	96	104	104	103	101	84	87	N
Merchants	-	1·65	-	-	-	-	-	1·7	%
	-	3	-	-	-	-	-	4	N
Total large proprietors	50·8	54·65	44·4	42·4	44·0	42·6	42·0	38·2	%
	66	99	104	104	103	101	84	91	N
Shopkeepers, dealers	28·5	24·9	33·3	31·8	36·3	34·2	21·0	21·0	%
	37	45	78	78	85	81	42	50	N
Building trades	1·5	1·65	-	2·4	1·3	1·3	-	1·3	%
	2	3	-	6	3	3	-	3	N
Total small proprietors	30·0	26·5	33·3	34·3	37·6	35·4	21·0	22·3	%
	39	48	78	84	88	84	42	53	N
Named merchants	2·3	2·2	5·1	3·3	1·3	2·5	5·5	10·9	%
	3	4	12	8	3	6	11	26	N
Agents	-	-	-	2·4	-	0·4	1·0	1·3	%
	-	-	-	6	-	1	2	3	N
Other businessmen	0·8	2·8	4·3	2·85	0·85	4·2	6·5	2·1	%
	1	5	10	7	2	10	13	5	N
Total all proprietors	83·8	86·2	87·2	85·3	83·8	85·2	76·0	74·8	%
	109	156	204	209	196	202	152	178	N

	%	%	%	%	%	%	%	%
	N	N	N	N	N	N	N	N
'Gentlemen'	14·6	7·7	6·4	6·9	7·3	6·3	12·0	12·2
	19	14	15	17	17	15	24	29
Professionals	1·5	6·1	6·4	7·75	9·0	8·4	12·0	13·0
	2	11	15	19	21	20	24	31
Others	–	–	–	–	–	–	–	–
Total all non-proprietors	1·5	6·1	6·4	7·75	9·0	8·4	12·0	13·0
	2	11	15	19	21	20	24	31
N =	130	181	234	245	234	237	200	238

Notes See table 3.

wealthy merchant, manufacturer, influential banker and director of the
Manchester Chamber of Commerce; Thomas Agnew, founder of the nation-
wide firm of art dealers Thomas Agnew & Sons, and a proprietor of *Punch*;
R. E. Mottram, one of Salford's leading brewers; James Worral, junior, head
of the factory that dominated Ordsall; and David Chadwick, an accountant,
who, by 1864, claimed to have become 'a very large employer of labour . . .
concerned as a proprietor in some of the largest manufacturing establishments in the kingdom, [employing] 42,000 people'.[5] The council also
included Samuel Armitage, a rather somnolent member of the glittering
Armitage family, whose factories and mansions dominated the Pendleton
district, and six of whom, between 1835 and 1881, took on the burdens of
municipal office.[6]

A very similar picture emerges if we turn to Bolton. Manufacturers
regularly constituted between 50 and 72 per cent of the Little Bolton trustees
for all but the final two years of that body's twenty-year existence from 1830
to 1849.[7] More scattered evidence suggests a very similar situation among
the Great Bolton trustees. Meanwhile, as is evident from table 4, between 36
and 53 per cent of Bolton councillors were various sorts of manufacturer.
Indeed, manufacturers remained the largest occupational group until the
mid-1880s, when they were overtaken by the shopocracy.

Some sources — notably the Tory *Bolton Chronicle* when lugubriously
contemplating the council in its Liberal phases — tended to assert that really
wealthy men shunned local legislative honours.[8] As with Salford, a precise
estimate of wealth is difficult. Nevertheless the evidence seems to contradict
such assertions. At one time or another, members of nearly all Bolton's
leading firms seem to have passed through the council and/or boards of
trustees — even if they did not stay very long.[9]

Again, a snapshot of the council may help provide a sense of its economic
character. In 1860-61 it included James and T. H. Arrowsmith, father and
son, members of a wealthy cotton spinning family controlling at least two
firms (Arrowsmith & Son and P. R. Arrowsmith & Co.); Edward Barlow, a
machine maker who laid uncontradicted claim to be 'the heaviest employer of
labour in this borough';[10] R. M. Haslam, owner of two cotton mills, and
again a member of a locally famous cotton family whose activities seem to
have extended into most branches of the trade. Haslam's partner, W. W.
Cannon, like his father, Walter Cannon, was also on the council. So too were
Richard Haworth, a sizer, and John Hodgkinson, cotton spinner — men who
owned two factories apiece. Finally, among the council's 'gentlemen', there
was, first, Robert Heywood, sometime owner of a Bolton factory and an
extensive Salford bleachworks. One of Bolton's richest men, his frequent
charitable donations came in dollops of several hundred pounds. Secondly,

and even more resplendently, there was S. T. Chadwick, a long-serving doctor to the poor, who, after migrating to Southport in 1865, outdistanced every other local philanthropist by leaving £23,000 to found an orphanage and a set of model dwellings.

However, by far the most consistent and impressive example of the legislative strength of great property is provided by Rochdale. Of the 156 individuals who combined membership of the improvement commission, between 1844 and 1853, with occupations which can be identified with reasonable certainty, around eighty (51 per cent) were engaged in mercantile (mainly woolstapling), or manufacturing, activity.[11] Rochdale's council was even more copiously blessed with men of substance. Table 5 reveals that manufacturers filled over 50 per cent of the seats for three of the six quinquennia between the council's formation in 1856 and the end of our period in 1880. Indeed, they remained the largest occupational group until the turn of the century. If those designated as merchant or woolstapler are added, we have a large proprietorial category which never falls below 52 per cent before 1880, and rises as high as 65·5 per cent in the council's first quinquennium.

As noted in chapter 1, Rochdale's factories were, on average, smaller than Salford's and Bolton's. Nevertheless all the town's leading firms and families had members on the improvement commission (1844-53) or the council at one time or another, and at any given legislative moment it was possible to find representatives of many of them. Perhaps the best example of the overlap between economic and political leadership is to be found among the thirty founding officials of the Rochdale Chamber of Commerce elected in 1869.[12] Three of the four vice-presidents were council members. So too were four of the chamber's own council. The officials also included seven ex-councillors and/or improvement commissioners, and three who were related to such individuals.

So far we have concentrated on the all-purpose legislative bodies. At least one of the two *ad hoc* authorities — the education board — seems to have exerted similar pull on the economically well-upholstered. In Salford manufacturers, merchants and bankers occupied nine of the thirteen seats on the board elected in 1870, and seven on that elected in 1873. The equivalent institutions in Bolton and Rochdale regularly contained at least six or seven large proprietors.

The boards of guardians also included significant numbers of men of substance among their members, but more intermittently. In fact small proprietors — shopkeepers, millers, shoemakers, builders, etc. — seem to have emerged in strength at a much earlier stage on these bodies than in the councils. In Salford, whilst large proprietors were heavily represented until

Table 5. Quinquennial occupational analysis of Rochdale Council, 1856–80

	1856–60	1861–5	1866–70	1871–5	1876–80	
Manufacturers	55·5	51·9	44·7	48·1	51·0	%
	95	107	84	91	98	N
Merchants	9·9	8·7	8·0	6·3	7·3	%
	17	18	15	12	14	N
Total large	65·5	60·7	52·65	54·5	58·3	%
proprietors	112	125	99	103	112	N
Shopkeepers,	19·3	22·8	25·5	25·4	25·5	%
dealers	33	47	48	48	49	N
Building trades	2·3	1·0	-	2·6	3·1	%
	4	2		5	6	N
Total small	21·6	23·8	25·5	28·0	28·6	%
proprietors	37	49	48	53	55	N
Named merchants	1·75	-	4·25	5·3	2·6	%
	3		8	10	5	N
Agents	-	-	-	-	-	
Other businessmen	1·75	2·4	3·7	1·05	-	%
	3	5	7	2		N
Total all	90·6	86·9	86·2	88·9	89·6	%
proprietors	155	179	162	168	172	N
'Gentlemen'	5·8	8·25	9·6	7·9	7·8	%
	10	17	18	15	15	N
Professionals	3·5	4·85	4·25	3·2	2·6	%
	6	10	8	6	5	N
Others	-	-	-	-	-	
Total all	3·5	4·85	4·25	3·2	2·6	%
non-proprietors	6	10	8	6	5	N
N =	171	206	188	189	192	

Notes See table 3.

1853, the shopocracy seems to have taken over from then on. Even in Rochdale small proprietors had at least 45 per cent of board seats by the late 1860s, as compared with a maximum of around 38 per cent for the larger proprietors. However, the picture is complicated by the intermittent character of the occupational data available, and in the case of Bolton and Rochdale by the board's wider, and substantially rural, administrative area —

one consequence being the presence, as guardians, of significant numbers of farmers.

Anyway, it seems likely that most of the foregoing calculations are under-estimates. Many of those categorising themselves as 'gentlemen' were probably retired manufacturers. Nor have we taken into account the significant numbers of professionals on at least Salford and Bolton councils, many of whom (particularly those of the fee-earning kind like solicitors, engineers and doctors) were only hazily divided from large proprietors (among whom they dwelt, and from whom they earned their living) in terms of wealth, and even ideological ethos. Finally we may note that many of the shopkeepers on these legislative bodies, whom we are classifying as small proprietors, were probably the more substantial of their kind. Certainly this seems reasonable if the fairly frequent ownership of two shops and/or a separate house in the more salubrious parts of town is to be taken as an indicator.

On most of the governing bodies of all three towns, therefore, we discover considerable overlap between economic and political leadership. In fact this overlap tends to increase as one shifts one's gaze up the municipal ladder. In Rochdale, as table 6 suggests, large proprietors are much more heavily represented among aldermen than among councillors. Indeed, with an average large proprietorial representation of 85·8 per cent for the period 1856–80 compared with 58·3 per cent for the council as a whole, the aldermanic bench seems ready to collapse under its burden of ratable value. Bolton's aldermen do not show the same characteristics, but there is some concentration of large proprietors among committee chairmen.

Not surprisingly, chief officers of the three towns were more weighty still. The boroughreeves and constables of both Bolton and Salford were almost always wealthy manufacturers or merchants, as were nearly all Rochdale's chief constables. The same picture emerges after incorporation with regard to mayoral incumbents. Twenty-seven of Bolton's forty mayors up to 1880 were large proprietors (many of them massively so). So too were at least twenty-one of Salford's thirty-six mayors up to the same date, whilst all but one of Rochdale's first twenty-five chief citizens were similarly impressive.

'. . . and standing'

If there is a marked overlap between economic and political leadership in the three towns, and if men of substance seem to possess clear advantages in political recruitment, the link with social leadership, and the apparent advantages thereby gained, is even more pronounced. If we take, as an indicator of social leadership, participation in the vast network of philan-

Table 6. Percentage of large and small proprietors among councillors, aldermen and committee chairmen

BOLTON

Large proprietors

Period	CW	C	A	CC
1843–45	50.8	50.0	51.7	–
1846–50	54.65	56.9	40.9	–
1851–55	44.4	38.8	63.5	–
1856–60	42.4	45.9	34.5	–
1861–65	44.0	49.7	17.8	48.0
1866–70	42.6	47.7	25.0	38.2
1871–75	42.0	43.7	37.9	57.1
1876–80	38.2	35.4	46.7	54.0

Small proprietors

Period	CW	C	A	CC
1843–45	30.0	33.4	20.7	–
1846–50	26.5	27.0	25.0	–
1851–55	33.3	37.7	19.2	–
1856–60	34.3	37.7	30.9	–
1861–65	37.6	33.5	50.0	42.0
1866–70	35.4	33.2	41.7	47.3
1871–75	21.0	23.7	13.6	14.3
1876–80	22.3	27.5	6.7	14.0

ROCHDALE

Large proprietors

Period	CW	C	A	CC
1856–60	65.5	56.9	100.0	–
1861–65	60.7	49.3	94.2	–
1866–70	52.65	39.4	88.2	–
1871–75	54.5	47.1	74.5	–
1876–80	58.3	52.6	71.9	–

Small proprietors

Period	CW	C	A	CC
1856–60	21.6	27.0	0.0	–
1861–65	23.8	31.8	0.0	–
1866–70	25.5	34.3	2.0	–
1871–75	28.0	31.1	19.6	–
1876–80	28.6	32.6	19.3	–

Note These figures represent percentages of the whole council (CW), of the whole number of councillors (C), of the whole number of aldermen (A), and of the whole number of committee chairmen (CC). A dash indicates that figures are not available. It has not been possible to calculate figures for Salford thropic and sociable activities of the nineteenth-century town, the connections between the political and social worlds rapidly become evident. Of many examples, three may suffice. Among the stewards advertised in the local press to preside over the annual junketings celebrating the Queen's birthday in the three towns, past or present members of the various local authorities generally constituted a majority. Similarly, the president of Bolton's Floral and Horticultural Society in 1838 was Alderman Robert Heywood, and of the twenty-one vice-presidents and stewards twelve were either councillors or had been members of the two boards of trustees.[13] Finally, Salford's 'Relief Committee', established in 1862 to cope with the social consequences of the cotton famine, included fourteen councillors.[14]

Many local legislators participated in philanthropic and sociable activities to a remarkable extent. Indeed, we can find the names of some councillors prominently displayed among the patrons of virtually every local institution or project. Meanwhile, given the scope for social activity, it is not surprising that a large majority of a council at any given time can be found involved in this way. Thus at least twenty of the thirty-member Salford Council of 1844-45 can be discovered participating in institutions ranging from the 'Queen's Birthday Dessert' to the Salford Royal Dispensary, the Mechanics' Institute and the Manchester and Salford Juvenile Refuge. At least twenty-three of Rochdale's forty-man council of 1857/58 were involved in a similar range of activity. Finally, all but fourteen of Bolton's forty-eight council members for 1860/61 can be identified among the patrons of such institutions.

The context of leadership

The legitimising theory

So far, in trying to demonstrate the relationship between economic, social and political leadership, we have concentrated mainly on quantitative material. Yet if we are properly to understand why men of property and standing should have had such advantages in political recruitment, and in being accepted as legitimate once recruited, we need to turn to more qualitative evidence. For, as we shall now see, the political significance of economic and social substance is comprehensible only in the context provided by the nineteenth-century industrial town — the legitimising theory that it produced, and the highly visible arena that it provided for its leaders, giving their power an intensely personal quality.

There was certainly a widely accepted ideology[15] justifying the 'due weight of property' in local politics. As we shall see in chapters 7-11, it had greater sway in Bolton and Salford than in Rochdale, but it gave political advantage to men of substance in all three towns. The theory can be discovered flavouring a host of newspaper editorials, letters to the editor, nomination and election speeches. Among the last of these one might even find long calculations terminating in heady conclusions like the following, in Bolton in 1873:

The total rateable value of the property of the three Liberal candidates was £859 10*s* against £51 10*s* paid by the Conservative candidates. With such facts before them [the electors] . . . there could be no doubt . . . as to the result of the election.[16]

Underlying such sentiments was the belief that only those with the largest accretions of property could fully understand the problems of a borough. They were the only men with enough time and breadth of view. This was partly so because the skills of the substantial businessman were felt to be peculiarly appropriate to the management of municipal government, particularly since that government was simply business on a very large scale. Thus nomination meetings were often reminded that candidate 'was a good businessman. He had managed his own affairs well . . . and that . . . was a very important qualification for managing the town's affairs.'[17] Similar views were expressed more brutally in a letter to the *Salford Weekly News* in 1864:

All comprehensive schemes of fiscal reform, national or local, are emanations of minds qualified by education or practice to solve intricate questions of finance. It would be as unreasonable to expect the small trader, who deals in units of ten, and seldom reaches three figures, to comprehend sums involving some hundreds of thousands as it would be to expect a man ignorant of geometry and mathematics to calculate the distance and density of Saturn.[18]

The theory also held that the greater the amount of rates paid, the more likely was the man paying them to see his own interests as co-terminous with those of the borough. It was partly for this reason that councillors were apt to express such unbounded delight when, as in Salford in 1847, they could survey a mayoral nominee who was

the proprietor of a considerable manufactory, . . . the employer of a great number of hands. His sympathies were consequently connected with the prosperity of the borough. One of the largest ratepayers . . . his son was also a large ratepayer.[19]

What also enhanced the great proprietors' position in the recruitment stakes was the assumption — again, more prevalent in Bolton and Salford than in Rochdale — that ratable property granted particular value to political opinion. Since the point will receive further attention in chapter 3, one example will suffice here. In 1843 the *Manchester Guardian* seemed to feel that Salford's incorporation was assured after discovering that the petition in favour had 'already been signed by a great number of the most respectable inhabitants, and large ratepayers, including nearly all the occupiers of mills, and other extensive establishments'.[20]

Salford, indeed, is perhaps the best illustration of the impelling nature of these ideas. One major reason why the borough — in spite of repeated rebuffs — sought to incorporate Pendleton and Broughton was the hope of gaining access to a veritable gold mine of the best sort of political talent. This hope was enshrined in the eventual amalgamation agreement of 1853, giving the smaller, but far richer, populations of these townships a combined council representation equal to that of Salford township. And as late as 1867 the hope was still expressed of finding 'men . . . so circumstanced that they might be eligible for becoming aldermen . . . and mayors. Salford people looked to Pendleton and Broughton to return such men.'[21]

The theory did not go unchallenged. Even in the socially quiescent years of the mid-century small proprietors, particularly in their more paranoid moods, could sometimes express sentiments that approached a total rejection of the special claims of 'gentlemen . . . who care not one farthing for us'.[22] Yet the important point to note is that few even came close to advancing an alternative rival theory about the special claims and skills of men other than large proprietors. Justifications, like the following for William Brocklehurst in Rochdale in 1867, stand out for their sheer rarity: 'a tradesman dependent upon the general public for patronage, and thus more likely to conscientiously represent the interests of the burgesses . . .'.[23] Moreover small proprietors like this often partially sold the pass by electing the most economically substantial of their number (and sometimes even large proprietors) as leading officials in their defence organisations.

It is also true, as we shall see from chapter 6 onwards, that party labels often rivalled economic weight in political recruitment. Of the three towns, only in Salford, and only between 1848 and 1867, was it possible consistently to consider selecting candidates 'with not the slightest attention to . . . political creeds but solely on account of . . . the amount of their rates assessments'.[24] Yet it remained everywhere a high priority in each party, and the increasing complaints in Bolton and Salford about the difficulty of persuading wealthy men to come forward seem, until near the end of our period, to have been as much a tribute to the appetite for them as a mark of their real scarcity.

In any case, the popular acceptability of the theory, and its utility for purposes of recruitment, were underpinned by the dominant economic position of the large proprietor, particularly the factory owner, in the neighbourhood where he conducted his business and in the town at large. Manufacturers did indeed provide a large part of the revenue from the rates; they also contributed heavily to the profits of the gas and water undertakings where these were municipalised. More important, perhaps, the factory owner was the centre of a network of dependency stretching out to his workforce, their families and probably also to many of the local shopkeepers. As we shall see shortly, he was often a very personal figure, and his relationship with his workforce distinctly familial. This gave him considerable potential influence over their political behaviour and opinions, and there is evidence that it was exerted.[25] Fear of such influences led Rochdale's radicals to opt, in 1856, for three large wards for the newly incorporated borough rather than five or more smaller ones, where 'you would be placing in the hands of a few mill owners the choice of the town council . . . '.[26] Anticipation of being able to use those influences caused most employers-turned-politician to wish to represent the ward in which their works were situated, and to become decidedly jumpy when their position seemed threatened by a revision of ward boundaries.[27] Though employers' influence in this area can be exaggerated, there is no doubt that dependency gave them a head start in the processes of political recruitment and election.

The urban arena

However, the legitimising theory and the economic relationship that gave it credence could achieve their full political effect only the context of the special environment provided by the nineteenth-century town. It was this environment also that lent political significance to charitable and other social endeavour. For what was important was not merely that an individual should be a substantial businessman, or an active philanthropist, but that he should personally be seen to be such by a large, attentive and admiring audience. As we shall now see, places like Rochdale, Bolton and even Salford (for all the influence of Manchester) provided leadership of all kinds — social, economic and political — with an arena that was autonomous, intimate and highly visible.

Although larger than anything before, the nineteenth-century town was far smaller, and geographically more distinguishable, than its twentieth-century successor. National events and politics undoubtedly impinged to an important extent. But for most citizens for most of the time the town and its constituent neighbourhoods probably represented the circumference of their economic and social vision, the places wherein they lived their lives, drew their liveli-hoods, and observed others doing the same.

As a result of this autonomy the town's environment was also intimate and absorbing. Most reports in the local press assume in their readers an attentiveness, and an intimate knowledge of persons and places, that is entirely absent today. At a prosaic level we see this in September 1873, when the Reverend Walter Chamberlaine wrote to the *Bolton Chronicle* complaining about 'a set of ruffians in my neighbourhood' who were wont to celebrate any wedding by rushing to the church with 'an indescribable vessel full of spirits and water to share amongst their friends.' Significantly, the purpose of the letter was to act as 'a gibbet in a manner most likely to degrade them'.[28] In a similar spirit, there is a long and furious correspondence, paraded before the *Rochdale Observer's* 10,000 readers during September and October 1869, between Miss Maria Nicholson and Miss Barber (along with assorted relatives of both). The battle centred on a gesture Miss Nicholson alleged Miss Barber to have made at her on a public footpath — a gesture which the complainant, after a battle with her sense of delicacy, eventually revealed as 'putting her thumb to her nose with the fingers extended'.[29]

What is significant about both these incidents is the assumption that the town provided an arena where even lowly 'ruffians' might be persuaded into propriety by public shaming; the assumption also (by the editor as well as the participants) that, in that arena, the reputations of even relatively humble persons, like the Misses Nicholson and Barber, were of wide interest.

Not surprisingly, this sense of attentiveness is even more pronounced on grander occasions when the elite themselves were on show. The frequent town processions — to open public buildings, erect statues, celebrate anniversaries, etc. — invariably attracted huge crowds and provided magnificent opportunities for the leading men to parade themselves. Bringing up the rear of every procession — and thus perhaps reinforcing the deference that was their due — were 'the gentlemen of the town four abreast'. Their names, and the details of such occasions, were always lovingly recorded in the press, and again in a way that implies great knowledgeableness on the part of readers. Thus, in Bolton on Coronation Day in 1838, we learn from the *Chronicle* that

Deansgate presented a most cheerful appearance. Mr Heaton, Mr Scowcroft, Mrs Lomax . . . Mr French and others . . . exhibited their loyalty by displaying the most beautiful and imposing banners.

Down this street came 'the Grand Procession', in which, the paper observed,

the men from the Union Foundry . . . led by Mr Peter Rothwell, and other gentlemen with a number of flags and ingenious devices . . . Mr Hick's men of the Soho Foundry made a most splendid display of flags and banners . . . The same may be said of Mr Dobson's machine makers . . . [and] Mr Albinson's engineers.[30]

As this suggests, it needed only Christian name and surname to identify the great, and even not so great. Addresses, still less personal histories, were unnecessary. Significantly, the only exception occurred when there were two figures with the same name in the town. Then each individual's house was identified. Thus the two William Jenkinsons which Salford boasted in the 1840s were simply distinguished as William Jenkinson respectively of 'Mount Pleasant' and 'of Adelphi'. No more, it seems, was required.

The use of such identification marks was perfectly natural, for the magnificent mansions of local celebrities contributed much to their visibility, particularly as they tended to be concentrated in groups within, and (in Bolton and Salford) more frequently on the fringes of, the towns. A Salford writer in 1900 delved lushly into his memories of the 1880s and recalled Eccles Old Road as the 'Mount Zion of Liberalism . . . beautiful for [this] situation. Like brethren, they dwelt together in unity . . . Wright Turner, J. B. McKerrow, Thomas Bradford, J. H. Agnew . . . Henry Bailey . . . Alderman Tysoe . . . .'[31]

However, as much of the above suggests, what helped to make the local arena so compelling for the watchers was the nature of the figure that members of the elite were cutting there. For the best way of understanding the political strengths of a leadership that, as we have seen, combined social and economic with political resources is to see it as a self-conscious and self-confident urban squirearchy.

At the centre of this role, and of the analogies with the rural situation, was the position occupied by the employer — particularly his relationship with his workforce and their dependants. The employer, whether local politician or not, and particularly in the age before the limited company, was an intensely personal figure. Like his rural counterpart, the stages of his life — marriage, births and anniversaries of his children, and even the simple passing of the years — were occasion for organised celebration by, and for, his workforce. Significantly, so too were the stages of his elevation up the political scale, with tea parties often marking his election as councillor, alderman and particularly mayor. The very fact of such celebrations is important in itself. So too are the details of them, and the copious way in which they were recorded in the local press.

Two examples will make the point more clearly. For the first, we must return to Bolton on Coronation Day in 1838. In the evening, in common with several other employers,

Mr Rothwell entertained his men with a hearty dinner, provided in one of the spacious rooms of the Union Foundry. About four hundred sat down. Beef pudding and ale constituted the most prominent items . . . Mr Cubitt [the manager] . . . proposed the health of Mr Rothwell, a toast which was responded to with vociferous alacrity, the whole of the men standing. Mr Rothwell, in reply, said nothing could gratify him more than the conduct of his workpeople on that day. He drank their health not only for their kindness in drinking his . . . but for the honour reflected on that establishment by their orderly and admirable behaviour . . .[32]

Equally infused with benevolence was a celebration in Rochdale twenty-four years later. In September 1862 600 employees, 'their wives and sweethearts', plus many council members, sat down to a dinner provided in the factory by its owner, Alderman John Tatham, on the occasion of his son's twenty-first birthday. There were speeches from the Tatham family, councillors, foremen and representative workmen. The lucky twenty-one-year-old was presented with an illuminated address from the employees. It was composed in part of what can best be described as a loyal lecture, expressing the hope that 'the master mind . . . has not neglected the important duty — the cultivation of the mind of his son with the same zeal for success'. It also hoped that, by following his father's policies, the son would 'merit the same unmistakable attachment' from the workforce, and 'transmit to your sons (should you be blessed with any) the name of Tatham as pure and unsullied as you inherit it . . .'. After several other speeches Rochdale's vicar weighed in. He provided some clue to the occasion's significance by regretting the loss of close feudal relationships, and seeing 'kind actions' like the present dinner as the only way 'we can make masters and men feel a mutual tie'. After toasts to the Tatham family, Rochdale's 'town and trade' and the corporation there began 'the most racy enjoyment', which the *Rochdale Observer* contrived to describe in the manner of a sedate Roman orgy. For 'the workpeople . . . passed to the room below where they began the worship of Terpsichore' until 4.00 a.m.[33]

Such examples — selected from among many — suggest a relationship between employer and employee that was not merely paternal but familial. Moreover we get a sense, particularly from the speeches at the Tatham junketings, that like the family it was based upon two-way obligations. We can also see the way in which this relationship in the economic field was being linked implicitly (explicitly where mayoral elevation, for example, was celebrated) to the political sphere. Both Rothwell and Tatham were active local politicians, and Tatham's dinner was attended by many council members. In this way other members of the elite could share in the paternal and familial political benefits.

Such evidence is somewhat suspect, filtered as it is through journalistic spectacles tinted wishfully by Victorian ideology. Certainly we are seeing only part of the picture. However, the reports are too frequent and too detailed for wish-fulfilment to produce more than fairly minor distortion. Moreover the fact that such events were invariably reported in this detailed and admiring way probably helped powerfully not merely to enhance the elite's visibility but also to increase and generalise the legitimacy thus gained.

In any case, in the context of the nineteenth-century urban arena, the political effects of this economic strand of urban squirearchy were greatly reinforced by the elite's immensely visible philanthropic and sociable role. Social and charitable activities were generously reported in the local press, and lists of patrons and donors regularly and prominently appeared in front-page advertisements. Such conspicuous participation again created a dependent relationship with the recipients, and reinforced the elite's benevolent image among the population at large.

We can also note that many others besides those having a direct economic relationship with a workforce could through such activities bask in the legitimising glow. Many merchants, professional people and even shopkeepers got in on the act. Perhaps the most spectacular example was G. S. Chadwick, a doctor who practised in Bolton from 1837 to 1863. During this time he had been honorary surgeon to the Bolton Dispensary, and had run a surgery for ear and eye complaints which by 1860 was treating 1,500 a year, 'all of the poorest class'.[34] As we have seen, Chadwick was hugely philanthropic in other fields too, eventually endowing an orphanage and model dwellings. He was also a councillor for many years.

The reputation 'this glorious man'[35] gained by such activities was extra-ordinary even by contemporary standards. In 1873, ten years after he had moved to Southport, a statue was erected by mass subscription. It was unveiled in lonely splendour outside Bolton's huge new town hall, after a day on which most factories were closed, and a procession of 5,000, consisting of trade unions, friendly societies, Volunteers, the police and fire brigade, the mayor and corporation, plus 'a marvellous number of brass bands, paraded to the site'.[36] However, Chadwick's actual departure in 1863 had been quite as spectacular. He received a working men's testimonial, signed by 7,380, in the form of a specially commissioned portrait. He also attended afternoon service at the workhouse and distributed 'treats' to the inmates, who filed out gratefully intoning, 'I know that my redeemer liveth'.[37]

It is clear that the economic and social roles of urban political leadership were, given the nature of the nineteehth-century town, sources of consider-able political advantage. This situation was symbolised and probably enhanced by the character of the mayoralty. Indeed, nowhere were the style and values of urban squirearchy more evident or more persuasively legitimised. The mayor was a prominent figure in the nineteenth-century town, so much so indeed that Rochdale Council thought it worth decorating his mansion with 'two ornamental pillars', removing them 'to the residences of future mayors as they should be elected'.[38] Mayoral activities and rituals were invariably undertaken in a blaze of publicity, and they turned the incumbent into a sort of industrial super-squire. He was expected to be, and almost invariably was, a great and 'benevolent' employer, and a generous philanthropist — a man in whom 'the weak will always find a counsellor, and the poor a friend'.[39] He was expected to typify the virtues the elite wished to transmit to the rest of the population — industry, thrift and self-help. According to W. W. Cannon, inspecting Bolton's mayoral nominee in 1869, the ideal mayor 'should be a man of business abilities . . . of good moral character . . . undoubted social position . . . and . . . like a bishop, given to hospitality'.[40]

The open elite

The comparison, then, between urban and rural squirearchy is fairly close. Yet in one important respect urban leadership was different — a respect that has considerable implications for the character of municipal politics. What will be argued in this final section is that the municipal elites in Rochdale, Bolton and Salford — however great the advantages accruing from economic and social activities, and however restricted by minimum property qualifications — were recruited from a wider group than their rural counterparts.

The key to the situation lies in the open-ended nature of social leadership, and in the relationship between it and political leadership. It is true that political leaders were generally also social leaders — in that they had access to a formidable network of philanthropic and sociable activity, and that, partly as a result, they were objects of respectful attention from many more lowly citizens. Yet this did not mean that the ranks of either sort of leadership were restricted to those 'to the manner born' — i.e. to members of leading families whose wealth and standing were of two generations or more.

Those involved in political recruitment certainly drew on such men, and did so eagerly. This helps explain the presence in each town of a number of political families — several generations of whose members participated in local legislative life. In Salford there were the Armitages, no fewer than five of whom followed Sir Elkanah (the founder) into municipal politics. Their example was paralleled in varying degrees by the Cannons, Haslams and Arrowsmiths in Bolton, and by families like the Tweedales, Fishwicks, Brights and Heapes in Rochdale. For later members of such minor political dynasties, social position, like economic substance, was inherited. As a result, political recruitment was often both early and automatic.

However, the pool of such talent was limited and constantly thinned by rural migration. It was also lessened by the frequent reluctance of such people to contest an election, or to stay long even if elected.[41] In any case, the number of offices to be filled at any one time, particularly taking into account such lowly but important positions as those of overseer, etc., was sufficient to ensure that demand always far outstripped supply.

Thus local political leadership — though clearly drawn from a minority even of the electorate of Rochdale, Bolton and Salford — could never be restricted to a social caste. For reasons of both necessity and ideology, politics were open to the self-made, and the self-improved, man.

It is true that nineteenth-century individualism was markedly over-optimistic about the real prospects for individual mobility.[42] Indeed, this produced a certain wishful mistiness in the contemporary biographical material on which estimates of the openness of the elite must be based. Nevertheless there were a few men on every legislative body in these towns who seem quite genuinely to have been self-made — albeit with the help of appreciable good fortune. Sir Elkanah Armitage — the son of a Failsworth hand-loom weaver, and by 1860 the owner of four factories in the Pendleton district of Salford — was the most legendary example of the breed.[43] Yet there were others: like George Piggott, agent to the Earl of Bradford, Great Bolton trustee, Bolton councillor and Poor Law guardian, but apparently also 'the son of humble parents';[44] or Alderman William Stewart — a wealthy retired flannel manufacturer, at one time or another chief constable of Rochdale, mayor and vice-chairman of the board of guardians, yet who had come to the town in 1813 as a travelling draper.[45]

Such men shaded into a much larger group who were self-improved in that they had risen from a lower to a substantially higher economic position. They included the brothers John and Richard Harwood of Bolton. Sons of a Heaton farmer, they had commenced activity as a draper and a cabinetmaker respectively. By the 1860s they were involved in separate cotton spinning partnerships, and each became mayor of Bolton in the same decade. More spectacular perhaps was James Barlow, mayor of Bolton from 1867 to 1869. The son of a hand-loom weaver turned small weaving manufacturer, Barlow himself, after one failure, emerged as a quilt manufacturer in 1846 and by 1878 was part owner of five cotton mills employing 2,000 people.[46]

Here we begin to see something of the contrast between urban and rural leadership. Although in the foregoing cases municipal recruitment was still based upon economic substance and social standing, social position was not so much inherited as earned. The ranks of urban social leadership, and political leadership also, were as open as the economic network itself.

Yet municipal politics were not just open to those who had already climbed the economic and social ladder. Partly for ideological reasons, and partly because of the shortage of more elevated talent, they were also open to those who could be construed as in some sense on their way up. Thus the stated occupation of quite a number of individuals in all three towns changed in an upward direction during their municipal careers. Both Harwood brothers, for example, were recruited to the council whilst still apparently small proprietors.

If one could mix economic elevation with a political career, this was equally true of progress up the social scale. It was possible even for small proprietors to augment considerably their social visibility and position during, and as a result of, successful municipal careers. If, as before, we take participation in the philanthropic and sociable network as an indicator of social standing the point emerges clearly. For it is noticeable that, whilst the participation of many individuals had begun substantially before their entry into local politics, for a significant number the reverse was the case.

A snatch of Salford biography may help clarify the argument. William Lockett was a silk mercer who retired from business in 1831. He became a police commissioner in 1832, overseer in 1835, chairman of several important commissioners' committees from 1836, constable in 1837, guardian from 1840, boroughreeve in 1842 and finally Salford's first mayor in 1844. Yet Lockett's entry into the social sphere apparently did not come until 1838, when he had already held several important offices. In that year he figured as a 'Steward' organising the 'Coronation Dessert', and became a committee member of the Salford Library and Newsroom. From then on his patronage was altogether more in demand. In 1840 his name was prominent among those called together to decide Salford's celebration of the Queen's birthday. In 1843 he became a 'Patron' of the Salford and Pendleton Royal Dispensary and, by virtue of his position as boroughreeve, president of the Mechanics' Institute.

In these circumstances even men of relatively modest economic substance could rise to the top of the social and political ladder — doing so by political effort. We shall investigate the internal legislative implications of this in chapter 4. However, one indication of social elevation worth noting here is the way sociable and philanthropic activity among local legislators was always far more widespread than the ranks of legislative large proprietors. Another indication is the respect accorded small men who did succeed politically. In Salford Thomas Davies, a retired draper, was elected mayor for a record three years after an effective career as chairman of the sanitary committee. Richard Stockdale, a retired shopkeeper, became mayor of Bolton in 1865 amid doubts about his fitness for such high office. Yet when, a few months later, there were moves to form 'a gentlemen's club' the new mayor was included among the select fifty invited to the inaugural meeting.

None of this necessarily contradicts our earlier argument that social prominence was a source of political power. What can be said, however, is that it was almost as likely to be an adjunct to an on-going political career as it was to be a reason for the commencement of that career.

In fact this symbiotic relationship between social and political leadership pervaded municipal politics at all levels. Recruitment to every office —

including the mayoralty — was not just a recognition of social standing but in itself an act of social elevation. Often, too, it was a recognition that such elevation was warranted by political effort — whether within the legislature or outside (the award of an aldermanic seat in return for party services, for example). Indeed, the various positions in, or connected with, the council (aldermanic bench, mayoralty, borough magistracy) were often used to mark the successive stages of social elevation gained in this way. The fact was touchingly recognised by Councillor G. Wolstenholme when he refused Bolton's mayoralty because 'he thought himself not entitled to [the] honour'. Although happy to accept office in the future, 'he felt he did not at present hold a position fitting him to fill the position . . . he had been appointed borough magistrate and begged they would wait and see whether . . . he performed his duties . . . for the public good'.[47]

The fact that municipal recruitment and promotion were acts of social elevation was recognised in behaviour and ritual. The councils of Salford and Rochdale, though not of Bolton, both absolutely refused to countenance direct recruitment of prestigious outsiders to the aldermanic bench or mayoralty. Meanwhile, in all three towns, there was a strict ritual surrounding the process of recruitment. It was the inviolable norm that, however ambitious, one should never openly seek political office. This was 'a little too previous'.[48] Rather one settled down to await the 'unexpected' receipt of a large petition or respectable deputation begging one to stand. As one Broughton nomination meeting was reminded in 1853,

Gentlemen would decline to stand if they were waited upon by a person who simply said, 'Will you stand if I propose you? . . .' But the meeting would probably appoint a committee to wait upon those nominated, and the positive recommendation of so numerous and respectable a meeting would no doubt cause those selected to accede.[49]

In one sense this ritual emphasises the parallel between urban and rural squirearchy. For 'the duties and burdens' of urban local office were often undertaken with a strong sense of *noblesse oblige*. Yet such coyness also once more highlights the limits to the parallel. The ritual provided a crucial means of drawing attention to the act of social elevation that was taking place — to the fact that the stages of social elevation were being marked and confirmed by those whose opinions mattered. In their invariably well publicised acceptances of nomination, candidates time and again continued to stress that their initial reluctance had been overcome only by the entreaties of 'numerous and influential deputations', 'influentially signed requisitions' or, as in Rochdale in 1875, a petition 'signed by over one hundred influential and large ratepayers'.[50] One sitting councillor, initially intent on private life, noted that he had changed his mind after being 'pressed by his friends' and 'spoken to by people who he thought were not his friends'.[51] Even a reluctant mayor could declare himself moved 'when he was waited upon at his house by such a deputation from the council, and heard their arguments, and read the address with its long list of names attached'.[52]

Perhaps the ultimate sign of the way in which these elites were open, compared with their rural counterparts, can be found in a funeral. It also seems an appropriate point to conclude a chapter on urban leaders, because the deaths of such men summarise so much of what we have been saying about their power in life.

Local leaders died with enormous panache. The final exit of those who had reached the very top was often accompanied by the closing of shops and factories. Large crowds turned out and, as on other similar though less tragic occasions, many of the still extant leaders took the opportunity to put themselves on show. The funeral procession in which they took part would meander imposingly around the town before reluctantly depositing its burden in the graveyard.

Given the significance of such occasions, it is doubly indicative that the greatest funeral of the whole period in any of the three towns should have been that of Thomas Livsey in Rochdale in 1863. Livsey, a small manufacturer for a while, and then railway company agent, was the son of a blacksmith. He was a lifelong Chartist, with an enormous hold upon Rochdale's working classes. During a twenty-year political career he held nearly every major office in the town, and was an immensely influential figure, politically and socially. When he died the *Rochdale Observer* appeared, for the first time, with black borders, and his funeral procession was attended by the mayor, the entire council, many corporation officers, and the board of guardians — along with an estimated 40,000 people.[53] There could be no greater tribute to the rewards that might await men of modest economic endowment but great political energy.

Notes

1 The possibly generous estimate of those championing the £30 qualification. Opponents estimated it still more modestly. See respectively Mr Barton, *RO*, 10 May 1856, p. 3, and Thomas Livsey, *RO*, 27 April 1856, p. 3.

2 Thomas Livsey, championing £15, *ibid*.

3 This, moreover, on a burgesses roll thought to be artifically low.

4 For an attempt to do so see W. Rubinstein, *Men of Property: the Very Wealthy in Britain since the Industrial Revolution* (London, 1981). Also relevant is V. A. C. Gattrell, 'Labour, power and the size of firms in the Lancashire cotton industry', *Economic History Review*, vol. 30, No. 1, February 1977.

5 *SWN*, 10 December 1864, p. 3.

6 Sir Elkanah, constable 1835, boroughreeve 1837 and later mayor of Manchester; Elkanah, councillor 1855-59; Samuel, councillor 1858-62; Elkanah junior, councillor 1866-69; V. K. Armitage, councillor 1871-7; Benjamin, councillor 1875-81.

7 Calculated as a triennial average of those elected.

8 See, for example, *BC*, 5 November 1859, p. 5.

9 See chapter 4.

10 *BC*, 1 August 1863.

11 This includes several (hat manufacturers, dyers, etc) whose operations were probably on a relatively modest scale. However, in terms of both capital and employees they were altogether more substantial than those of most shopkeepers, for example.

12 *RO*, 12 June 1869.

13 See *BC*, 28 August 1838, p. 1.

14 See *SR*, 9 August 1862, p. 3.

15 For its prevalence elsewhere see Hennock, *op. cit.*, p. 308.

16 William Bamber, *BWJ*, 18 October 1873, p. 7.

17 Councillor Wood, *BC*, 21 October 1876, p. 2.

18 *SWN*, 16 July 1864, p. 4.

19 Thomas Agnew on William Jenkinson, *MG*, 10 November 1847, p. 6.

20 *MG*, 14 January 1843, p. 2.

21 William Jenkinson, *SWN*, 9 November 1867, p. 3.

22 Letter from 'H', *SWN*, 31 October 1863, p. 3.

23 John Howe, *RO*, 17 August 1867, p. 5.

24 *MG*, 25 October 1848, p. 6.

25 For a sensitive if long-winded expansion of these points and their political consequences see Joyce, *op. cit.* As will become evident, I feel Joyce's picture of factory-owning 'power' to be somewhat overpainted.

26 Peter Johnson, letter, *RO*, 10 May 1856, supplement.

27 See exchange between Messrs Snape and Frankenburg, *SR*, 19 December 1891, p. 4.

28 *BC*, 20 September 1873, p. 3.

29 *RO*, 5 September 1869, p. 4 ff.

30 *BC*, 30 June 1838, pp. 2-3.

31 James Richardson, *SR*, 1 September 1900, p. 5.

32 *BC*, 30 June 1838, p. 3.

33 *RO*, 1 March 1862, p. 5.

34 *BC*, 30 June 1860, p. 5.

35 Letter, *BC*, 4 January 1868, p. 5.

36 *BC*, 2 August 1873, pp. 5 and 8.

37 *BC*, 9 May 1863, p. 5.

38 *RO*, 3 December 1859, p. 3.

39 Working men's address to T. B. Willans on his becoming mayor, *RO*, 24 December 1869, p. 7.

40 *BC*, 13 November 1869, p. 7.

41 See chapter 4.

42 For an estimate see J. H. Fox, in S. P. Bell (ed.), *Victorian Lancashire* (Newton Abbot, 1974).

43 See J. A. Garrard, *Leaders and Politics in nineteenth Century Salford* (Salford,

1976), p. 45; also obituary, *SR*, 2 December 1876, p. 3.

44 *BC*, 23 February 1867, p. 5.

45 *RO*, 24 September 1870, p. 5.

46 *BWJ*, 1 June 1878, p. 4.

47 *BC*, 16 November 1850, p. 5.

48 Letter, *SR*, 26 September 1896, p. 5.

49 James Lofthouse, *MG*, 26 October 1853, p. 6.

50 Robert Clough, *RO*, 23 October 1875, p. 1.

51 Councillor Bromley, *BC*, 21 October 1871, p. 7.

52 Alex Ross, *MG*, 11 November 1854, p. 9. For an analysis of the wider national significance of these emotions see J. A. Garrard in Garrard Jary, Goldsmith and Oldfield (eds.), *The Middle Class in Politics* (London, 1978).

53 *RO*, 30 January, 6 February 1864.

3

The power of municipal leadership

Chapter 2 suggested that economic weight and social prominence were an important advantage in the processes of political recruitment and legitimation. We now need to look at power in the wider policy-making sense. The chapters that follow will place considerable emphasis upon the limitations on power. In the interests of balance, it therefore appears sensible here to highlight the areas wherein local political elites seem to have been undisputedly powerful.

As implied in chapter 1, two of the book's most central issues are: (1) the power of elective leadership and the extent to which it stemmed from the accumulation of social and economic resources; (2) the power of the leading economic groups from which the largest section of municipal leadership was drawn. Here we shall be concerned with both issues. It will become evident that, in many fields, nineteenth-century urban political elites could successfully look after their own interests, and also do things conceived to be in the interests of others (or at least good for them) on their own initiative rather than in response to pressure from the beneficiaries. This stemmed not merely from advantages gained through political conflict and decision but also from advantages in less conflictual, less conventionally political and less observable areas.

Decisions

We can start with some pointers forward. Chapters 6-11 will show that, however extensive public involvement was in some issues, there were others where councils could initiate, and carry out, their policies without the participation of those most intimately affected. Sanitation is an obvious example. There was effective intervention from groups like the Manchester and Salford Sanitary Association and, on the other side, property owners.

There was none from the thousands displaced by the closure of unfit dwellings. These were 'the residuum': they were not politically mobilised, and their participation was not regarded as legitimate. In 1874 the editor of the *Rochdale Observer*, himself a councillor in a Liberal elite that prided itself on its democratic principles, suggested that cellar dwellers were there by choice and not by virtue of poverty. Thus 'their objections need not be considered for another hour'.[1] Such overt brutality was rare, and, as we shall see, all three councils often moved with caution in such matters. Yet, even where such hesitancy stemmed from more sympathetic views of the plight of slum dwellers, those views resulted from philanthropic concern rather than from fear of the political penalties that such victims might exact.

What was true of particular issues was also true over time. While there were some periods where municipal leadership was subject to intense outside pressure, there were others where their deliberations were altogether less disturbed. Moreover, while leadership was often paralysed by internal conflict, a really determined and united local elite, using all the political resources that stemmed from its social and economic position, could operate with impressive power. This will become evident when we examine Salford's incorporation battle between 1842 and 1844, and Bolton's municipalisation of the water supply in 1850.

If powerful actions are observable from elective leaders, we can see similar trends emerging from conflicts and decisions involving the well-padded socio-economic groups from which those leaders were primarily drawn. Chapter 5 will show that councils experienced greatest difficulty in their dealings with the world beyond town boundaries. Yet it must be admitted that, though relative socio-economic weight was only one of a number of variables determining the outcome of such conflict, the most successful opposition often came from large landowners, railway companies and substantial manufacturers. Moreover, where such dealings involved attempts at boundary expansion, areas with far smaller and richer populations than the existing municipality were offered considerable advantages as inducements to entry. For example, in 1853 the relatively well-heeled inhabitants of Pendleton and Broughton were seduced into incorporation only by the promise of a combined council representation equal to that enjoyed by the far more numerous population of Salford. They were also guaranteed that individual townships should generally only pay for the remedy of problems within their own borders. Normally they were not obliged to contribute towards projects or problem-solving elsewhere in the town — however much wealthy suburbanites might use townwide facilities, and however justifiably problems might be argued to have been generated by the economic activities of businessmen living in the 'out-townships'. Although its impact steadily lessened, the 1853 agreement long continued to influence council operations,[2] and gave an inbuilt, albeit negative, advantage to the wealthy outer fringes of the town.

Subject to important qualifications to be drawn out later, similar points can be made about the broad general policies followed by the councils of Rochdale, Bolton and Salford. Though normally justified in terms of wider community benefit, most major decisions could be interpreted as being in (and were certainly never against) the interests of manufacturing and mercantile men. Municipalisation, for example, increased the efficiency of major services like gas and water, and thus ultimately reduced the marginal costs of manufacturing. Urban improvement was a crucial part of municipal activity. Yet, in Rochdale and Bolton as elsewhere,[3] it was quite as likely to take the form of building opulent town halls (projects dear to the heart of businessmen interested in prestige and trade) as of transforming the slums or cleansing the river.

None of this is surprising. As chapter 2 showed, it was not an age which calculated the merits of men and issues solely in terms of the 'mere numbers' supporting them. Although outside pressure might come, as we shall see, from a variety of sources, there are indications that for many local legislators it was worthy of serious consideration only if sanctioned by men of substance and standing. Certainly contemporaries often behaved as if this were so. For example, when there was pressure for a recreation ground in Bolton in 1863 its council proponents drew attention to the weight and prestige of those heading the petition in its favour in a way that suggested that this might crucially sway the minds of significant numbers of their colleagues.[4] Meanwhile the absence of such support was, for some, positively damning. When, one month earlier, a petition for a similar project had been received by the same council, signed only by vicars, 'tradesmen and workpeople', one councillor scathingly suggested that someone 'had better read the names. I don't think they have much responsibility attached to them.'[5]

Even if wealthy men outside the local legislature did not volunteer their opinions, their views were actively sought prior to the taking of at least some important decisions. When in 1850 Bolton's council was considering a change in the proposed site for the new market, one member explained that the new proposals had been 'shown to many influential and very heavy rate-payers . . . who consider them better'.[6] As we shall see, similar procedures were followed at crucial stages in the building of Bolton's town hall.[7] Of the three towns Bolton was probably the most instinctively hierarchical. Yet even in Rochdale's much more radical environment it was possible to find Thomas Livsey, the town's moderate Chartist chief constable, asking a parish meeting in 1852 to postpone consideration of the site for a new cemetery 'to give the churchwardens . . . the chance of consulting the wealthy and influential rate-payers . . . .'[8]

Lacing municipal discussion in all three towns are constant references to 'men of influence and standing'. If a political scientist were let loose in any of them, armed only with reputational methods of locating influence, he would probably produce a picture of a small and wealthy group exercising autonomous and exclusive power. This, as we shall see later, would be grossly over-painted. Yet we must note that such phrases referred to areas beyond decisions, conflicts and even conventional politics. They draw attention to wider aspects of power that we must now consider.

Non-decisions

One of the main charges elitist political analysts level at their pluralist counterparts is that their concern with issues and decisions cooks the books in their own favour. If one concentrates purely upon conflict, then, almost by definition, one arrives at pluralist conclusions — if only because one is studying areas wherein rival interests become mobilised, and where negotiation is therefore likely. Elitists urge the need to examine those areas where conflict does not take place, where problems do not become issues and where decisions are not taken, but where power is nevertheless exerted. There is no political activity in the senses defined above, precisely because some individual or group is controlling the political agenda, exercising an explicit or implicit veto over the development of political issues. This might be done by the occupancy of key positions within the political process (such as a committee chairmanship), or less directly by what one champion of the thesis has called 'a reputation for power'.[9] In the latter case, the fortunate holder of such a reputation may never need to enter the political arena at all. He is believed to possess such power that causes likely to evoke his opposition are simply not taken up in anticipation of failure.

More significant still for elitist analysts is the possibility of groups controlling the political agenda by heavily influencing the whole intellectual framework in which political debate takes place — exercising ideological hegemony such that disadvantaged groups never see themselves as having grievances, or fail to recognise their problems as fit matters for political discussion or governmental remedy. They are therefore never mobilised. In these and other ways power is exerted, interests are safeguarded and benefit is derived by those in control of the system — and it is all achieved without conflict or identifiable governmental decisions.

Pluralists have countered by arguing that the concept of 'non-decisions' is useless for analytic purposes because it is untestable. One can never know whether they are present precisely because there is no measurable activity. It is also difficult to establish whether those who benefit from the system do so intentionally (and thus as a result of some clear exertion of power) or inadvertently in a situation where power is arguably not involved. Moreover, it is suggested, the concept places its champions in an intellectually arrogant position — imputing interests which people do not recognise themselves as having. Finally, it is sometimes argued, non-decisions are an unnecessary tool of analysis, pluralist methods being perfectly adequate for the discovery of power centres in capitalist society however well hidden.[10]

These objections, though often overstated, clearly raise acute problems for anyone using the non-decision concept for analytic purposes. Some of the methodological ones are probably insoluble, and particularly so for the urban historian. The participants are dead, and cannot be interviewed even had they been willing to speak. The possibility of historical anachronism makes the task of allotting people interests that they did not recognise at the time even more hazardous than usual — and the problems are not really solved by the historian's unique ability to know whether or not disadvantaged groups did recognise such interests at a later stage. Moreover the problem of testing phenomena so essentially discreet and inactive as non-decisions is peculiarly acute in a situation where (as is so often the case in local, as distinct from national, history) nearly all the available sources are public, and geared to the recording of processes that are public, active and visible. Local newspapers seem *prima facie* to be unlikely places in which to discover private, non-political inactivity.

Some of the difficulties will be raised in a more detailed way towards the end of this chapter and in later ones. Nevertheless, however great the problems, it is difficult to feel that any picture of power in a nineteenth-century industrial town can be complete without some idea like non-decisions. Even if one believes them ultimately untestable (and perhaps because one does), the possibilities thus revealed need, at the very least, to be borne in mind amid the long-winded public noises emitted by Victorians engaged in local political conflict. In fact the case can be made more strongly. The concept of non-decisions draws attention, as we shall now argue, to certain key features of nineteenth-century industrial and urban life and politics.

Political routines

It alerts us firstly to the extent to which local legislatures served the interests of men of property and substance, not merely by the great decisions outlined above but also by what Geraint Parry and Peter Morris[11] have called routines and routine administration, and furthermore by simply not doing, not enforcing and leaving well alone. Though the room for important initiative was far greater in the nineteenth than it is in the twentieth century, routine administration still represented a large chunk of local government work. It is difficult not to see this as being involved to some degree in 'system maintenance', or at least in the perpetuation of situations of advantage. The day-to-day functioning of the New Poor Law — even given the relatively relaxed way in which boards of guardians came to operate in the north — nevertheless fulfilled some of the social control functions envisaged by its originators. Though the workhouse test was never really applied in the three towns,[12] the Poor Law probably retained enough 'less eligibility', in Bolton and Salford at least, to induce a desperate sort of self-help among the respectable poor, whilst supplying sufficient aid to the 'undeserving' to prevent resort to violence.[13] Meanwhile, though some of its sense of purpose may have been blunted by the pluralistic pressures with which it was sometimes faced,[14] the local bench of magistrates was also arguably engaged in the business of social control. Certainly it provided its wealthy incumbents with opportunities to attempt to suppress some of the social (and political) trends among the lower orders of which they disapproved — vagrancy, intemperance, immorality and offences against property, etc.

However, local government routines also helped perpetuate the advantages of those near the top of the socio-economic scale in more prosaic ways. Rates were (and are) a regressive form of taxation. Moreover, as a tax on the rental value of property, they bore most heavily on those (normally relatively small men) whose income was derived primarily from this source[15] rather than upon the great factory owners. The administration of utilities, even after municipalisation, also tended to work to the advantage of the better-off. In all three towns water, and particularly gas, were supplied at markedly higher discounts to large than to small consumers. For example, in Rochdale in 1865 those consuming more than 800,000 cubic feet of gas per annum were offered a fivepenny discount (on a basic price of four shillings) per thousand cubic feet. This compared with a penny discount for those consuming between five and ten thousand cubic feet per annum, and no discount at all to the smallest consumers.[16] Furthermore, in Bolton and Salford (though, significantly, not in Rochdale) gas was far more likely to be supplied to the houses and commercial premises of the wealthy and relatively wealthy than to those of the poor.

Meanwhile there were also important fields of municipal responsibility where, though a problem was recognised, no action was taken — regulations not being produced, not being enforced or deliberately being framed so loosely as to be unenforceable. Moreover this torpor probably existed at least partly because factory-owning councillors were regulating their own kind, or because of 'the reputation for power' possessed by important groups or individuals outside the council.

We shall see in chapter 5 that, in their dealings with areas beyond municipal boundaries, councils often failed to follow preferred paths because they anticipated formidable opposition from large factory owners and landowners. Such individuals often had no need to move overtly. It was enough simply to be in the way of some proposed municipal project, and thought likely to mount parliamentary opposition, for their interests to be anticipated by inaction.

Power of a similarly inactive and reputational sort is also evident within borough boundaries. Generally, for example, the activities of large proprietors were less closely regulated than those of smaller men. Admittedly factories, mines and railways came less under the purview of local (and more under that of national) government than those of builders and the like. The difference was also always one of degree rather than kind. Nevertheless it was marked, and one of the factors involved was again the formidable 'reputation for power' possessed by manufacturing men.

By the end of our period all three councils had taken detailed powers over the building and drainage of new houses and were setting minimum standards for old ones. Often they were not enforced. Nevertheless they became steadily more detailed, enforcement was at least intermittent, and non-enforcement against 'the Ishmaels of social life' (as one paper significantly called slum builders) was often regarded as execrable.

Restriction of the anti-social side of industrial activity, on the other hand, was even less rigorous, less legitimate and less optimistic of success. This was particularly evident in Bolton,[17] but all three towns show a similar trend. Regulations over the tipping of noxious waste into the rivers (mainly an industrial sin) were never enforced. Even where sewage rather than industrial effluent was involved, schemes for alleviation often faltered because of anticipated opposition from 'parties interested in the waters'[18] for industrial purposes. Attempts to curb smoke pollution were even more half-hearted. They rarely went beyond regulating the size of new chimneys. Clauses regulating their emissions were merely pious declarations of desirable virtue. Fines were tiny, and enforcement was always based on 'co-operation'. Discussions of non-enforcement tended to degenerate into giggling comparison of polluting sins between factory-owning councillors. Many factors were involved in such weak-kneed behaviour, but one was certainly the (largely implicit) threat by manufacturers to move their operations to less regulated climes beyond borough borders. The fears induced are suggested by Salford council's advice to its health committee about a recent infringement:

while they desire that . . . manufacturers should conduct their works so as to cause the least . . . annoyance . . . yet looking at the importance of manufacturing to . . . this borough, this council desires that it may be only after the most mature . . . consideration that anything should be done . . . to cause the removal of important manufactures . . . [19]

Some of this argument about local government routines and inaction cuts two ways. It certainly provides evidence of the power of those at the top of the socio-economic scale. Yet where a genuine municipal wish for action was frustrated by outside opposition it also shows the severe limitations upon the power of local legislators, however well endowed with political resources.[20]

The political agenda

However, the concept of non-decisions also alerts us to a second inactive form of power, this time at the disposal of local legislators themselves: the possibility that the agenda of local institutional politics might have been controlled or manipulated by individuals in strategic positions, either in those institutions or influencing access to them. Corporation committees, and particularly their chairmen, represent one point where issues could be prevented from coming to a decision or even debate. We know that committees, because of their specialist character, were important centres of power whose deliberations (or lack of them) were only occasionally success- fully challenged by the council as a whole.[21] Chairmen could often, though did not always, become very powerful. However, it is difficult to get beyond these generalities because of shortage of evidence. Perhaps significantly, despite pressure to publicise their proceedings, committee deliberations remained largely hidden from view.

A more examinable point for possible control over the political agenda is to be found in the electoral process — or rather at the points of candidate selection. Nineteenth-century local elections seem particularly worth investigation, since, unlike the situation since 1945, the number of contests was often limited. From incorporation up to 1880 the average proportion of council wards contested in Salford, Rochdale and Bolton was 61, 39 and 39 per cent respectively. The boards of guardians and, even more, the school boards could be similarly non-conflictual. Such quiescence generally resulted from compromises arranged between the potential contenders on the ostensible justification of 'saving the ratepayers the expense of a contest'. Sometimes underlying such excuses was an identifiable intention to curb public discussion of issues regarded as dangerously exciting, and to keep such discussion within the legislative circle. We get a hint of this from the oft- repeated justification for compromise in terms of a wish 'to obviate the bad feeling and excitement which a contest is sure to engender'.[22] Sometimes compromise resulted from a desire by those already elected to control recruitment to the elite, to ensure themselves a quiet life or to ensure that legislative issues were not 'distorted by public and party controversy'.

Nowhere are these motivations clearer than in the determined attempts from the 1870s onwards to prevent contests in school board elections. In 1870, very typically, a group of Rochdale's leading men, drawn from all parties and religious persuasions, attempted to draw up an agreed and uncontested list of candidates. One of the group, himself a councillor, explained that they wished to prevent educational questions being 'agitated'. This was bad for the town, and anyway the board's work needed to be done by 'men . . . who all saw precisely alike'.[23] A second councillor explained why clergymen and teachers had been omitted from the list: they would want to talk about religious ideas and educational theories, and would never get anything done. It was therefore 'a wise decision to take out . . . from the school board anything of a debatable character'.[24]

Bolton's new education board was the subject of a similarly motivated attempt in the same year. Although more charitable towards the political claims of clergymen (the nominators included them), this move by 'the best men of all parties and creeds' represented 'an expression of opinion that the election of a school board was a matter which they might arrange in a spirit of forbearance . . . without the revival of controversies'.[25] Overall, as was explained after a similar attempt at compromise in 1879, the trouble was that education boards tended 'to keep the educational questions in a continuous state of unwholesome ferment amongst us'.[26]

The motives for such contest-avoidance are rarely so clearly identifiable and, as we shall see towards the end of this chapter, they often seem not to have been directly connected with agenda control at all. Nevertheless, whether intended or not, the result of such compromises was often seriously to curtail public discussion of issues, and electoral choice between alternatives — and thus to lend greater autonomy to the deliberations of the political elite.

Extra-political power

The third and most important thing the non-decisions concept helps focus attention on is the crucial fact that in the nineteenth-century, even more than in the twentieth, power has to be understood in much more than political terms. The economic and social roles of the local political elites that we reviewed in chapter 2 were not just sources of political power; that is to say, they did not just produce clout in political institutions. They also represented potential areas, in their own right, for the exercise of power.

This is so in at least three interconnected senses. First, the formidable charitable network, in which so many of the elite were influential participants, represented an area in which decisions could be taken that affected intimately the everyday lives of large numbers of people. Most important — particularly given the number of philanthropic institutions concerned with the relief of poverty — was the ability to give or withhold benefit. In a situation where there were likely to be few detailed rules about how aid was to be given, and to whom, there was considerable room for discretion, even caprice.

Second, the extra-political roles of members of local political elites, and of the classes from which they were drawn, provided an important potential basis for the exercise of social control. From the evidence in chapter 2 it seems that the relationship between factory employer and workforce was often, particularly by mid-century, one of paternalistic dependency. Moreover the possibilities of influencing conduct and attitudes thus offered may well have extended to the entire family, owing to the widespread employment of women and children in the textile industry.[27]

Similar opportunities for mass influence also existed in the social and philanthropic sphere — especially when so many employers reinforced their paternalistic image by involvement in such activities. In the autonomous atmosphere of the nineteenth-century industrial town, the giving of charity induced dependency of a highly personalised kind. Moreover the potential for inducing not merely social deference but desired attitudes of a broader kind was particularly strong because 'the gift', being discretionary, could be withheld. Finally, such possibilities were strengthened still further by the sheer range of the field. A survey of the social and philanthropic activity of local elites in any of the three towns shows that it included, among other things, poverty relief, aid to the sick and handicapped, Sunday and ragged schooling, adult education, leisure, temperance and thrift inducement. Men of property and standing were often eagerly sought, too, as patrons of building societies, working men's clubs and even co-ops.

Meanwhile, if these economic and social roles provided a strong basis for influencing mass conduct and attitudes, there is clear evidence in Rochdale, Bolton and Salford (as elsewhere) that members of the local elites saw, and strongly desired to use, them in this way. Sometimes the desire amounted merely to expressions of pious hope about the benevolent social consequences of philanthropic effort. Frequently, on the other hand, there were deliberate efforts at the transmission of values. Sometimes it was merely hoped to make the working classes nicer and more civilised; yet such aspirations shaded imperceptibly into concerns about values whose spread was seen as crucial to social stability.

At the level of pious hope are the *Bolton Chronicle*'s comments in 1866 on the beneficial effects of the town's new park:

The deplorable want of courtesy . . . amongst the working classes . . . arises chiefly from the want of rational pleasures . . . it is a . . . fact that the lower orders when assembled in large bodies, intermingling with a sprinkling of betters are much more courteous than at any other time . . . It is in sociality . . . that politeness can be found.[28]

More ambitious about what was the masses might learn from such institutions was the paper's attempt to persuade recalcitrant members of the upper classes to subscribe to the projected public baths: 'Nothing could . . . more . . . destroy that rancorous jealousy which at times shows itself in threatening aspects amongst the working classes than a spirit . . . of care for their well-being on the part of their masters.'[29] Celebratory factory dinners might provide opportunities for heavier persuasion. After one such jamboree at Messrs Barlow Goddy & Jones in 1852 in Bolton, 'that distinguished and able advocate of teetotalism, Edward Grubb, Esq., delivered a most appropriate . . . address occupying three quarters of an hour to the workpeople'. Suitably instructed, the latter 'were allowed to indulge in the recreations [of] their tastes . . .'.[30] Attempts to 'dry out' working people can also be found in Rochdale, where in 1846 Messrs John Bright & Bros held a tea meeting under the patronage of the Total Abstinence Society.[31]

Evidence of a self-confidence leading to even harder selling with wider ambitions appears in the *Bolton Chronicle*'s criticism of leading Conservatives for not patronising the Mechanics' Institute. In answer to excuses that it was dominated by radicals and Chartists, the paper commented, 'even be this so, the Conservatives are rich . . . and powerful enough to rectify the evil . . . If the people are misled; if they are supplied with . . . mischievous exhibitions instead of more solid mental food, does not the guilt reside [with] . . . those who have the power but will not intervene?'[32]

Equally ambitious expectations are displayed in the stated aims of Luke Boardman's Ragged School as announced to potential patrons in 1858: 'by habits of cleanliness and the supply of plain suitable clothes, as well as by constant industry, moral training and religious instruction, the committee endeavour to foster habits of order, cleanliness, industry and self-respect'. In the long term the committee hoped that, as the result of its efforts, 'our churches, chapels and schools may be filled, and our prisons and workhouses empty; that peace, harmony, love and concord may reign amongst us; that we may be able to pass through our streets without insult, injury or robbery'.[33]

Such hopes and fears will be familiar enough to anyone who has looked at the growing literature on social control.[34] There seem indeed to have been

few institutions or activities in the Victorian industrial town which do not
have the transmission of appropriate values as part of their intended or hoped-
for function. The role of social control in philanthropy was generally
accepted; disagreements tended to centre upon the utility, or otherwise, of
given institutions for these purposes. Thus the Sunday opening of reading
rooms might be championed as a means of keeping working men away from
the pubs and in 'a much better state of mind . . . to enjoy the religious
services of the evening', or attacked because library attendance would 'keep
them out of church'.[35]

Even political institutions were seen to have functions in this area of extra-
political power. We have already noted it to be the case with boards of
guardians. Moreover, as I have argued elsewhere,[36] urban parties were not
just political bodies: their activities, particularly after 1867, extended far
beyond propaganda. They attempted to touch a much wider part of their
members' lives through an impressive network of clubs, lectures, galas,
excursions and even friendly society activities. The aim was the production of
'political fitness' in its widest sense. Local parties were concerned to ensure
that those admitted to the national political system after 1867 were rational
and well informed — and, equally important, that they accepted the social
and economic *status quo*.

As with the other institutions examined here, ambitions varied. Sometimes
local party leaders were concerned simply to secure civilised behaviour. Thus
political clubs were believed to have 'a refining influence on the manners of
the members because the discipline of life is always best taught in crowds'.[37]
J. L. Barrett hoped that the Pendleton Constitutional Club facilities would
enable members to 'spend a comfortable evening, and afterwards go home,
and enjoy the company of their wives and sweethearts . . . what they learned
at that club would have the effect of making young men good husbands in the
future'.[38] As this suggests, party leaders often saw political clubs as 'places
where you shall improve yourselves'.[39] Among other things this meant
intellectual improvement, because it was impossible that 'men possessing a
great amount of political power could be too well-informed'.[40] Clubs were
urged 'to do all they could to improve the mental tone of the people at the
bottom of the social order'.[41] It also meant the promotion of self-help,
sobriety and thrift. Club members were regularly lectured about the self-
helping virtues of great men. They also heard rather frequently about the
national drunkenness statistics from local leaders who predicted:

By such institutions . . . with the means [they] afforded for improvement and rational
amusement, by keeping young men from the public house, and teaching them to
respect themselves, to put their money into their own pockets instead of those of the
publicans, they would accomplish a very great good.[42]

Meanwhile, for some at least, such concerns stemmed directly from more general worries about the social order — worries that led one wealthy Conservative to proclaim that 'the object of the [Salford] Constitutional Association was to prevent the lower classes combining with the rough class, and governing those above'.[43]

How successful all these attempts at value transmission were is open to doubt on grounds that we shall review in the final section of this chapter. However, it is clear from what has been said that the intention was there, and the potential for social influence was extensive. Moreover, if at all successful, such activities must be seen as providing local elites with important channels for the exercise of power over conduct and attitudes, and through these over the political agenda. For if they did help induce large numbers of working people to take an individualist view of their lives and problems, then their organisers clearly had the ability to prevent certain problems from becoming political issues at all — by making them seem inappropriate for governmental remedy.

Private politics

Before examining the problems involved in such generalisations, we can note a third and more measurable way in which the social and philanthropic network provided local political elites, and others of their class, with channels for the achievement of intended effects. In nineteenth-century towns there was a form of private philanthropic politics that could be utilised when normal public institutional channels were blocked — either because of irreconcilable and paralysing conflict, or because a particular project seemed inappropriate for governmental action. As we shall now see, private politics depended upon the highly visible arena provided by the nineteenth-century town.

Though the process varied over time and according to issue, certain basic elements were almost always present. A few wealthy and prestigious individuals, interested in some project like a park, library or baths, would ask the mayor to call a public or semi-public meeting of 'friends of the undertaking'. This appointed a large committee of notables, and set going a subscription list led by high contributions (normally ostentatiously donated at the meeting itself) from the mayor, MPs and other top persons. Then would begin a process of persuasion on other members of the local elite and those immediately below. This sought to exploit pressures towards social conformity, and the widespread wish to demonstrate generosity to those below, in the interests of social peace. It also exploited the desire for public inclusion among the town's men of standing — or at least to bask in their reflected light. Thus the committee would start 'a canvass of the town'. As soon as the subscription list seemed long and prestigious enough to start a bandwagon effect, it would be published (with names and amounts) on the front pages of the local newspapers — hopefully growing longer week by week. With luck, these pressures were reinforced by the local press itself, not just by publicity but also through editorial comments that 'It is a subject of much conversation . . . that the names of several gentlemen of station and wealth . . . are still absent from the . . . subscribers'.[44] With a large project of obvious benefit to the poor, attempts were often made to involve the whole community. Early in the period factory owners or foremen might be persuaded to canvass 'their workpeople'. Later trade unions and friendly societies were invited to fulfil the same role. Either way, the frequent inducement was that 'the more earnest . . . the industrious populations show themselves . . . the greater will be the . . . encouragement from the opulent'.[45] Here, too, lists of 'contributions from working men' were published in the press. The names were exhibited on a works basis, often with the name of their employer — presumably exploiting the sense of dependence and competitive *esprit de corps* that often seems to have characterised factories in towns like Bolton, Rochdale and Salford.[46] If successful, the process often ended with an opening ceremony, preceded by a 'grand procession' of the town's elite, trade unions, friendly societies and massed bands — a great ritual affirmation of the exercise in communal consensus that had just been concluded.

Private philanthropic politics were common in all three towns. Mechanics' institutes, parks, libraries, public baths, ragged schools, infirmaries and infirmary extensions were often started by these means, or some variation of them.

The process was sometimes embarked upon when public institutional channels were blocked. Here it becomes evident that members of the elite were able to use not merely social but also economic channels to achieve their ends. For example, in Bolton in 1836 there was extensive Liberal dissatisfaction with the service provided by the Great Bolton Gas Company. The Great Bolton trustees (the local authority) were a closed corporation and, like the company, Tory-dominated. They were therefore unsympathetic to taking the company over. The Little Bolton trustees were Liberal-dominated and more open, but prevented both by the time available and by their terms of incorporation from applying to Parliament for power to supply gas on their own account. Liberal manufacturers in Little Bolton therefore attempted, via a well orchestrated public meeting, to establish a rival gas company for the township in the hope that the Little Bolton trustees could eventually take it over.[47]

As this suggests, politics quite often moved from public into private channels, and then back again — the resort to private politics sometimes being used to pressurise the public sector. This probably happened in Bolton in the early 1840s. Several attempts to form a private water company seem to have been prompted by the desire of the Liberal section of the elite to persuade the existing company to lower its rates. They were also probably part of a successful longer-term campaign to persuade the old company to consent to municipalisation.[48] This style of politics came naturally in towns presided over by leaderships combining political, social and economic prominence.

The resort to philanthropic politics was actively encouraged by some national enabling legislation. The council could organise a poll or public meeting to authorise the collection of a limited rate for a project like a park or library. However, the remaining money had to come from private sources. Bolton's Library and Museum was started in this way in 1852 — and it may illustrate some of the points made here if we briefly tell the story.

In February the corporation adopted the Museums and Libraries Act. A subsequent poll authorised a halfpenny rate, realising £250. With the enthusiastic support of the local press, the new Museum and Library Committee called a meeting of sympathetic notables, inside and outside the council, to organise an appeal for subscriptions. This, in turn, decided that the mayor and Robert Heywood (probably Bolton's wealthiest social and political leader) 'should wait upon parties assessed to the rates [at] more than £500 per annum', whilst two slightly less celebrated figures should 'call on those assessed at £200 to £500'.[49] By November such ritualised arm-twisting had produced £800, and the mayor called a public meeting. Here two hours of prestigious oratory set going a public subscription. From December onwards two growing lists of contributors appeared in the *Bolton Chronicle* — one marshalled by the Museum and Library Committee, the other consisting of works contributions organised by an 'operative committee' appointed at a separate working men's meeting. The library was opened in October 1853.

Before the final section of this chapter a few words of summary may be helpful. It seems obvious that, if only because of the influence of *laissez-faire*, the sphere of governmental politics, which will be analysed from chapter 4 onwards, was much more circumscribed in the nineteenth than in the twentieth-century town. The 'non-political' or private political sphere was very important, and municipal elites (along with other members of the class from which they were primarily drawn) had disproportionate access to it. More generally, in both the political and social aspects of non-decisions, we come across important areas where these elites seemed largely able to get their way — precisely because they could call upon resources of economic and social, as well as political, leadership.

Some qualifications

This said, we need to add some final notes of caution and qualification. For in the sphere of discreet and private politics — just as in that of public politics (as we shall see later) — the configuration of power was more complex than the simple picture painted so far.

First, however much the important decisions of the local legislatures might be construed as operating in the interests of the great proprietors (as was suggested at the beginning of the chapter), they were rarely seen in that way by all members of this group. In fact, as will become evident in chapters 6-11, local decisions, great and small, were often the subject of intense conflict, embracing members of the socio-economic elite as much as other groups. This was one factor obliging local politicians to appeal for support further down the social scale. As a result, great decisions had at least to be publicly justified in terms of community interest.

Second, non-decisions were often more complex than so far suggested. For a start, as we shall see in later chapters, small ratepayers as well as large could possess a sort of inactive influence through their 'reputation for power' in the electoral process — by local politicians anticipating their hostility to the prospect of increased municipal expenditure.

Furthermore, while governmental routines might perpetuate a *status quo* serving the interests of dominant economic groups, this did not necessarily mean they were uncontroversial. For example, in Rochdale gas prices were the centre of intense conflict both inside and outside the council, with differentials between large and small consumers subject to continual adjustment under shifting pressures from these groups.[50] Meanwhile, quite apart from large consumer pressure, there was a perfectly respectable case for offering price concessions to this group on straightforward economic grounds. The overheads of installing and maintaining the supply to big customers were proportionately lower than for small consumers. The more gas the former could be encouraged to consume the greater the eventual rewards to the corporation and (if profits were devoted to improvement) to the town.

Moreover, whether controversial or not, political routines could offer access and advantage to at least some groups besides the great proprietors. For example, though building regulations became far more rigorous than those on smoke emission, there were plenty of instances of the former remaining discreetly unenforced for long periods of time. Salford councillors from the late 1860s onwards prided themselves on having the toughest building byelaws in the country, yet throughout most of the '70s they seem not to have enforced them.[51] The interests being discreetly catered for here were not large proprietors but small speculative builders and landlords — many of them, to judge at least by their own propaganda, only a few precarious rungs above the working classes.

Assumptions that certain groups controlled the political agenda also meet other sorts of problems. It is certainly true that successful electoral compromise often *resulted* in the elimination of issues from that agenda, and this undoubtedly made the political elite more autonomous of outside pressures. Yet this outcome seems to have only sometimes been due to deliberate *intention*. Thus one arguably crucial ingredient of power was often absent. Attempts to curb public discussion were quite common in school board elections, but much less so in those for the council and board of guardians. Here motives varied. Sometimes compromise was prompted by a desire to avoid 'unpleasant feeling' between otherwise friendly members of the political elite,[52] and to attract into that elite the many businessmen who disliked the rough-and-tumble of electoral contest. This perhaps shades into the desire for legislative autonomy. However, compromise was often portrayed as a response to the mood of the electorate itself. It was justified in terms of 'preventing . . . useless expenditure'[53] and saving the ratepayers' money. The local press often saw contest avoidance as an expression of the burgesses' 'satisfaction'[54] with their representatives. Anticipating a compromise in 1863, the *Salford Weekly News* commented that 'A quiescent feeling and a disposition to wait patiently for the return of more prosperous and bustling times seem to have taken possession of the burgesses'.[55] In 1860 a Bolton correspondent complained that there were important issues that were not being discussed in the current quiescent council elections but noted sadly that 'the ratepayers appear quite apathetic'.[56] The numerous cases where no contest took place because one party anticipated defeat might also be seen as responses to electoral opinion, though they might equally have resulted from something altogether less democratic — the other party's successful manipulation of the registration process.

Even where agenda control was intended, the ultimate compromise might be the result of a long process of bargaining to ensure 'fair representation' for most of the politically relevant groups. This was often the case in school board elections. In Bolton in 1870, for example, the final list was carefully devised to include representatives from all religious groups and all classes. It even contained two rather dubious 'working men', one nominated by 'two of the most influential gentlemen in this town',[57] and both present because 'it was deemed essential that the working classes should have representatives of their own order . . . in a matter so vitally affecting their . . . welfare'.[58] In this respect the process was paternalistic, but the elite had clearly done their best. The *Bolton Chronicle* benignly described the overall result as 'a bill of compromises where parties had to submit to little sacrifices to make it agreeable to all'.[59]

Moreover even bargaining as careful as this did not always work. School board compromises, in particular, were always precarious. For example, in 1879, a carefully arranged compromise in Bolton was blown wide open by the incursion of one trades council and two friendly society candidates. Fighting on the sensitive issues of compulsory school attendance and board expenditure, and exploiting the cumulative voting system, the trades council candidate was returned at the head of the poll.

Meanwhile the broader issue of agenda manipulation through social control runs into difficulties of another sort. As we have seen, it is easy enough to establish the existence of networks available for the transmission of values; it is also fairly easy to establish evidence of an intention to transmit. It is even possible to find apparent evidence that working-class attitudes conformed to the model envisaged for them by those attempting control. Skilled trade unions, friendly societies and co-ops in Rochdale, Bolton and Salford made the same individualistic noises after the mid-1840s that they have been discovered to have made in other towns.

The real problem lies in establishing that middle-class transmissions led to working-class attitudes. Here there is considerable dispute amongst historians, and it seems relevant to summarise their arguments from the viewpoint of our present concerns.

Some have argued for considerable middle-class influence. Foster,[60] for example (writing mainly about Oldham), sees the collapse of working-class militancy in the mid-nineteenth century primarily as a result of conscious bourgeois effort at 'liberalisation'. Consequently the skilled working class was first defeated, and then drawn into the authority structure of the factory as low-level work organisers. Thus the key working-class element was bought off, and the rest effectively neutralised.

Patrick Joyce,[61] though rejecting the notion of ideological hegemony to which Foster[62] seems sympathetic, nevertheless sees the influence of the factory and factory owner on the working class as amounting to domination. For him, the key is the paternalistic role of the large employer, and the way the factory thus came to dominate the whole day-to-day pattern of working-class life and experience. The result was not so much an attachment to bourgeois values as an enthusiastically deferential attachment to the person of the factory owner. This produced a situation where 'work got under the skin of life', not just for a working-class elite but for the whole working population in the Lancashire factory districts.

Though both writers would postulate explicit or implicit limits to employer influence, the burden of their arguments points towards high levels of extra-political power. In our terms, both imply considerable control over the political agenda by the manufacturing elite. Even though Joyce insists upon cultural rather than ideological hegemony, the net result was a situation wherein the working class did not perceive their problems as fit matters for governmental remedy, and did not do so as a result of policies at least partially *directed* towards that end.

Other historians see the situation in less hegemonic terms. T. R. Tholfsen[63] argues that the central ideas of working-class radicalism were rooted, like those of middle-class radicalism, in the eighteenth-century Enlightenment. However, they were refined through different channels and experiences, and came to serve different needs. Thus, although the working-class ideal might use the same terms as its middle-class equivalent, and therefore be subject to strong middle-class influence, it nonetheless was, and remained, partially separate. Even at the height of 'bourgeois hegemony' working-class ideas and prescriptions still meant something different to those who followed them from what was meant by those who urged working men to adopt the middle-class version. For example, for the middle class, respectability was linked into the whole panoply of ideas surrounding upward individual mobility, but to 'respectable working men' it often indicated notions of self-respect and dignity.

Tholfsen is still prepared to allow considerable middle-class influence on working-class attitudes. Geoffrey Crossick, in his study of nineteenth-century Kentish London, on the other hand, paints a culturally more autonomous picture. He argues that the attitudes and ideas of the skilled working-class elite arose naturally from experiences gained from workplace, family, and the social structure of the geographically isolated and rather inward-looking part of London in which it lived. The skilled worker's attachment to his own version of ideals like self-help, respectability and independence stemmed mainly from his own efforts to make sense of his local world. There limited upward mobility was possible; the local middle-class elite sympathised with the artisan's aspirations, but its influence was limited by the fact that it did not employ him. At best, that influence lay 'not in imposing a new set of values . . . but rather in encouraging those strands in artisan ideology of which it approved'.[64]

Given that social control is not the central topic of investigation here, one can draw only tentative conclusions from the foregoing arguments for the configuration of power in the three towns. The sort of working-class autonomy described by Crossick seems unlikely in Rochdale, Bolton and Salford. In that factory context some appreciable level of hegemony appears more plausible. This is particularly so given the formidable philanthropic network described earlier, and the willingness to use it for value transmission.

On the other hand, there were clear limits to social control. Even Foster and Joyce allow that they existed. In fact Joyce's picture of hierarchical factory communities seems to me somewhat overpainted. The reasons will emerge in subsequent chapters. However, two points can be made here in reference to agenda control. First, even leaving aside Tholfsen's arguments, it seems plausible to suppose that many working men (skilled or otherwise) might have arrived at pretty individualistic prescriptions for themselves and their families simply by consulting their interests in the context of life in, or near, the slums of the three towns. Certainly one not unreasonable mode of survival was to set up some personal standard of respectability, however precarious, and to follow rules of sobriety, thrift and at least mutual self-help.

Second, even the apparent adoption of middle-class prescriptions about life and society did not necessarily produce total identity of views about the detailed issues of local politics — public or private. Our main emphasis here has been upon working-class attitudes. However, it is worth noting a phenomenon illustrated in later chapters: the shopocracy was led by its enthusiastic acceptance of individualism, as well as by the impact of the rating system, into far more parsimonious ideas about the proper role of local government than many more socially elevated political participants.

Such 'economical' attitudes are also sometimes evident among the working class. We have room for only one piece of evidence. However, it serves our purpose well, since it neatly illustrates how working-class attachment to self-help did not automatically produce consensus with entrepreneurial politicians about the role of local government. Significantly, the example comes from Rochdale — the town where the retail co-operative movement was most influential, and the place most frequently quoted by middle-class politicians as evidence that the working class had sufficiently accepted the socio-economic system to be considered 'politically fit'.

In 1870 the council decided to recommend adoption of the Public Libraries Act. Though ultimately successful, the move was bitterly opposed by the Rochdale Pioneers. In spite of massive efforts at persuasion from the dominant Liberal elite, the co-operators resisted. They claimed that a library would be expensive, and pointed out that the Pioneers had already provided both libraries and reading rooms for their members, and had therefore 'already taxed themselves for education purposes'.[65] They demanded to know whether 'people who subsist by daily toil are to be called upon to pay . . . for the sole benefit of shopkeepers'.[66] Some were prepared to concede that the library's advantages might spread a little more widely, but even then only to 'the trading, shopkeeping, middle and upper classes who are able to pay for their own without taxing those who have already taxed themselves'.[67]

Our final note of caution against making over-simple assumptions about the discreeter forms of power concerns the sphere of philanthropic politics. What will now be suggested is that, while members of the social and political elite may have been able to utilise this channel to a far greater extent than other, lowlier groups, they did not have exclusive access. Nor did they by any means totally control what happened there. Whilst it was invariably they who initiated in the private sphere, others could veto, or successfully demand conciliation.

There were several problems standing in the way of success. One was division within the elite itself. The religious and particularly party conflicts which, as we shall see, hampered successful municipal activity could also spread destructively into private politics. An attempt in 1845 to establish public baths in Bolton through philanthropic channels took more than a year to get off the ground (much longer, counting an earlier, aborted attempt in 1841). The *Bolton Chronicle* ascribed the delays to 'the disputes that irritated the two political parties in the borough' and suggested that 'if this matter had been kept clear of party the list of subscribers would have long since been filled up'.[68] As one mighty philanthropist noted in another context, even in private politics 'the mixing together of parties' was always likely to result in 'a complete defeat of the object they had in view'.[69]

Religion often reinforced such conflicts and caused considerable problems. In 1846 certain members of Bolton's elite tried to establish an Athenaeum. Their attempts foundered. This was partly due to party cleavage (some Tories holding back because of the promoters' connection with the Mechanics' Institute, which the former saw as a radical hotbed). They also ran into difficulties over whether the new institution should include a day school. The promoters agonised for some time but, rightly fearing conflict over religious education, decided that it should not — only to find day school champions threatening to withdraw support.

Attempts to found a public park in Bolton in 1850 in commemoration of Robert Peel were more successful. Nevertheless they took over six years. A major problem was the issue of whether the park should be open on Sundays. The proposal aroused considerable hostility from the clergy, and led one pious soul to advocate a cemetery as a more fitting memorial and place of Sabbath resort — particularly given the 'subdued cheerfulness' characterising such places.[70]

Partly because of party divisions, philanthropic politics were also subject to some of the pluralism often found in the public sphere. In 1862 the dominant Liberal section of Rochdale's elite established a committee to administer relief during the cotton famine. It decided to distribute relief in kind rather than distributing tickets to be spent in the local shops. Not surprisingly, the move infuriated Rochdale's grocers and provision dealers, who saw themselves as 'trespassed upon by the gentlemen of this town'.[71] The row continued for several months. The relief committee, whilst insisting on the continuance of aid in kind, hastened to conciliate the shopkeepers. The mayor assured them, 'I have always expressed a strong desire to do something for your body,' whilst the committee offered financial aid while the slump continued.[72] Such conciliation was necessitated by local Tory attempts to exploit the issue and take the shopkeepers' side. Here, as elsewhere, public and private channels overlapped, since the Tories hoped to gain municipal advantage by this gesture.

Rochdale's elite were confronted with stranger problems in the late 1860s when there was a move by local notables of both parties to establish a hospital. Initially the process went smoothly and pluralistically along, with the promoters attempting to consult 'every class and every section and every creed and every party'.[73] At the obligatory public meeting, motions supporting a hospital were enthusiastically passed, and a subscription list was set going. Then Alderman W. Robinson persuaded the meeting to support the establishment of a homeopathic ward in the projected institution. At this point, to the uncomprehending astonishment of the entrepreneurial elite, the town's entire medical fraternity rose up in insensate fury. A letter to the *Rochdale Observer* from some twenty doctors declared that 'the medical faculty of Rochdale are treated with . . . contempt. It . . . seems as if doctors are looked upon as a sort of utensil . . . for their opinions are set at naught, their susceptibilities derided and their education despised.' The doctors threatened to boycott the hospital if a homeopathic ward was established, and ended by observing that 'The plutocrats . . . may now consider themselves in a dilemma . . .'.[74] There ensued a ferocious debate over several weeks between allopaths, homeopaths and anyone else who cared to join in. Several denounced the doctors' 'arrogant' behaviour, suggesting that 'medical men are as plentiful as blackberries'.[75] Yet, despite such contempt, Rochdale's elite was eventually forced to abandon the scheme altogether.

Even the mood of the working classes could become at least negatively relevant in the private political sphere. This followed from the emphasis on community participation in some of the projects undertaken, and from the fact that they were often seen as primarily for the working class, and therefore requiring some evidence of working-class enthusiasm to get them under way. The absence of such enthusiasm or support could therefore prove crucial. For example, one reason for the non-appearance of Bolton's Athenaeum was the withdrawal of working-class support following allegations of middle-class 'dictation' over the aims of the proposed institution.[76] Similar problems beset the equally unsuccessful attempt to found a Public Institute in 1860. Considerable efforts were made to drum up working-class enthusiasm and financial support, first at the workplace by foremen and factory managers and then, when this significantly failed, by house-to-house canvassing organised by a separate working-class committee. Nevertheless the move was eventually abandoned, partly because 'the working classes as a rule took [not] the slightest interest . . . but rather treated it with ridicule'.[77]

None of the foregoing is intended to deny that the elite derived considerable power from its advantageous position in the sphere of discreet politics. Nevertheless it does suggest that others had access to such channels, could demand conciliation or exert vetoes. Moreover, though private and inactive politics were important, the activity and conflicts centring on public institutions were crucial, and seen to be so. It is to this sphere that we must now turn.

Notes

1 *RO*, 29 August 1874, p. 4.
2 See chapter 11.
3 See A. Briggs, *Victorian Cities* (London, 1968).
4 See p. 202.
5 W. Makant, *BC*, 15 August 1863, p. 7.
6 M. Dutton, *BC*, 16 February 1850, p. 7.
7 See p. 200.
8 *MG*, 29 September 1852, p. 7.
9 M. Crenson, *op. cit*.
10 See R. Wolfinger, *op. cit*.
11 *Op. cit*.
12 Or elsewhere in the north. See D. Fraser (ed.), *The New Poor Law in the Nineteenth Century* (London, 1976); N. C. Edsall, *The Anti Poor Law Movement, 1834-44* (London, 1971).
13 Perhaps less so in Rochdale; see chapter 8.
14 See p. 177.
15 See E. P. Hennock, 'Finance and politics in urban local government, 1835-1900', *Historical Journal*, VI (1963), pp. 212-25.
16 See *RO*, 8 April 1865, p. 6.
17 See chapter 10.
18 Bolton Sanitary Committee, *BC*, 18 July 1868, p. 7.
19 *SWN*, 6 February 1869, p. 3.
20 See chapter 5 onwards.
21 See p. 72.
22 *RO*, 29 April 1859, p. 3.
23 Thomas Schofield, *RO*, 19 November 1870, p. 7.
24 W. Simpson, *ibid*.
25 Rev. Davidson, *BC*, 19 November 1870, p. 3.
26 Canon Powell, *BC*, 6 December 1879, p. 5.
27 See Joyce, *op cit*., pp. 111 ff.
28 *BC*, 26 May 1866, p. 4.

29 *BC*, 2 August 1845, p. 2.
30 *BC*, 10 January 1852, p. 5.
31 *MG*, 17 January 1846, p. 8.
32 *BC*, 25 April 1846, p. 5.
33 *BC*, 4 December 1858, p. 1.
34 The most direct example is A. P. Donajgrodski, *Social Control in Nineteenth Century Britain* (London 1973) However, all the writers mentioned here — Joyce, Foster, Tholfsen, etc. — are concerned with the issue at one level or another.
35 Council debate, *SWN*, 8 April 1871, p. 4.
36 See 'Parties, members and voters after 1867: a local study', *Historical Journal*, 20, 1 (1977), pp. 145-63.
37 W. H. Bailey, *Manchester Examiner*, 15 December 1881, p. 3.
38 *SWC*, 30 January 1875, p. 2.
39 C. E. Cawley, *SWC*, 27 January 1872, p. 2.
40 Mayor of Rochdale to Cutgate Liberal Club, *RO*, 29 November 1873, p. 3.
41 Jacob Bright, *BC*, 23 December 1871, p. 7.
42 John Milne, *RO*, 29 November 1873, p. 8.
43 John Snape, *SWN*, 7 February 1867, p. 3.
44 *BFP*, 23 August 1845, p. 2 (on public baths).
45 *BC*, 3 August 1850, p. 1 (on proposed public park).
46 See P. Joyce, 'The factory politics of Lancashire in the late nineteenth-century', *Historical Journal*, 18, 3 (1975), pp. 525-53.
47 See *BC*, 17 and 24 December 1836; also Little Bolton Trustees Minutes, pp. 142 f.
48 See especially *BFP*, 2 August 1845, p. 2.
49 *BC*, 14 April 1852.
50 See p. 150.
51 See p. 219; also Local Government Board report on Bolton, reproduced *BC*, 11 May 1872, pp. 5 and 7.
52 See William Jenkinson at Board of Guardians, *MG*, 7 April 1849, p. 7.
53 *MG*, 19 October 1853, p. 7.
54 See, for example, *SWN*, 22 October 1859, p. 2.
55 *SWN*, 24 October 1863, p. 4.
56 Letter, *BC*, 29 September 1860, p. 3.
57 J. K. Cross, *BC*, 19 November 1870, p. 3. They were both shopkeepers.
58 Editorial, *ibid.*, p. 5.
59 *Ibid.*, p. 3.
60 Foster, *op. cit.*
61 *Work, Society and Politics*.
62 Along with other writers, not all of them Marxists. See H. Perkin, *Origins of Modern British Society, 1780-1880* (London, 1969).
63 *Working Class Radicalism in Mid-Victorian Britain* (London, 1976).
64 *An Artisan Elite in Victorian Society: Kentish London, 1840-80* (London, 1978), p. 253. See also comments by R. Q. Gray on problems of the general concept of social control in *The Aristocracy of Labour in Nineteenth Century Britain* (London, 1981).
65 J. R. Shepherd, president of Rochdale Pioneers, *RO*, 28 May 1870, p. 5.
66 Letter, *RO*, 14 May 1870, p. 6.

67 Letter, *ibid*.
68 *BC*, 13 September 1845, p. 3.
69 Mayor Robert Heywood at meeting to establish a society for poverty relief, *BC*, 22 February 1840, p. 3.
70 Letter, *BC*, 5 October 1850, p. 7.
71 Jon. Milne, *RO*, 21 February 1863, p. 5.
72 *RO*, 31 January 1863, p. 4.
73 *RO*, 6 February 1869, p. 5.
74 *RO*, 13 February 1869, p. 4.
75 *RO*, 20 February 1869, p. 3.
76 See meeting reported *BC*, 27 March 1847, p. 8.
77 Mr Edmondson, *BC*, 29 September 1860, p. 7.

4

Power within local authorities

In Chapter 2 we saw that men of property and standing enjoyed considerable advantages in political recruitment, and in being accepted as legitimate once recruited. In chapter 3 we investigated the ways in which the possession of such impressive political resources also enabled them to achieve desired ends not merely in the political/institutional sector but also in the pervasive non-political areas of life.

I now want to examine the areas where the situation is altogether more complicated, and to begin here by analysing some of the factors determining the location of power within the local authorities of the three towns. At the end of chapter 3, we had begun to get a sense of this greater complexity. There we suggested that urban political leadership, however resourceful, was open in certain important respects: first, it was open to anyone who could make — or at least be construed as making — his way up the economic scale; second, political leadership, even for the man of relatively modest economic substance, was itself an important road to social prominence. I now want to argue that this had important consequences for legislative life. Partly because of this rather fluid relationship between social prominence and political leadership, partly because of the impact of the increasingly complex urban environment upon municipal life and functions, power within local authorities was determined by factors besides the relative economic weight of the participants. It was determined particularly by the desire and ability to work, and to gain expertise. This had three consequences: first, councillors who gained the greatest power were those best able to make themselves expert; second, professional servants emerged as increasingly crucial helpers and even rivals to elected councillors; third, councillors' growing helplessness in the face of complex and conflicting information led to the hiring of outside professional consultants.

Power among councillors

We are not arguing that economic substance played no part. Awareness of it clearly exerted considerable influence upon municipal minds. There is certainly evidence that being 'one of the greatest ratepayers in the borough', particularly given the pervasive ideology examined in chapter 2, may have added considerably to the seriousness with which a man's opinions were received by his colleagues. Whenever 'special committees' were appointed — to negotiate on the corporation's or improvement commission's behalf with railway companies, public utilities or neighbouring local authorities, to press the town's case in Parliament, or simply to investigate corporate efficiency — large proprietors were always heavily represented. Also, as seen in chapter 2, men of substantial property were disproportionately represented (in Rochdale) on the aldermanic bench, and (in Bolton) among council committee chairmen. We further noted that the chief officers of the three towns — chief constables, boroughreeves and mayors — were almost invariably drawn from the ranks of active, or retired, manufacturers and merchants.

This last fact is important because, in Bolton and Salford at least, such positions (particularly the mayoralty) seem often to have been centres of political initiative over quite wide ranges of important issues. At the beginning of his term of office practically every mayor gave what amounted to a 'state of the union' message, often recommending council action in important areas of policy — most commonly in the field of sanitary reform, but also in finance and administration.[1] Some submitted specific schemes for reform — like William Jenkinson's plan for a new system of rate collection in Salford in 1848.[2] Mayoral nominators frequently emphasised the executive qualities of the office,[3] and there are references to a co-ordinating role for the mayor among the conflicting desires of the various committees.[4] Meanwhile, in all three towns, the mayor was seen as a crucial figure in safeguarding borough interests in negotiations with neighbouring towns, and in Parliament. One of the more persuasive reasons for Rochdale's decision, in 1855, to seek incorporation was the belief that 'the town suffered by not having a mayor to represent its interest . . . .'.[5] William Jenkinson, mayor of Salford in 1848, put the matter even more strongly in noting that in this area 'almost everything devolved upon him'.[6]

Such a role was not unnatural, given that the mayor was frequently a managing entrepreneur. Indeed, it was one of the central reasons why large proprietors were generally appointed. The role also resulted from the fact that, however vociferous their incursions into elections, political parties did not, in these nineteenth-century towns, play the sort of central role in directing legislative business that is commonplace in the twentieth century.

However, if economic weight could sometimes prove important, there is also much to suggest that it was in no sense the only, or even the most significant, factor determining the location of intra-legislative power. Committee chairmen, whether great proprietors or not, were rarely all-powerful. It was quite a common occurrence on all three councils to find such men rather wanly trying to persuade the council to reverse a committee decision taken against their opposition. Mayoral initiative, though acceptable and even expected, was decidedly limited in scope. More than one retiring incumbent declared himself 'conscious of the unfulfilment of many purposes and wishes with which he had entered ... office'.[7] In 1882 Salford's mayor, Richard Husband, declared the need for 'discretion ... for, if a mayor were to interfere too much with the business of any committee, he would soon find he was encroaching upon their rights and privileges ...'.[8] Overall, the situation, in Salford at least, is perhaps best summarised by Councillor Walker, who noted that council members 'honoured and respected their chairmen and deputy chairmen, but those gentlemen had to rule in justice and mercy ... They did not allow even mayors to be tyrannical ...'[9] Finally, the substantial role of the mayors and 'special committees' of financially well-upholstered council members in negotiations with the outside world was a delegated one. They followed courses prescribed by the legislature, with little room for discretion. Economic substance was simply used to add weight to corporate opinions.

Meanwhile there are signs that men of property found legislative life neither congenial nor easy. An indication of this is the high turnover of legislative personnel. The average triennial influx of new people (i.e. individuals who had not served any previous term) on to the Rochdale council between 1856 and 1880 was 31·9 per cent, with individuals spending an average of 10·5 years on that body. In Salford, between 1844 and 1881, the average triennial turnover of council members was 36·6 per cent, whilst in Bolton new legislators replaced old ones at the startling rate of 44·25 per cent, with an average life span of only 6·5 years. Many on all three councils survived less than two years, sometimes only for a few months. Such figures become even more significant when compared with the replacement rates of the altogether less propertied and more proletarian councils of the post-second world war era. In Rochdale, Salford and Bolton the average triennial influx between 1946 and 1970 has been running at the much lower levels of 29·8, 26·6 and 28·8 per cent respectively.

Moreover the tendency to get itchy legislative feet was not just confined to the councils of these nineteenth-century towns. The proportions of new to sitting candidates in the Salford police commissioners elections of 1837, 1840 and 1843, for example, was respectively 62·5, 52·5 and 37·5 per cent. Finally, on the evidence of the 181 individuals who passed through the sixty-man Rochdale Improvement Commission during its twelve-year existence, life there must have been more than most flesh and blood could stand.

We may also note that the strains which, as will be seen, were largely responsible for this legislative mobility seem to have been at least as acute for the large as for the small proprietor. In Salford the average legislative life span of a manufacturer or merchant between 1844 and 1880 was 8·9 years, compared with the small proprietorial council member's 8·7 years. 44·9 per cent of large proprietors managed fewer than six years on that body, whereas a marginally smaller proportion (41·3 per cent) of small proprietors did so. In Rochdale the picture seems, if anything, less favourable to men of substantial property. Between 1856 and 1880 their average council term was 10·2 years, compared with 12·4 years for their more lowly counterparts; and 39·2 per cent of them survived less than two council terms, compared with 38·2 per cent of the shopkeeping sort.

What we are seeing here seems largely to have been due to the strains that legislative life imposed on businessmen. This is suggested by the fact that most of the movement out of these councils resulted from voluntary retirement rather than electoral defeat. For example, of the thirty-seven members of the thirty-eight-man Bolton council of 1841–42 who had been replaced by 1845, twenty-seven had left voluntarily. There were, in any case, markedly fewer electoral contests in our period, compared with the years since 1918, and it is therefore doubly significant, given what we are saying, that legislative turnover should have been so much higher.

Such strains are suggested more directly by the constant chorus of complaint about the time taken up by legislative business. As early as 1832 one of Salford's overseers gloomily conjectured that 'it was impossible that any three overseers could manage the affairs of the town, as they would their own, unless they devoted to it the whole of their time during six days a week'.[10] Surveying his own overseership, Salford's wealthiest factory owner of the 1840s estimated that it had absorbed 'fully one third of my working time'.[11] Not unnaturally, in later years, mayors in particular were given to such temporal anxiety, and in Bolton one retiring incumbent observed that 'he had neglected both his business and his family to attend to the affairs of the town'.[12] It was a problem that also affected many council members, so much so that, in Salford at least, there were constant experiments from the 1860s onwards with the timing of council and committee meetings in an attempt to cater for the varying 'difficulties of mercantile men'. Meanwhile, in 1858, in an attempt to equalise the opportunities of members with business commitments and those without, Bolton council decided that no one should sit on more than three committees.[13]

The basic problem was that municipal business was, from the first, both complex and extensive — a difficulty compounded by Victorian verbal expansiveness. Thus it tended to compete seriously with the individual's economic activities. For those able to retire before assuming 'the burdens' of municipal service the problem of course scarcely arose, but the majority found it difficult to cope with. Symptomatic of this is the heartfelt cry from William Jenkinson, one of Salford's largest manufacturers. Appealing for punctuality, he observed, to the evident agreement of his council colleagues, that 'To rob a man of his time was practically to rob him of his money'.[14] Given that this was the problem, it is scarcely surprising that, time and again, we find even the most economically substantial individuals giving 'business reasons' for municipal retirement. Occasionally they were more explicit. G. H. Jones, a wealthy merchant, pointed out that 'the details of his business were increasing to such an alarming extent that it was ... necessary that he should give his personal attendance to it. The duties of a councillor were such that one had to forfeit a great mass of business arrangements.'[15] Even if the pressure of economic activities did not enforce retirement, it quite often seems to have seriously limited the amount of time businessmen could devote to legislative activity. Thus James Ormerod, one of Bolton's leading manufacturers, tried unsuccessfully to escape membership of the council's improvement committee in 1846 on the grounds that 'his duties were very onerous, and ... would prevent him being an efficient member ...'.[16] For one Rochdale councillor the problem seems to have been even worse, for he 'found it utterly impossible to attend the meetings of *any* committee'.[17] Yet perhaps the saddest comment on the political difficulties of businessmen came from David Skinner, who told a Bolton ward meeting in 1857:

When he went into the council, he had not the slightest idea of the time it would take, and that was one reason why a great many, in promising great things ... found that to accomplish [them] would take up a great deal of their time, and ultimately got weary ... and ... neglected to fulfil the expectations of their constituents.[18]

However, whilst some men clearly had difficulties in managing any sort of effective legislative activity, others seem to have found life more congenial — remaining for periods of twenty, thirty and, in two Salford cases, over forty years. Indeed, it may be possible to divide legislative members into two rough groups. One, much the larger, entered and left the local legislature rather quickly, and had little time to amass much political influence. There also seems to have been a second, smaller 'inner circle' who had the leisure and inclination to master municipal business, and to remain for much longer periods.

If the latter group existed in the councils of these towns, relative economic weight appears to have played little part in its composition. Certainly, if one examines those who managed to remain councillors for long periods, small proprietors at least held their own. Of the fifty-one individuals surviving life on the Salford council for fifteen years or longer, twenty-six are identifiable as large proprietors and thirteen as proprietors of a more modest sort.[19] These represent 22 and 20·6 per cent of the total number of individuals in their respective categories. Rochdale's shopocracy seems to have done even better. There were thirty council members who remained for fifteen years or longer, of whom fifteen were manufacturers or merchants and thirteen small proprietors. Whilst the former represented only 20·5 per cent of the total number of individuals in the large proprietorial category, the latter represented 37·2 per cent of their total.

Thus the discrepancy, evident in chapter 2, between large and small proprietors in overall council membership may have been evened out in practice by the burdensome effects of municipal life. The possibility is reinforced by a look at the yearly rosters of council attendances. These are not entirely reliable indicators of the work done by council members, but they do seem to support the trend indicated by the evidence examined so far. Thus, on Bolton's council of 1856/57, for example, there were twenty-four manufacturers or merchants, fifteen variously classifiable as small proprietors, three professionals, three 'gentlemen' and one broker. However, of the twenty-five managing to attend forty or more council or committee meetings, eleven were shopkeepers, builders and the like, two were professionals, three were gentlemen and only nine were large proprietors.

If the balance of power within the legislature evens out in the way such evidence indicates, and if competition between economic and political life was more acute for large proprietors, this is likely to have been due to differences in the business necessities of each group. Large businesses, unlike perhaps landed estates, did not run themselves, particularly in an age that was yet fully to discover the virtues of the manager. Shops and other small businesses, on the other hand, could probably be safely left in the hands of another family member, or an assistant. However this may be, it seems likely that the composition of a legislature's 'inner group' was determined by other (and probably more important) factors besides relative economic weight. Indeed, the most significant influence was probably the ability and inclination to work. Its importance was reinforced by legislative attitudes and norms. Publicly at least, council members tended to talk in terms of 'assistance' and 'help' as much as 'influence' when describing or desiring contributions from colleagues to some legislative project or committee. Admittedly this trend was partly symptomatic of the tendency to see municipal service in philanthropic terms. However, it was also a commentary upon the necessities of a legislative life that was becoming increasingly complex and time-consuming.

The trend towards an industrious, rather than industrial, elite inside the legislative chamber was also reinforced by the tendency to apply industrial codes of conduct to behaviour within the municipal situation. Beliefs about the virtue of simple industriousness, for example, spiced the resentment which non-attenders induced among those who did attend council. There was constant sarcasm about 'the present council, or the working men in it'.[20] Once backsliding was perceived, not even past services or high position could necessarily save the offender from attack. In Salford in 1847 Aldermen Lockett, Kay, Harvey and Gardiner — all well up the social and economic ladder, and all of long political service — found that their continued absences had been perceived by the General Purposes Committee, which sarcastically wrote 'to know which of the annual committees it will be convenient for them to attend.'[21] One rather pathetic indication of the importance that committee attendance held in some members' minds is the not infrequent complaint that they 'had been known to go out of one committee room to another, and, having got their names entered, return to the first'.[22]

That such bizarre behaviour could seem necessary is a commentary on the fear that sanctions might be visited upon the non-attender. The first Bolton Council elected after incorporation in 1838 decided who was to be the first to rotate out of office, and thus face the voters entirely on the basis of legislative assiduity. In a regular and long continuing attempt to whip the backsliders into line, an ignominious league of council attendance was published in each town just before the November elections. As a result, attendance sometimes became an election issue, or the pretext for refusing nomination. The Rate-payers' Retrenchment Association, which held virtually undisputed sway over nominations in the central wards of Salford[23] from 1853 to 1861, placed heavy emphasis upon the likelihood of industriousness in its candidate selection. It was prepared to refuse nomination, even to long-standing councillors, if their attendance was considered inadequate. Meanwhile Bolton's electorate was asked to contemplate the following astonishing calculation:

Eighteen Radicals make 1305 attendances in the year; eighteen Tories make 868 attendances in the year. The four best radicals make 393 attendances in the year; four best Tory councillors make 337 in the year . . . As wards become represented by Tories, the attendances become fewer . . . If you want the business of the town neglected, vote for Tories . . . [24]

If wickedness could be punished, the kudos attaching to industrious virtue was considerable. When Councillor J. W. Stead, a Salford shopkeeper, died in 1875 he was posthumously congratulated upon being 'very assiduous in attention to council matters; although not gifted with eloquence . . ., he was always thoroughly practical in his ideas, and was frequently consulted upon questions of importance'.[25] Alderman Bromiley died some years later. One of his colleagues again brought dubious powers of arithmetic to bear upon 'one of the best workers' and produced the startling fact that 'from 1868 to 1878, Mr Bromiley attended 154 council meetings, 1,070 sub-committee meetings, making a total of 3,304 attended by the late alderman'.[26] In 1850 there was an indication that more concrete accolades might come the way of the industrious living when the 'unostentatious labour' of Salford's Councillor Fuller was 'warmly eulogized'. This was accompanied by the confident prophecy of a council leader that Fuller was 'silently preparing himself for the highest honours of the Council'.[27]

Remarks like these, implying as they do that positions of influence could be earned by simple industry, certainly tie in with what seem to have been remarkably open channels of entry to the executive offices of local legislatures in the three towns. Competition between economic and political activity seems to have resulted in replacement rates among committee officers even higher than for the legislature as a whole. Between 1832 and 1844, for example, fifty-two people were chairmen or vice-chairmen of the six or seven committees of the Salford Police Commissioners. Similarly, the turnover among equivalent officers of Salford council committees was around 45 per cent every five years from 1844 until well beyond 1880. The quinquennial replacement rate among committee chairmen on Bolton Council seems, on the evidence of the only period for which evidence is available (1860-80), to have been even higher — ranging from around 45 to as high as 85 per cent. It is finally notable that, to judge at least by Salford's pattern, promotion to these offices was rapid. Between 1850 and 1875, for example, councillors had to wait an average of only 4·4 years to attain their first office (normally a vice-chairmanship), often as little as a year.

Power within the legislature was thus determined not merely by economic weight but also by the ability of legislative members, whatever their occupational background, to labour industriously. This became increasingly important as the needs of a complex urban environment made legislative business steadily more burdensome. This, in turn, ensured that a further qualification for admission to the municipal 'inner circle' was not merely work but expertise and specialisation.

As noted in chapter 2, the theory legitimising municipal participation by the business elite held that the skills and understanding its members acquired in running their enterprises would automatically equip them to cope with a set of council activities that were merely private enterprise writ large. In fact from the moment corporate functions went beyond law enforcement and the management of corporate property into fields like sanitation, building regulations and running public utilities, the real situation became increasingly at variance with the model. Whilst the skills acquired in large-scale economic life might give confidence and a certain breadth of view, the only way to acquire the increasingly specialist and technical knowledge needed to cope with things like gas and water supply, river conservation, public health, etc., was by intelligently working in those fields.

Perhaps the most dramatic initial illustration of this point can be found in the area of gas administration. No field of municipal activity aroused greater controversy both within and outside the councils. Gas supply, and, even more, gas prices produced regular council debates of the most windy kind. Yet it was also an extremely technical subject, and the character of such debates shows that the economics of gas administration (for example, the buying of coal and cannel, or the relative profits to be derived from different pricing policies) was something most council members found very difficult to understand, still more to master. During one particularly heated controversy over gas prices in 1866 the *Rochdale Observer*, then owned by a leading council member, attempted to set its readers right in a long editorial. By the following week, however, the paper had to admit to 'an unaccountable oversight' and was ignominiously forced to publish a second equally long editorial seeking to clarify the misunderstandings raised by the first, which had been 'confused by many important mistakes'.[28] Two years later, perhaps warned by the *Observer's* experience, Rochdale's new mayor poked gingerly about him, and declared his intention of attending some committees during his term of office, but not 'for instance, the Gas Committee — it would not be the least use of my attending . . . It would take me all my time to understand the question of gas . . . and to be of any service . . . would be beyond my power.'[29] His sentiments were ruefully echoed by Alderman W. Robinson, one of Rochdale's largest manufacturers and gas consumers, who, during a characteristically rambling debate on the subject, complained that 'those who were not on the Gas Committee found it impossible to understand all the details which [were] set before them'.[30]

These remarks might equally have been applied to areas like sanitation, water supply and even finance; as Robinson's comments imply, such a degree of technicality gave a crucial role from the start to the specialist committees of the improvement commissioners, council, etc. So much was this so that many participants believed that it was here that 'the real labour and business of the council was done'.[31] Indeed, the specialisation required in many spheres of activity was such that committees soon began to delegate much of their work to sub-committees — to a point where in the eyes of one Bolton councillor in 1857 'they had been going too far in the direction of subs. It was sub-committee this, and sub-committee that, until it was almost impossible to . . . know who had done certain things.'[32]

As these comments imply, the power rapidly being acquired by committees was the subject of considerable periodic disquiet — not surprisingly, when some were found to be 'quite out of the control of the council'.[33] In Salford, particularly, this led to a whole panoply of measures designed to facilitate some control over their activities — culminating by 1867 with the decision that an objection from any council member to any part of a committee's proceedings would entail its whole monthly report standing over to the next meeting.[34] Committee proceedings were also generally read out in full — an experience which led one hardened stalwart to the slightly masochistic conclusion 'that they had not had a more interesting council meeting for a long time'.[35]

Such feelings were shared by many others, to judge by the frequency with which committee proceedings were subject to questions and long debates in all three councils. It was also true, particularly at certain periods, that committee recommendations were subject to direct challenge and even defeat. Certainly they were regarded as less sacrosanct than in the more party-bound circumstances of the twentieth century. Spending committees seem to have been particularly subject to 'insults' of this sort. The early years of the Salford Baths Committee were described by its vice-chairman as being 'about as happy as that of a toad under a harrow'.[36]

Yet the lives of most municipal committees in the three towns normally remained undisturbed by such irritations. Most discussion of proceedings centred on points of detail, and many reports were passed *nem con*. Most challenges seem to have originated from defeated minorities taking their case to the whole council, or from territorial disputes between committees.

The increasing complexity of council policy thus meant that much of it was effectively decided in committees and sub-committees. It also meant that expertise was an important factor determining the respect accorded individual legislators by their colleagues. When Thomas Booth resigned as chairman of the Rochdale Gas Committee in 1869 the council refused to accept his resignation for two months because of his mastery of gas affairs and 'so that members of the committee would feel able to consult him on matters which they might not know in detail themselves so well as he did'.[37] Booth was a manufacturer, but the respect was for his expertise, not his economic weight. Another equally influential figure on the Rochdale Council, and for the same reasons, was Edward Taylor, a druggist, chairman of the sanitary committee, and the central figure in persuading the council to undertake a programme of sanitary reform in the late 1860s. It is obvious from the way his lengthy contributions to council debates were received that his influence stemmed from his increasing mastery of a subject that many colleagues found difficult.

Expertise rather than economic weight also determined the role of Bolton Council's two most influential members in the 1850s and '60s. The part played by Fergus Ferguson, a doctor and sanitary committee chairman, in persuading the council to allow the demolition of large numbers of cellar dwellings, and to start cleansing the nauseating river Croal, was based primarily upon his grasp of an immensely technical subject and his willing-ness endlessly to explain it to colleagues — impressing some and boring others into submission. J. R. Wolfenden retired as borough treasurer in July 1858. So great was the respect for his mastery of municipal finance that within three months he had been elected to the council, and had taken over as finance committee chairman. Two years later he became alderman and mayor. Wolfenden's understanding of the most intimate corners of borough finance was unique. It made him a central figure in the building of Bolton's opulent town hall. Only he had sufficient understanding of corporate finance to be able to convince an otherwise doubtful council that the decision to build, and continue with, a project of such accelerating expense could be taken without danger of bankruptcy, or even substantial rate increases. Indeed, unlike their reaction to Ferguson's medical lectures, council members seemed positively to enjoy Wolfenden's long excursions into financial statistics. Gleefully anticipating one such two-hour peroration, Councillor Richardson observed comfortingly:

With respect to the rate, they would probably hear from Mr Alderman Wolfenden what would be its amount [with reference to the town hall]. He [Mr Richardson] had had it explained to him, but he was not one who liked to dwell long in connection with figures when he was to be followed by Mr Alderman Wolfenden.[38]

The role of professional servants

In fact Wolfenden's rapid rise from borough treasurer to such a central council position also gives us a clue to a further phenomenon born of the complexity of municipal business — the increasing influence of professional servants and outside experts. This is normally assumed to be a twentieth-century phenomenon.[39] Yet, to judge by Rochdale, Bolton and Salford, such influence — and the worries about it — began substantially earlier, at a time when the economic elite's position in local politics was at its most striking.

Many of the strains thus engendered are revealed in a telling episode in Bolton in 1869. The council, under pressure from the Local Government Act Office, decided to take up the long delayed question of cleansing the river Croal of raw sewage. Two schemes were submitted to the streets committee: one for an intercepting sewer, from the borough engineer; another, simpler and temptingly cheaper, from one of its own members, Councillor Lomax. The committee decided in favour of the Lomax scheme in spite of contrary pressure from the Local Government Act Office and opposition from the borough engineer. The latter, although anxious to refute the charge that was 'gaining ground amongst the council generally' that he was 'opposing the scheme because I am not its author', nevertheless declared that the Lomax scheme 'will result in failure and disappointment'.[40] There ensued a long and angry debate in which the borough engineer's supporters called attention to his expertise, whilst his opponents indignantly refused 'to abdicate their functions to an engineer, however eminent'.[41] Eventually the council decided to submit the two plans for adjudication to a local engineer — and then, under further government pressure, to 'an eminent London consulting engineer'. It did so in spite of angry charges from Lomax that 'they were abdicating their responsibilities to an outsider'[42] and from Streets committee members that 'they had not entered into the merits of either scheme but . . . had thrown [their] committee overboard merely because it differed from the . . . Borough Engineer'.[43] There was also the hopeful suggestion that they ought to be able to decide the matter for themselves by 'common sense'.[44] The majority feeling, however, was less stirringly but more realistically expressed by Alderman W. Rushton, a wealthy Bolton banker, who

did not feel confident himself to determine which was the best scheme but . . . had confidence that [the consulting engineer], who had been impartially selected from a distant place, of great engineering ability, and great powers of mind and understanding, would be able to do so.'[45]

A week later the London engineer pronounced in favour of his borough counterpart, and the council obediently began work.

This episode tells us much about the increasingly tense relationship developing between council members and professional experts of all kinds from at least the late 1850s. It shows the growing influence and assertiveness of professional servants and the increasing reverence in which they were held by some leading councillors. It also reveals the resentment many councillors felt against the officials, and the not unrealistic sense that their traditional functions were being usurped. Finally, it shows the increasing tendency to supplement the expertise of leading corporation employees with that of outside consultants. We will examine other manifestations of each of these aspects in turn.

The increasing role and self-confidence of paid officials was revealed in several ways. It was shown by their tendency to defend themselves and their departments against attack by indignant letters to the press.[46] Some even used this means to advance policies they were pushing in the council. In the mid-1870s Salford's medical officer of health and borough engineer engaged in a vigorous public correspondence championing rival forms of privy that they wanted to make obligatory throughout the borough.[47] Occasionally public officials joined in wider controversies — with Rochdale's waterworks manager passionately opposing the public park at the town meeting in October 1864.[48]

Their influence is also revealed by a trivial but significant incident in 1867. In that year the Bolton council discovered that a two-storey house, costing £2,000, had somehow been erected in the new Spa Fields Park for the under-gardener. The plans originally sanctioned by the council had been for a one-storey building. The chairman of the parks committee scruffed around in his memory and 'recalled something of the alteration', but most members, both of the committees and the council, could not remember 'how they came to get a second storey'. One explained that

the building had been erected under the superintendance of Mr Baylis [the borough engineer], and, knowing it was in the hands of a man who understood his business, he had not troubled in looking after it. Allowance must be made for the committee . . . they had not the same time to spare for the examination of plans as Mr Baylis, and . . . they were led astray . . . they merely took Mr Baylis's word.

Alderman Stockdale tried to shed further light by explaining that council members, 'not having a practical knowledge of engineering or architectural matters brought before them, must put some confidence in their servants'.[49] In this last remark Stockdale appeared to be broadening his comments to include relationships with other corporation servants. Quite rightly so, because apart from the borough engineer there were other increasingly influential professionals, notably the town clerk, the gas and water engineers, the borough treasurer and the medical officer of health.

The town clerk was a crucial figure from the start. He was accorded considerable respect within the council and outside. His legal expertise gave him an important role in shaping local improvement Bills — a source of advice not merely on the wording of particular clauses but more generally upon what powers could be obtained from Parliament, and how (ie. whether the corporation should shape its own clauses, or incorporate parts of existing national permissive legislation).

In fact his role went much further, as Salford's general purposes committee found when it considered reducing the salary for the incoming town clerk on the grounds that 'his duties were strictly confined to municipal business':

in their inexperience . . . the committee quite forgot that, though inclined to be quiet themselves, people might not be disposed to leave the Corporation alone — that . . .

they would have to fight on all sorts of subjects whether with those who wished to bring a railway through the borough, or to promote some other private object.[50]

Furthermore, as councils moved increasingly into the land market to find sites for town halls, baths, parks and cemeteries the town clerk became an important, and often sought after, source of advice on complex and confusing issues like the ground landlord's legal title, the position of existing lease-holders, and so on. Rochdale's leading official, for example, was quite crucial in the corporation's negotiations with the vicar of Rochdale and the Church Commissioners to purchase church lands for a park, public baths and a town hall. So important did his role become, in a situation where the vicar's right to sell the land appeared hazy, that the mayor was driven to exhort his colleagues that 'this is a very important matter ... upon which most of us are quite at sea, and I hope you will listen quietly to the Town Clerk's explanation'.[51]

In fact Rochdale's town clerk (Zach Mellor) felt sufficiently confident to rebuke his employers periodically. When attacked he was wont to remind councillors of the difference between his expertise and their experience. Thus the drafting of a Bill 'required time and consideration, and was not like buying or selling a piece of cotton goods ... '.[52] He sometimes complained that councillors were 'attempting to interrupt me with irrelevant observations'.[53] When asked to speak up by no less a person than the chairman of Finance, he issued a general, and significantly well received, rebuke to his errant masters:

if members ... would not carry on a conversation while he was [speaking], they probably would hear quite well. (Hear! Hear!) But when there was a buzz of conversation and it was evident that members were not paying the slightest attention to what he said, it was not likely that they would hear (laughter and Hear! Hear!).[54]

Gas managers were also important and visible figures in all three towns. Even more than town clerks, their position was enormously enhanced by the sheer technicality of their field, and by the confusion that many felt in its presence. Thus they seem to have played an important part in decisions, for example, to enlarge the municipal gasworks — and, faced with opposition, could prove less than respectful to those who employed them. As early as 1847 we find Rochdale's manager responding to opposition to his plans for gas works expansion by accusing some improvement commissioners of 'entertaining prejudices against myself'.[55] Such frankness was symptomatic of growing influence. By the end of our period one Rochdale alderman was opposing an increase in the salary offered to candidates for the same post on grounds that spoke volumes for the balance of power between gas manager and councillors:

His fear was that if they got one of those big men he, like a new broom, would be desirous of sweeping very clean . . . while Mr Hunter [a previous manager] was here, something like £100,000 was spent on remodelling the works, and if they had another big man . . . he did not know where he would land them.[56]

Samuel Hunter, the individual rather fearfully mentioned in this passage, had by this time taken himself off to Salford. There he took the role of manager to spectacular limits. By the mid-1870s many councillors were complaining of rudeness. Hunter's relationship with the gas committee seems to have been positively dictatorial. It was suggested that committee members were not informing themselves of the details of gas administration and

went like automatons to meetings and sat and listened and voted, and went away . . . they were more under the control of the officials than any other committee in the Council. There were four aldermen . . . and the Gas Manager had them all under his . . . thumb.[57]

Such accusations were given spectacular substance when it was discovered in 1887 that this committee of wealthy businessmen had sat somnolently by whilst their chief official decorated the gas office entrance with a wrought iron version of his monogram, graced the tower of the gasworks with a carved bust of himself, ran up a bill for cabs which, according to one critic, suggested that he 'went to bed in a cab'[58] and drove through the streets in a carriage headed by a servant in livery. They also failed to notice that, during his twelve-year period in office, Hunter accepted bribes for municipal contracts to the tune of £11,000, purchased a Cheshire hunt on the proceeds and spent up to two months at a time away from his office touring Europe. The committee failed to notice these activities purely because he had achieved the one thing that they as businessmen were particularly well equipped to appreciate: he ran the gasworks at a profit.[59]

Salford's gas scandal is admittedly an extreme example of the relationship that could arise between councillors and officials. It also occurred at a time when the political elite was already in decline. More typical perhaps is the role played by the medical officer of health in the three towns from the 1860s onwards. In Bolton, for example, from the moment of his appointment in 1867 this official was a deciding influence over the direction of sanitary reform. His regular, copious and often highly technical reports on the town's sanitary condition set the framework within which problems were discussed. He also decided which houses were unfit for human habitation, and therefore to be demolished by the sanitary committee. He successfully pressed the committee to insist on ashpit privies in all new houses (1874) and on the compulsory notification of infectious diseases (1879). Less successfully, throughout the '70s, he pressed the council to establish an isolation hospital and day nurseries.[60]

Though those reviewed so far were the most influential, other corporate employees were also becoming important. As early as 1852 Salford council was having trouble with its chief constable. The watch committee requested his resignation on the grounds that 'instead of devoting himself solely to the performance of duties ... he frequently interfered with other matters contrary to the expressed and often repeated orders and expostulations of the committee'. The committee's request was successful. Nevertheless it occasioned 'considerable excitement in the town', and the sacked official published a pamphlet 'full of accusations and personal charges against members of the committee' on his way out.[61]

Lowlier officials could also acquire autonomy. Ironically, Bolton's medical officer was first appointed because the corporation's two sanitary inspectors 'could not be brought to do their duty ...'. By 1873 the medical officer was experiencing the same difficulty: one inspector was said to be perpetually drunk and 'stank like a polecat', whilst the other 'carried himself as if he knew more than anybody else, [and] ... more than all the [Sanitary] Committee put together'.[62] Two years later the streets committee found similar problems in controlling the humbler officials in their employ. It emerged that 'young men in the Surveyor's office [were] making plans in their spare time' — drawing them up, at a fee, for buildings projected by private individuals to ensure that the buildings would be passed by the streets committee.[63]

The borough surveyor himself was indulging in something on the side, for he was trading in land. Here Bolton's experience had been extensively anticipated in Rochdale. In 1858 the late borough surveyor was said 'by his blandness of manner [to have] overcome many of their councilmen, and thus had been enabled to carry out his own crotchets'.[64]

Some of the foregoing also suggests that, while many leading councillors displayed considerable respect, even deference, for corporation officials, others increasingly resented their alleged intrusions. Moreover they expressed their resentment in ways that said much about the patterns of influence that were emerging. It may be that such irritation was one factor fuelling the frequent battles in all three towns over attempts to raise official salaries. If so, the feeling is evident right from the start of our period. However this may be, the resentment certainly becomes overt from at least the 1860s. As early as 1858 there was a revealing discussion in the Rochdale council about what sort of man should be appointed as borough surveyor to replace the one recently sacked. Some were happy enough to appoint 'an educated surveyor who could advise them as to the best means of doing anything ... who would be respected in Parliament ... not a mere clerk'. Others were clearly suspicious at the prospect of another professional, and seemed to hanker after someone very like the way they saw themselves. Councillor Petrie felt that 'they must avoid getting an engineer instead of a surveyor, or a gentleman who could talk, instead of a man who would work', whilst Edmund Ashworth suggested that 'what Rochdale wanted was not an engineer, but a man of ... industry, integrity and efficiency'.[65]

In Bolton in 1867 such suspicions were more explicitly stated. Councillor Pilling, a substantial manufacturer, was clearly thinking in rather personal terms when he said it was 'a well known fact that there were several practical men in connection with the Council, whose advice again and again had been set at naught simply because the advice of the servants overruled'.[66] Later he referred to 'a large amount of jealousy' on the part of councillors 'with regard to our servants'.[67] By the late '70s there were complaints of decisions being taken between officials and leading members of committees 'without the sanction of the committee', and predictions that soon 'the Council would be called upon to sanction things after they had been carried'.[68] There were even suggestions that council business 'would come to be conducted by [a few members] and their officials'.[69] Equally revealing complaints could be heard in Rochdale. In 1873 one councillor asserted that 'there was a certain kind of autocratic management on the Gas Committee, what with the manager and what with the chairman'.[70] All this tells us much about the relationships that were emerging, and about the feelings of councillors who were thus excluded from influence.

Another expression of the difficulty in which councillors found themselves was the increasing tendency to call in outside experts on a consultancy basis. Often — as in the case of Bolton's river purification scheme with which we started — the decision seems to have been a confession of helplessness in the face of technology. Nor did consultation always help the situation. These points are perhaps best illustrated by Rochdale's confused attempts to solve the problems of instituting a proper sewage system, particularly of where to run its main sewer. This had been a subject of agonised debate since at least the early 1850s, and had been made infinitely more intractable by the surprise insertion of a clause into the 1853 improvement Act, by the House of Lords, which effectively prevented running the sewage into the river Roche.[71] As early as 1854 'practical men had been called in' (particularly Manchester's borough engineer) by the improvement commissioners in an unsuccessful attempt to find a solution. This pattern, once begun, acquired its own momentum. Indeed, by 1869 the council's paving and sewering committee had amassed at least four other reports on the subject: one from its own borough surveyor, two from separate consulting engineers, and another from its special sub-committee set up to see what was happening in other towns. The committee had also visited a sewage conference in Manchester. The

paralysing problem was that the experts disagreed. The two engineers had
come to diametrically opposed conclusions, thus ensuring that 'practically so
far as the ultimate disposal of the sewage was concerned, these reports
amounted to nothing . . .'.[72] The sub-committee had found 'considerable
diversity of opinion amongst the practical men in every town visited', and the
Manchester conference had posed the same difficulty. Consequently 'the
Committee were at a loss to know what to recommend'.[73]

Such problems are equally evident where the construction of public
buildings is concerned, though here outside experts did not so much confuse
councillors as seduce them. Both Bolton and Rochdale built town halls whose
ultimate cost far exceeded the money allowed when the specifications were
drawn up. There were several reasons, but one was certainly the relationship
built up between the relevant council committee and the architect employed
to design the building. G. L. Ashworth, with the air of one whose virtue lay
in ruins about him, accounted for yet another jump in the estimates for
Rochdale's astonishing edifice by explaining that 'this subject had grown
upon the committee as they had discussed it . . . The more they came into
contact with artistic and professional men, the more they felt tempted to
gratify their taste.'[74]

In the foregoing, we have argued that work and expertise, rather than
economic weight, increasingly determined the way power was distributed —
firstly among elected representatives, and secondly between them and their
paid experts. Because of the growing scope and complexity of corporate
functions in the urban setting, and the continuing pressures of business
responsibilities upon members of the political elite, councils were finding it
increasingly difficult to control their specialist committees. For the same
reasons, committees were themselves experiencing severe problems in
keeping tabs on those they employed.

In some respects the problem went beyond even this; for, as may be evident
from the foregoing, the policy process in these towns sometimes acquired a
momentum of its own — even reaching a stage where no one, whether
councillor or official, seemed to control it. In 1875, for example, Bolton
Council discovered that 'every department of the corporation was in a very
disorganised state'[75] and set up an investigation committee. This uncovered
large-scale and long-term incompetence and some corruption — particularly
in the gas and water departments. The main trouble appears to have been the
whole system of corporation accounting, which was 'defective in system and
slovenly and inaccurate in execution'.[76] The borough treasurer was blamed
and removed, and he in turn laid the responsibility at the door of 'the novices
in power' on the finance committee. Bolton, in fact, at that time appeared to
have a financial system that no one controlled, still less co-ordinated.

The possibilities are more dramatically illustrated by the building of Rochdale town hall. The intention in January 1864 had been to produce 'a neat elegant building' rather than anything 'fanciful and extravagant', and the cost was estimated at £20,000.[77] By May 1865 the town hall committee was asking the council to find an extra £5,000 for the foundations and £7,000 for improvements to the design.[78] By January 1866 the estimated cost of the 'mere building' had risen to £41,000 — and the gross cost to nearly £60,000. Though there were protests, including one from a member of the town hall committee itself, the general opinion was that, whatever the mistakes, they could not go back now but 'must go on'.[79] In 1872 there was a revealing debate about overspending and unauthorised work. Some ascribed it to the architect, who had apparently admitted to doing 'extra work on his own . . . authority'. Others suggested that, whenever enquiries were made, 'the members of the General Purposes Committee were like schoolboys when the windows were broken — no one knew who had done it'. The mayor admitted that 'the committee had been days and nights anxiously delibera-ting' about 'who authorised the work in excess of the contracts . . . they had all more or less authorised it'.[80] The final cost of a building which some described as 'one of the finest in the North' and others as being 'covered with monkeys in all stages of colic', was well over £110,000[81]

In none of all this are we suggesting that the situation, even by 1880, had reached that of today. Nineteenth-century municipal officials had fewer advantages *vis-à-vis* councillors than their twentieth-century counterparts. Though often formidable as individuals, they were not a self-conscious group: their numbers were too small and, below the ranks of the top officials, professional training and qualifications were rarely required. The municipal hierarchies wherein decisions are taken that twentieth-century councillors know little about, though clearly emerging, were still at an early stage. The national organisations of professional officials, now so important as networks for the circulation of privileged technical information, the creation of professional *esprit de corps* and negotiation with central government were scarcely evident at all.[82]

Moreover, in some respects, nineteenth-century municipal officers were different figures from their successors. Again the high visibility of the local arena is important: corporate officials could become social leaders in the same way as their employers. Indeed, some were successful local figures before acquiring their posts: the town clerk was often a leading solicitor, and remained so after appointment. Certainly all the major officials, if they stayed long enough, and were sufficiently active and sufficiently philanthropic, could reach a stage where they and their carriages were instantly recognisable in the town. To some extent, therefore, their influence was derived from the same source as that of their employers, and they were part of the local political elite rather than its rivals.

Nevertheless municipal officials were also different. Many — particularly engineers, managers and medical officers — were outsiders, moving about in a developing career structure that extended beyond the town and its region. Moreover, whatever their social position, they were appointed because of their expertise and derived their influence from the possession of much-sought-after technical knowledge. Many councillors saw them as different from themselves, even rivals. Certainly, if they wished to control, match or even know what 'our servants' were doing they had to strive to become like them. Increasingly, many failed.

One fact made councillors more likely to fail than their twentieth-century successors. Though often highly important, party conflict had a more limited impact upon local elections than it does now. Councillors therefore rarely arrived with a mandate; practically never with a collective one. This aside, many had no very clear sense of what they wanted to accomplish beyond social advancement and the fulfilling of civic duty. There might thus be very few, apart from professional officers, with clearly defined objectives.

Overall, it is clear that any idea of an elite serenely controlling municipal affairs by the exercise of skills and knowledge derived from occupational life is erroneous. The complexity of the urban environment being administered by local councils, etc., increasingly impinged upon them, and affected their internal configurations of power. This will become even more evident as, in the remaining chapters, we turn to the relationship between municipal bodies and the outside world.

Notes

1 By way of example see H. D. Pochin's speech to the Salford Council, *SWN*, 10 November 1866, p. 3.
2 See *MG*, 15 April 1884, p. 9.
3 See Thomas Thomasson, for example, *BC*, 12 November 1853, p. 6.
4 See Richard Husband, *SWC*, 9 September 1882, p. 3.
5 Thomas Livsey, *MG*, 10 August 1855, p. 4.
6 *MG*, 4 March 1848, p. 9.
7 H. D. Pochin, *SWN*, 14 November 1868, p. 6.
8 *SWC*, 9 September 1882, p. 3.
9 At Liberal meeting; *SWN*, 17 November 1877, p. 4.
10 Quoted by Mr Bury, *MG*, 17 November 1832, p. 3.
11 Holland Hoole, *MG*, 6 November 1840, p. 3.
12 Stephen Blair, *BC*, 15 November 1845, p. 3.
13 See *BC*, 13 November 1858, p. 7.

14 *MG*, 10 November 1847, p. 6.

15 *SWN*, 10 October 1882, p. 3.

16 *BC*, 14 November 1846, p. 3.

17 Jonathan Nield, *RO*, 22 October 1859, p. 4. Emphasis in text.

18 *BC*, 31 October 1857, p. 5.

19 There are also nine professionals and two 'gentlemen'.

20 J. J. Parker, *MG*, 31 October 1849, p. 1.

21 *MG*, 11 December 1847, p. 10. All had been prominently involved in the struggle for incorporation, and Lockett had been Salford's first mayor.

22 Councillor Smalley, *BC*, 13 November 1858, p. 7.

23 See chapter 11.

24 *BC*, 7 November 1868, p. 3.

25 Obituary, *SWN*, 5 June 1875, p. 3.

26 *SWN*, 11 January 1878, p. 3.

27 *MG*, 14 September 1850, p. 3.

28 See *RO*, 8 and 15 September 1866, p. 4.

29 *RO*, 14 November 1868, p. 6.

30 *RO*, 4 September 1869, p. 7.

31 Councillor James Worral, junior, *MG*, 17 July 1847, p. 10. See also, for example, Councillor Neill, *RO*, 22 October 1859, p. 4, and letter, *BC*, 8 November 1856, p. 8.

32 Councillor Parkinson, 16 May 1857, p. 3.

33 Town clerk, *MG*, 10 November 1858, p. 3, on Salford watch and water committees.

34 See *SWN*, 5 January 1867, p. 2, when there was an unsuccessful attempt to rescind the order.

35 Richard Husband, *SWN*, 25 January 1862, p. 3.

36 W. H. Bailey, *SWN*, 8 September 1878, p. 3.

37 Alderman G. L. Ashworth, *RO*, 6 February 1869, p. 7.

38 *BC*, 20 January 1866, p. 3.

39 See particularly J. M. Lee, *op. cit*. The role of nineteenth-century municipal officials is largely unexplored, though useful comments can be found in Hennock, *Fit and Proper Persons*, *op. cit*., and in A. Sutcliffe, *Towards the Planned City: Germany, Britain, the United States and France, 1780-1914* (Oxford, 1981). For the growing literature on present-day municipal bureaucracies see M. J. Goldsmith and P. Baxter, *S.S.R.C. Urban History and Politics Study Group: a Bibliography of Professions in British Local Government* (Salford, 1981).

40 *BC*, 12 June 1869, p. 7.

41 Councillor Crook, *BC*, 17 July 1869, p. 7.

42 *BC*, 7 August 1869, p. 7.

43 Councillor Crook, *ibid*.

44 *BC*, 17 July 1869, p. 7.

45 *BC*, 7 August 1869, p. 7.

46 See, for example, James Tweedale's complaint about corporation servants, *RO*, 3 July 1875, p. 6.

47 See, for example, *SWN* during January 1875.

48 *RP*, 29 October 1864, p. 5.

49 *BC*, 17 August 1867, p. 7.

50 E. R. Langworthy, *MG*, 27 February 1852, p. 2.

51 *RO*, 23 April 1864, p. 6.
52 *RO*, 23 September 1871, p. 6.
53 *RO*, 23 April 1864, p. 6.
54 *RO*, 2 November 1878, p. 6.
55 *Sp* February 1847.
56 Alderman Tweedale, *RO*, 3 July 1880, p. 7.
57 Councillor Walker, *SWN*, 7 September 1878, p. 3.
58 Councillor Phillips, *SR*, 12 February 1887, p. 5.
59 For details of scandal see *SWN*, February–March 1887; also reports of special committee of investigation beginning *SWN*, 11 June 1887, p. 5. After four years in prison Hunter eventually emerged as a country squire in a Cheshire village.
60 For role in London see A. S. Wohl, in H. J. Dyos and M. Wolff (eds), *The Victorian City: Images and Reality* (London, 1973), vol. II.
61 Quoted in *MG*, 23 June 1852, p. 3.
62 Alderman Greenhalgh, *BC*, 13 September 1873, p. 3.
63 *BEN*, 18 March 1875, p. 3.
64 Thomas Whitworth, *RO*, 23 October 1858, p. 3.
65 *RO*, 4 November 1858, p. 3.
66 *BC*, 14 September 1867, p. 7.
67 *BC*, 19 October 1867, p. 7.
68 Councillor Brimelow, *BC*, 19 January 1878, p. 7.
69 Councillor Brimelow, *BC*, 22 December 1877, p. 7.
70 James Tweedale, *RO*, 10 October 1874, p. 6.
71 See later, p. 101.
72 Alderman Stott, chairman, *RO*, 9 April 1870, p. 8.
73 Alderman Stott, chairman, *RO*, 9 October 1869, p. 8.
74 *RO*, 6 January 1866, p. 5.
75 *BC*, 13 March 1875, pp. 5 and 7.
76 Outside accountant employed to examine corporate methods, *BC*, 16 October 1875, p. 7.
77 *RO*, 9 January 1864, p. 5.
78 *RO*, 27 May 1865, p. 4.
79 *RO*, 6 January 1866, p. 5.
80 *RO*, 6 July 1872, p. 6.
81 *RO*, 3 December 1870, p. 5.
82 Such organisations were emerging in Germany by the 1870s. See Sutcliffe, *op. cit.*, chapter 2.

5

Local authorities and the outside world

I. The world beyond the municipal borders

In the following chapters we shall be examining the relationship between municipal bodies and their environment. We start here with the area wherein the power of elective elites, however well-heeled, was at its weakest and least predictable: the relationship with the world beyond the formal town boundary. We shall soon see that the local autonomy highlighted in chapters 2 and 3 was not total. Though it was important in the senses that the elite moved within a visible local arena, and that municipal authorities possessed considerably more power to act without reference to a national legislative framework than they do now, Victorian towns were nevertheless economically, socially and politically interdependent with their surrounding districts. As a result, elective leaders were constrained, as we shall see in the first section, by influences emanating from beyond municipal boundaries and frustrating the achievement of municipal aims both within and outside those boundaries. It will become evident in the second section that the power of local leaders was periodically deeply affected by what happened in London — particularly in parliamentary committees dealing with improvement Bills. Thus there were important constraints upon even the most generously endowed political elites,[1] and we shall argue that such limits stemmed partly from factors connected with the very nature of the endowment — the fact that they were men of property operating in an atmosphere strongly influenced by a general attachment to local control.

The influence of neighbouring areas

Several factors influenced relations between the urban local authority and its immediate hinterland: the fact that municipal boundary expansion could never keep pace with urbanisation; the impact upon the town and its problems of what was done or not in the surrounding area; the municipality's need to impinge upon its hinterland in search of water, land for its sewage

schemes, extra customers for its utilities, and sometimes simple administrative control. All this meant that the local authority required co-operation
and consents from the surrounding area in order to operate effectively. As we
shall now see, economic and political considerations determined that neither
was readily forthcoming.

Manchester and Salford

The most dramatic example of the effect of such factors can be found in the
considerable problems caused for generations of Salford's leaders by her
relationship with Manchester. Salford was the third largest town in north-
west England throughout the nineteenth century. Yet to countless outsiders
she appeared 'a mere suburb', and even, to a few unpatriotic insiders, 'the
mere lapel of our great neighbour'.[2] This was not surprising, for Salford was a
town in the shadow of a city just across the Irwell — a city moreover that was
the social and economic focus for south-east Lancashire and, certainly until
the 1880s, the regional capital of the north.

Industrialisation increases urban interdependence in various ways. However, Salford's relationship with Manchester was extreme — altogether more
like economic and social dependence. The town never developed many of the
urban institutions that one might expect in a place half the size. The two
towns were visually indistinguishable, and Salford's centre — so far as she
ever possessed one — was tucked away in the south-eastern corner, only a
few hundred yards from the centre of Manchester. Salford's first newspaper
did not appear until 1859, and then only because the Manchester papers had
been giving the town minimal coverage — counting it neither as part of
Manchester nor as sufficiently distinguishable to appear in the 'District
News' columns. Over the years Salford came to be trisected by two thick
swathes of railway line, which, having 'occupied some of her fairest
portions',[3] and having tipped her a few token stations, terminated magnifi-
cently in Manchester. There was considerable travel between the two towns
and many of Salford's inhabitants, particularly from the middle classes,
conducted their economic, and some of their social, activities in the neighbouring city. This was hardly surprising, since, as late as 1875, Salford was
reputed to possess 'The postal accommodation of most villages'.[4] Moreover,
as one citizen traitorously noted, 'where are our markets — our Exchange —
our Free Trade Hall — our theatres — but on the other side of the Irwell?'[5]
As a result, Salford could never be as self-sufficient as were many other
Victorian towns. Though much more than a suburb, she was heavily
dependent upon her neighbour.

In a rational world the two would have been united under a single local
authority. Indeed, throughout our period they uneasily shared a common but

separately administered water supply. However, although there were many attempts at permanent amalgamation, any prospect of union with 'a mere mushroom creation of the day'[6] was always successfully resisted by the majority of Salford's elite. All her political institutions remained totally separate.

Yet Salford's leaders still had to face the fact that the town 'could not live by itself alone'.[7] The relationship with Manchester restricted their freedom of action in at least three interrelated and important ways: it considerably inhibited their ability to carry out desired courses of action; it helped make Salford less governable; and it created split loyalties in the bosoms of many Salford legislators.

Most important were the inhibitions. The corporation was often unable to act without Manchester's co-operation. Mainly for this reason, it was felt desirable that Salford's mayor 'should be well known in their great neighbourhood, and connected with the interests of that borough as well as those of Salford'; still better if he was 'a personal friend of the mayor of Manchester'.[8]

However, mayoral amity notwithstanding, such co-operation was rare. Instead, throughout our period, the two authorities fought pitched battles over a wide variety of issues — over the tolls on certain interconnecting roads, control of the fire services during joint operations, clauses in each other's improvement Bills, and over the building of bridges across the Irwell. (Here, as elsewhere, Salford suspected that it was commencing 'improvements for the benefit of other people'.[9])

In these and other battles the town frequently came off worse than the city. Three examples will make the constraints upon Salford's leaders clearer. In 1861 the Lancashire & Yorkshire Railway Company applied for parliamentary permission to widen substantially its existing line through Salford to Manchester. Salford Corporation opposed the company's Bill on the grounds that the proposal would involve considerable demolition and inconvenience in the most populous part of the borough; that the present line was sufficient, and that, even if widening were deemed desirable, the scheme should be much more limited. It also argued that the company should be compelled to provide a new road across the Irwell.[10] The House of Commons committee eventually granted the railway its improved line *in toto*, though insisting that it pay £25,000 for improvements in the area of Salford thus desecrated.[11] This was admittedly a substantial concession, and councillors hailed it as a great victory. However, the LYR contrived fairly rapidly to escape some of its obligations. Moreover Salford's sense of triumph was symptomatic of the fact that its aims had rapidly come to end at damage limitation. This, in turn, was partly because the corporation's negotiating stance had probably been considerably weakened by the attitude of Manchester, which stood to gain most of the advantages and little of the inconvenience from the new line. Shortly before the Commons committee meeting the city's corporation had publicly endorsed the scheme, threatened to adopt a favourable petition 'unless [Salford] became more reasonable',[12] and then adopted one anyway.

A longer-running illustration of the constraints imposed on Salford's municipal leadership by Manchester's proximity is the issue of river conservancy. In 1867, not for the first time, though more generously than before, the Irwell flooded, and distributed itself disgustingly over Lower Broughton. Salford Council established a river conservancy committee and appointed an inspector, who reported that the only effective way of preventing a repetition was to build a tunnel diverting the flood waters and costing £150,000. The new committee endorsed the scheme, and began negotiating with Manchester about a joint parliamentary application for the necessary powers, and to try to persuade the city corporation to prevent the tipping of rubbish into its part of the river. These negotiations — along with countless later examples — failed. For the next twenty years, apart from the building of an intercepting sewer by Salford, nothing happened. The deadlock was partly over apportioning costs for the various schemes between the two authorities. It was also partly because Manchester, largely unaffected by the floods, was pursuing, on its own later admission, a policy of 'masterly inactivity'.[13] The result was paralysis: in spite of the Irwell's frequent return to Lower Broughton, and strong pressure from outside, the majority of Salford's council never felt able to take independent action. Meanwhile, without effective action by Manchester (and other authorities along the Irwell), Salford's own stringent anti-tipping measures proved nugatory.

Similar problems arose over a proposal in the 1870s to construct a tramway through the town into Manchester. Salford delayed action for years because of the city corporation's refusal to come to a definite decision. Independent action was always rejected because 'Salford was only a suburb of Manchester and a tramway that was to terminate only in Salford would not pay'.[14] The comments of those advocating an independent course indicate the sense of frustrated impotence that gripped so many of the town's councillors when they looked across 'the sludge'. They demanded 'why should they dance attendance upon Manchester', and likened their more circumspect colleagues to 'little children waiting for the commands of their parents and if they could not stir a step without Manchester'.[15] Looking beyond the immediate issue of tramways to a more general pattern of behaviour, the *Salford Weekly News* alleged that 'the very name has only to be mentioned to produce a sort of . . . trembling throughout nearly the whole . . . council'.[16]

Meanwhile, Manchester's looming presence also contributed to the already marked centrifugal tendencies within Salford's political 'community' — making the town less governable. It contributed particularly to what was, as we shall see in chapter 11, the strong and (from the municipal elite's viewpoint) paralysing separatism exhibited by Salford's 'out-townships' of Pendleton and Broughton. Both had a long border with Manchester, and Broughton in particular had only become incorporated with Salford in 1853 under duress. For a considerable period thereafter its inhabitants often saw Broughton as 'the West End of Manchester'.

The separatist consequences of Manchester's presence can be seen in the byzantine arrangements governing water supply. Salford never had its own sources but received water first from a private company and then, after 1845, from Manchester. By 1850 Salford had taken over the pipes and installations, together with supply management within its borders. The situation was productive of almost constant mutual irritation, and was made considerably worse by the arrangements for Pendleton and Broughton. These townships were each supplied separately, and — partly at their own insistence — continued to be so after amalgamation with Salford in 1853. Broughton was supplied direct, in pipes owned by Manchester, and paid its water rates to the city. Pendleton was also supplied direct, but initially in pipes owned, and at rates levied, by Salford. The situation produced endless confusion and regular apoplexy. It reached a point in 1862 where Pendleton's section of Salford Council opposed a Salford Improvement Bill before a House of Lords committee on the grounds that some clauses altered its water relationship with Manchester. Eventually, after further angry conflict, Pendleton joined Broughton in acquiring its own district water committee, in paying for its own supplies direct to Manchester, and in surrendering the ownership of its pipes to the neighbouring corporation.

These centrifugal tendencies, and the obstructiveness they engendered, were probably reinforced by the fact that the townships invariably contained the residences of several Manchester councillors. These were not averse to interfering periodically in Salford's local politics. More than one alien legislator was accused of 'seeking to set the inhabitants of [Salford] against its municipal government'.[17] Sometimes it was justifiably alleged that they did so as agents of their own corporation. Thus Alderman Neill (of Manchester) led the opposition of Broughton inhabitants to Salford's Improvement and Consolidation Bill of 1862 at a time when Salford and Manchester were locked in parliamentary conflict over the Bill's water clauses. More lethally, Pendleton's petition against the same clauses was headed by Sir Elkanah Armitage — ex-Salford boroughreeve, currently chairman of Manchester's waterworks committee, and the owner of factories that dominated Pendleton's economic and social life.

Many leading Salford councillors waxed indignant about the insults to 'Salford's honour' resulting from Manchester's many sins. Yet, as implied by some of the foregoing evidence, Salford's anger was rather ambivalent. The problem was that many Salford politicians — along with other wealthy citizens — conducted their business activities in Manchester. As table 7 suggests, well over a third of the council regularly owned a house in Salford and a factory or business in Manchester. Added to this is the probability that many others transacted part of their business in the city, and used its commercial facilities. This meant that the primary focus of at least economic interest for many of Salford's real and potential political leaders lay in Manchester, and in the activities of the Manchester council, rather than in Salford.

Table 7. Location of residence and business of Salford Council members for seven specimen years

Council	House and factory, etc., in Salford	House in Manchester and factory in Salford	House in Salford and factory, etc., in Manchester	Not applicable*	Total council membership
1855-56	26	3	27	8	64
1861-62	27	3	24	10	64
1867-68	25	2	25	12	64
1873-74	21	10	13	20	64
1882-83	19	1	24	20	64

* This column includes those for whom only one address is given in the Municipal Year Book and (increasingly significant towards the end of the century) those with addresses altogether outside the Salford/Manchester boundaries.

Such divided loyalties help to explain the mouse-like results of the outrage against Manchester, and many Salford councillors' unwillingness to support independent action. It may also explain why there was always a significant minority of council 'traitors' willing to support the regularly produced schemes for amalgamation between the two towns. Indeed, such attitudes were probably reinforced by (and themselves reinforced) the ambivalent attitudes towards Salford of Pendleton and Broughton: the great majority of council members, residing in Salford whilst conducting business in Manchester, lived in, and represented, out-township wards. Not surprisingly, they were also the most prolific source of schemes for amalgamation with Manchester.

Rochdale, Bolton and their hinterland

Although Rochdale experienced occasional difficulties with Oldham, neighbouring municipalities produced far fewer problems for Rochdale's and
Bolton's elites. However, both experienced very similar and very considerable problems from areas which, although contiguous and often indistingish-
able from the two towns, were beyond municipal boundaries. Here a host of
difficulties and constraints stemmed from the fact that administrative expansion could not keep pace with either urbanisation or the towns' growing need
for resources.

Municipal elites experienced the greatest problems with the hinterland of
their towns in three related areas: in their attempts (1) to discover new water
supplies, (2) to discover new places to deposit sewage and ways of purifying
their rivers, and (3) to expand their administrative borders. As we shall now
see, the quest for all three almost invariably became intensely political,
bringing Rochdale's and Bolton's leaderships into acute conflict with neighbouring communities, with wealthy individuals in those communities and,
increasingly, with their local government. As with Salford's dealings with
Manchester, the prevailing impression left by such municipal activities is one
of weakness and vulnerability.

The search for water was, not surprisingly, a frequent source of conflict
with outsiders. Bolton provides the best example both of the scope of the
interests who could feel themselves affected and of how formidable their
opposition could prove. In 1863 the corporation sent an improvement Bill to
Parliament which, among other things, sought to expand its waterworks, to
obtain more water from their existing reservoir at Turton and to build new
reservoirs in specified locations outside the town. During the Bill's parliamentary progress these clauses were opposed by the commisioners of the
Turton reservoir, by landowners on whose property the corporation proposed
to construct its new reservoirs, and by the Bridgewater Canal trustees on
behalf of various local areas wanting access to Bolton's water supply. Before
and during the parliamentary committee hearings the corporation managed
to secure the withdrawal of most of the opposition by promising to insert
generous compensation and protection clauses for the landowners, and by
agreeing to the demands for water.

On this occasion determined negotiations obtained for Bolton's local
leadership most of what it wanted — perhaps because the opposition may well
have been motivated by a desire for more favourable compensation, for
supplies of water, or better prices for compulsorily purchased land. The
council had been altogether less fortunate with its 1854 Improvement Bill.
This also sought, in part, powers to expand the water supply by building

reservoirs in the Belmont and Longworth areas, four miles north-west of the town. The proposals aroused 'opposition . . . of a most formidable and influential character'.[18] — from local landowners, manufacturers and, most lethally, from a determined group of bleachers whose mill water was drawn from below the Belmont area, and who predicted disaster if the supply were interrupted. Parliamentary committee hearings dragged on for several weeks. Despite vigorous encouragement from the Commons committee, and the corporations's strong desire to compromise, all attempts at negotiation failed. The bleachers were satisfied neither with the water offered by the corporation in compensation for the lost supplies, nor with its price. Although the committee eventually imposed a solution largely-favourable to the council, the bleachers, 'much dissatisfied', carried their opposition to the House of Lords. Here their stories of manufacturing cataclysm fell on more sympathetic ears: the water clauses were annihilated. With the help of some equally unfriendly decisions on other clauses, the Bill was thus badly mutilated. The street widening powers that remained for royal assent had cost Bolton around £9,000.

The quest for decently distant places wherein to spread or process municipal sewage was equally productive of conflict and constraint — as were council attempts to prevent other areas from dumping theirs into rivers running through the town. Although the resultant problems are observable for both Bolton and Salford, Rochdale provides the best illustration. By the 1870s most of the town's households were equipped with tub privies — and the resulting 'night soil' was aromatically transformed into manure at a plant near the centre of Rochdale. However, some four hundred houses possessed water closets. The council was prevented from turning their output into the river Roche by a clause in its 1853 Improvement Act and, more immediately, by a court injunction. Therefore, in its 1871 Improvement Bill, Rochdale Corporation sought 1,300 acres in the Heap and Pilsworth area, several miles to the south-west, for a sewage farm — the raw material being carried thence by an intercepting sewer also projected in the Bill. Powers were also sought to prohibit the dumping of any solid or fluid material into the Roche or its tributaries, within or beyond borough boundaries.

Although the Bill already contained guarantees about the inoffensiveness of the sewage farm, and clauses excluding certain manufacturers from the dumping prohibitions, its sewage and pollution provisions raised a storm of protest. Opposition to the sewage clauses came from the ratepayers and local board of health in Heywood, through whose land the intercepting sewer was to run, and who characterised Rochdale's plans as a design 'to pour all their filth through the district'.[19] There were ominous rumblings from Cheetham Hill, five miles away from the projected sewage works. Even here 'the people

... were afraid lest they should be injured by the miasma'.[20] However, the most damaging opposition came in a parliamentary petition from the Earl of Derby — the owner of the lands upon which the sewage farm was to be built. His counsel claimed that Rochdale's proposals would ruin the bright financial prospects of land which had been specially converted for building purposes, and which was geologically unsuitable anyway.[21]

Meanwhile the river purification clauses aroused equally fervent opposition from the inhabitants and local boards of Milnrow, Crompton and Littleborough who had hitherto used the Roche as a receptacle for both industrial and untreated human effluent. Crowded ratepayers' meetings were regaled with visions of their sewage being 'bottled up', and of trade being damaged by a Bill that was 'a sad blow to manufacturers and consequently to the working classes'.[22] Hostile petitions also emanated from many mill owners, inside and outside the borough, who saw the pollution regulations as hampering their operations and the intercepting sewer as robbing them of water.

The council frantically tried to conciliate — by offering protective clauses, by promising manufacturers a generous period to adjust to the regulations, and eventually by half nullifying the latter through the removal of the prohibition on liquid pollution. However, most of the opposition was carried to Parliament. There, after hearing evidence, the Commons standing committee expunged the sewage clauses, though eventually permitting the corporation to construct the intercepting sewer, and carry it to a point five furlongs beyond the town boundaries. This would avoid Lord Derby's property, and, hopefully, enable negotiations to take place with local landowners about a different site for the sewage works.

In fact the revised clause allowed the sewer to stop slightly short of five furlongs — 'to avoid coming into contact with the property of the Heap Burial Board'.[23] Even this attempt to conciliate opposition before it arose proved insufficient to avoid further hostile petitions from landowners situated at the new terminating point and probably gleefully contemplating the possibility of exacting a high purchase price. The Lords committee refused to proceed further even with the revised sewage clauses unless the corporation first came to terms with one of the protesters. The latter — perhaps miscalculating what the market would take — refused to sell unless Rochdale bought his whole estate at a price of £63,000. Faced with this, the corporation's parliamentary committee gave up — not merely accepting the loss of the remaining sewage clauses but also voluntarily surrendering the river purification sections. They did so because they thought it wrong 'to inflict on themselves or their neighbours such a great penalty as would result from the carrying out of those clauses unaccompanied by the sewage scheme, and especially as they had excited so much opposition, both inside and outside the borough'.[24]

Corporate weakness, and a sense of just what had to be given to achieve even modest success against hostile outsiders, is even more evident when we examine municipal efforts at boundary extension. The wish to expand was itself often connected with the municipal elite's desire to influence the world immediately beyond its boundaries, and its failure to do so. This was particularly so with the problems just reviewed — expansion being linked with the corporation's desire to control areas from which it took, or wished to take, water; to which it supplied water or gas; which were, or wished to be, connected to the town's sewage system, or which polluted its rivers and thus nullified the effect of its regulations. More generally, the desire for expansion was linked with urbanisation, and the feeling that outsiders were increasingly using town facilities without bearing their share of the costs and respon-sibilities. A Rochdale councillor expressed the irritation of municipal leadership in complaining that

it was a monstrous thing that the council should have jurisdiction over an arbitrary circle three quarters of a mile in radius, when there were populous villages just upon the verge of the borough relying upon them for water and gas; and . . . have to submit to the smoke and other nuisances these outsiders caused without having control over them.[25]

Unfortunately for urban corporations, the areas upon which they cast hungry eyes rarely saw things the same way. Indeed, the very facts which persuaded councillors and other citizens of the necessity for amalgamation often provided outsiders with strong reasons for staying separate. Particularly in Rochdale and Bolton, many mills were being built just beyond the municipal borders in order to gain access to the towns' workforce, communications, gas and other facilities without incurring the costs of maintaining them. They also thus avoided, for example, municipal regula-tions about the use and abuse of stream water. Landowners too found adjacency without inclusion convenient. In such areas the demand for building land was high, and neither land prices nor building operations were inhibited by the building regulations in force inside corporation boundaries. Landowners also expressed fears about the absence of municipal provision for the lower rating of agricultural land.

Manufacturers and landlords lent considerable weight to outside opposition to expansion, but they were not the only ones aroused. Crowded and lively township meetings, and the signatures on parliamentary petitions, testify to the fact that others much further down the social scale could see the advantages of cheap rates and parochial control.

Some of the flavour of the resistance to amalgamation, and the motives and depth of feeling behind it, can be gleaned from the metaphors of rapine and violence that so often greeted attempts at expansion. In 1877 a 'ratepayer' characterised Rochdale's proposal to absorb part of Castleton as a plan to 'kidnap innocent outsiders for the purpose of forcibly taking their money'.[26] Five years earlier one reason why the town's plan to build a sewage farm aroused so much opposition was that the Improvement Bill also empowered the corporation to expand its boundaries. Thus even the inhabitants of Heywood, who were not threatened with absorption, peered suspiciously at the plans to run the intercepting sewer across their territory. Rochdale, they said, 'was approaching them by subterranean passages'. It was like the Indian tactic of raising siege on towns 'by throwing stinkpots over the walls and, having driven the defenders away, taking them over'.[27] In the same decade a counsel defending Great Lever from Bolton's imperialism asked a Commons committee, 'was there really . . . no limit to Corporations stretching out their octopus-like hands or claws, and drawing in some of their neighbours to pay their debts?'[28] Thirty years earlier Salford also had been likened to a set of animals that were as physically remarkable as they were biologically improbable. A Broughton inhabitant called the town's authorities 'sly snakes in the grass who wanted to put their hands in the pockets of the people of Broughton and, as soon as they got hold of them, . . . would pawn them'.[29]

Given these emotions, expansion was necessarily a hazardous undertaking. To achieve even partial success, much had to be conceded. Partly for reasons reviewed in the final section of this chapter, the process could easily escape control. The most illustrative example of the problems is Bolton's attempted expansion in 1876/77. It is worth examining at some length, since it not merely provides considerable insight into what could happen but is typical of the difficulties experienced by both Rochdale and Salford at other times.

The 1876 Improvement Bill was at least the fourth attempt at expansion in thirteen years. Two — in 1864 and 1871 — had been abandoned by the council as soon as it became clear that they were 'certain to provoke a powerful and costly opposition in Parliament'.[30] Meanwhile, in 1867, Bolton's elite had even avoided requesting the expansion of the *parliamentary* borough because of the certainty of massive opposition from those who saw this as the thin end of the *municipal* wedge.[31] A further attempt at municipal expansion was started in 1875 but temporarily abandoned after rejection by a town meeting.

The 1876 plan was to extend municipal limits by 6,694 acres, absorbing the townships of Great Lever and Tonge along with substantial parts of Darcy Lever, Turton, Sharples, Halliwell and Heaton. It was based upon the area's natural drainage, and would have increased the population by 20,000. Bitter experience had made the corporation cautious. It moved publicly only after exhaustive negotiations had apparently neutralised most potential opposition. The general purposes committee had invited the local authorities affected (the boards of health and the Bolton rural sanitary authority) to meet them. All except two had done so. Turton's local board was eased into neutrality by a promise to deal with its sewage. The proposed boundary was altered in an effort to remove the objections of Sir Charles Tempest, owner of most of the land in Heaton township — and similar negotiations were reputed to be going on with other relevant landowners. As a result the committee believed that it had secured assent, or at least neutrality, from all but five of those who felt themselves affected, and that there was 'pronounced opposition' from only three. On this understanding, at the end of September, the council applied to Parliament.

In the usual manner of such legislation, and in order to increase what would now be called its cost effectiveness the Improvement Bill also contained clauses empowering the corporation to establish new sewage works, new waterworks and a new cemetery, to expand the gasworks, improve certain streets, and to increase its own borrowing powers substantially. Ironically, this served to intensify opposition to municipal expansion. Fears were expressed about the closure of local churchyards, and the fate of those who had already booked their seats to Heaven by reserving graves. Many predicted invasion by sewage pipes, and many used Bolton's various plans as justification for claims about the financial profligacy of all urban corporations.

It rapidly became obvious that, for all the negotiation, Bolton was 'about to enter a struggle of a most formidable character'.[32] Several councillors, who were also out-township residents, moved into the opposition camp. By mid-October the Halliwell and Astley Bridge local boards had decided to oppose the Bill, and had been backed by enthusiastic township meetings. Crowded meetings in Tonge and in the part of Heaton excluded from the Bill had voted the same way. There were also signs of growing opposition from several local landowners. Most damagingly, in January 1877 the Bolton rural sanitary authority came out in open opposition.

This last move illustrates how unpredictable the expansion process could become, and how difficult it was to please everyone. When the Bill had first been mooted the authority had indicated that it would not object. Its opposition now was based partly on familiar fears about rate increases for those parts of its area included in the proposed municipal limits, and on the decline in its own ratable resources resulting from their departure. Opposition was also based upon a consideration of what the authority would be left with: apart from the remains of its original area, it was also to get the remains of other areas which the Bill proposed to include in Bolton. The authority claimed that the new territory would be 'much more difficult' both to finance and 'to deal with for sewage and other sanitary purposes as the ... watershed inclines naturally towards the ... districts which are proposed to be included'.[33] Significantly, also, the authority's opposition was led by James Fogg — a quarry master in Great Lever who had entered his own private plea for special protection from municipal regulations, and a man who combined the position of authority chairman with that of Bolton councillor.

By the time the Bill reached Parliament in March some thirty-one petitions were lodged against it[34] — almost exclusively against the expansion clauses. They came from local boards, manufacturers, landlords, railway companies and a socio-economic variety of 'ratepayers'. Most were merely tactical moves designed to get better terms of inclusion or special protection from corporation regulations if included. A few were objections to incorporation *per se*.

Two points can be made about the response of Bolton's municipal elite to all this opposition up to, and during, the parliamentary hearing. First, it was characterised by a frantic desire to conciliate almost anyone who appeared even slightly susceptible. Proposed boundaries were redrawn, where possible, to secure the compliance of landowners. Local boards were tempted away from starting their own sewage schemes in anticipation of the Bill's defeat by promises 'to deal efficiently with the sewerage of those districts without their having to incur a considerable proportion of the ... expenditure'.[35] Ratepayers currently within the rural sanitary authority were told that their contribution to any new corporation sewers would be 'only in proportion to rateable value', not the actual cost of construction.[36] The corporation negotiated with Lord Bradford, and secured the withdrawal of his opposition, and that of Great Lever and Darcy Lever (most of which he owned) in return for a promise that the borough rate for those districts would not exceed a shilling in the pound. The noble lord was also promised specially low rating for agricultural land within the borough in perpetuity. Finally, Halliwell's local board was given similar promises, and its proposed representation on the new council raised from five to eight.[37]

The second point is that the very process of conciliation could lead to further complications. The granting of special terms to particular areas, or individuals, soon led to expectations that the same terms would be granted to all. Moreover, in negotiating with the unfamiliar world beyond their boundaries, municipal elites could sometimes innocently exacerbate local social conflicts, thus making the process of negotiation more difficult. Perhaps the principal reason why opposition from some of Great Lever's inhabitants persisted was 'on account of the exceptionally favourable concessions granted to Lord Bradford whereby the manufacturing interests of the township have been sacrificed, as is alleged, to . . . the landed interest'.[38]

Eventually conciliation secured the withdrawal of all but three petitions. However, for reasons which we shall shortly examine, the Commons committee itself now took a damaging swipe at the Bill. Having heard testimony from around fifty variously expert corporation witnesses, it listened to the case for excluding Astley Bridge. Its response was to exclude from incorporation not merely Astley Bridge but most of the areas which had been successfully conciliated into acquiescence. Of those originally scheduled for inclusion, only part of Halliwell remained.

At this point the process threatened to get even further out of hand. In early May 1877 a crowded and thoroughly bad-tempered Halliwell township meeting decided against amalgamation — forcing the local board itself back into opposition. The move was prompted by fears that, in the now only moderately enlarged borough, Halliwell would have to bear a much greater share of the rate burden than if all the proposed districts had been included. The board demanded guarantees that Halliwell's borough rate would be 6d in the pound less than the rest of the borough for the next twenty years. Though the corporation refused, conciliation continued. Eventually Halliwell subsided contentedly when Bolton promised to pay all the costs of its parliamentary opposition and to connect it immediately to the town's sewage system at a charge proportionate only to its ratable value.

The rest of the Bill was now given an unhindered parliamentary passage, receiving the royal assent in December. However, instead of the planned increment to its ratable value of £135,000, Bolton received only £28,000. The expansion had originally been conceived partly as a means of supplementing Bolton's increasingly scarce supply of building land. Instead it was given the most populous part of Halliwell along with only one-seventh of that township's acreage. In all respects, therefore, the 10,000 population increment was something of a poisoned chalice.

Although municipal expansion, the search for water and the disposal of sewage were the principal sources of conflict, other corporate actions — such as tramway building or gas supply extension to areas beyond municipal borders — could also provoke outside opposition. Even an apparently internal matter like gas municipalisation might produce objections from outsiders fearful that corporate gas would prove more expensive than private gas.[39] In these as in the foregoing areas the position of municipal elites was one of weakness — and it is worth pausing briefly to examine why. This will lead logically into our final section.

There has been little in this chapter to suggest that the problems of nineteenth-century municipal leaders, in their dealings with the outside world, came from anywhere but the rest of the propertied classes. My contention is that acute difficulties stemmed partly from the very fact that economic standing and political office were so often combined.

Two points are worth making in this respect. First, Rochdale and Bolton's municipal elites — like that of Salford — were facing obstacles that were partly the result of ambivalence due to the very nature of their political resources. For they were not merely proprietors but often also the owners of *scattered* property — factories within and beyond the municipal border, or more frequently a factory on one side and a house on the other. Quite frequently, too, such individuals played dual political roles — as councillor and local board member.

The combined effect was to face urban leaders with conflicting political loyalties. We have already witnessed the effect in Salford and Manchester. We have caught glimpses of the same problem in Rochdale and Bolton. There are other examples. Bolton's 1876 amalgamation scheme was damagingly opposed not merely by Councillor Fogg (who, as we saw, was chairman of the rural sanitary authority) but by J. Wilkinson — also a Bolton councillor and an active member of the Astley Bridge local board. In 1872 Thomas Hesketh — a Bolton manufacturer and leading councillor but also Astley Bridge's largest ratepayer and an active member of its local board — appeared before a Commons committee and successfully argued that his township should be granted lower gas prices than those envisaged in the town's current improvement Bill. However, the individual best illustrating the political schizophrenia that we are referring to is James Taylor. In November 1864 Bolton Council discussed the extension of the borough boundaries. Having delivered himself of the following comment, Taylor abstained in an ambivalent heap.

He felt himself placed in a very peculiar position, for being a commissioner in Halliwell as well as a member of the Council, he felt anxious to do his duty to both his constituencies. . . . in Halliwell . . . there was the most determined feeling among the ratepayers to oppose the application . . . He felt reluctant to give a vote either [way] . . . if he voted [against extension] it might be supposed he voted for his own particular interest; and if he voted for [extension] he should be considered to oppose the interests of those who had placed him in office as a commissioner.[40]

Second, municipal leaders also faced obstacles stemming from the activities of other elites beyond their borders. Normally local boards, even more than councils, seem to have been composed of leading industrial proprietors in the area. Their activities, as we have seen, were often supplemented by those of local landowners — even better endowed with political resources.

Yet trouble did not emanate solely from other large proprietors. Out-township society was semi-urban, and thus socially and politically complex. It was often divided not merely by the landowning-manufacturing conflict witnessed earlier but also by the perennial clash between large and small ratepayers. The ultimate ruling bodies were often township meetings which all ratepayers could attend. Local boards were also elected by the ratepayers. By these means the participation of small ratepayers probably added considerable force to out-township opposition. After all, they had genuinely more to fear from rate rises than those further up the economic scale. Significantly enough, as we have noted, what seems to have been crucial in pushing Halliwell's local board back into opposition to incorporation at the last ditch in 1877 was a crowded and angry ratepayers' meeting.[41] To some extent, therefore, municipal elites were subject to the vagaries of other political systems in the same way that, as we shall see in later chapters, they were subject to those of their own.

Overall, the problems faced by urban leaders in their dealings with outsiders can be ascribed partly to a series of paradoxes. First, there is the point we came across in the last chapter: the very property and substance that gave certain men such advantages in political recruitment and legitimation also imposed constraints on them in certain aspects of political activity. Second, the local autonomy, so prized by municipal elites and so much a part of the basis of their power, was prized equally by others beyond the town boundaries. Third, in spite of the foregoing, there were some respects in which nineteenth-century towns were not at all autonomous. Because of urbanisation, and the interdependence that resulted, they and their elites were subject to influences from contiguous areas. They were also subject, as we shall now see, to what often seemed to be the capricious behaviour of the final arbiter in London. This was all the more true because, as is already evident, conflicts with surrounding areas, like those within the towns themselves, were often carried to the centre for solution.

The influence of the centre

Although local authorities enjoyed considerable independence in deciding what powers to take or not to take, Britain was in no sense a federal country. Local Acts were admittedly the main way of expanding, obtaining improvement powers or acquiring resources beyond municipal borders. But they had to be obtained from Parliament. Although central government increasingly impinged upon local decision-making during the century, by far the most important central institution in the life of an urban municipality was not government at all but the national legislature.[42] More particularly, it was the parliamentary legislative committee.

Improvement legislation was subject to private Bill procedure. The first and second readings were entirely formal, and the committee stage was crucial. Private Bill committees of the Commons and Lords were virtually in the position of American Congressional committees. They had almost total power not merely over the Bill's detailed clauses but also, through their ability to consider its 'preamble', over its principles. This meant that corporate elites were in the hands of legislative committees over which they had little influence — and which could often prove themselves quite as susceptible to the pleas of objectors as to the entreaties of municipal initiators.

In this situation urban corporations invariably sent deputations to Parliament composed of their most weighty and resourceful members — in social, economic and political terms. However, their role before legislative committees was at best to persuade, and more often simply to plead. Thomas Thomasson, one of Bolton's leading manufacturers, spoke from bitter personal experience when he explained to fellow councillors in 1854 that 'people who might think that they were very important in Bolton found themselves very little boys when in London . . . and had to deal with such men as Lord Redesdale, and they could not get all that they would like . . .'.[43]

Moreover the complexities of parliamentary procedure necessitated dependence upon lawyers for the presentation of the council's case. Since the same was generally true for objectors, the improvement process was normally 'very profitable to gentlemen of the long robe'.[44] It was thus also very expensive. As early as 1848 the average cost of guiding an improvement Bill through Parliament was estimated at over £2,000.[45] In 1854 the cost of getting the sorry remnants of Bolton's Bill to the point of royal assent was claimed without contradiction to be £9,000.[46] In 1877 witnesses and deputations in support of the Bolton expansion Bill alone cost £4,290.[47]

The expense might have been more bearable if the process had not been so fraught with risk. In 1854 the editor of the *Rochdale Standard* explained how difficult things were:

You have a host of parliamentary usages to observe, with which [only] parliamentary agents and lawyers are acquainted; and you are compelled to submit yourselves into their hands or submit to disappointment . . . Even when the Bill has passed the Commons, you may be left to the very last moment in fear and trembling as to whether or not you can get before a Committee of the Lords at all; and, if you do not during the session, you must being *de novo*.[48]

He was describing Rochdale's experience over its 1853 Improvement Bill, when, after a parliamentary petition from two Conservative manufacturers, this predominantly Liberal town was foist with the notorious clause 96. The clause prohibited the depositing of sewage in the river Roche above a certain point. Together with subsequent court injunctions based on the clause, it seriously hampered attempts to dispose of Rochdale's sewage for the next thirty years. Precisely how the clause came to be inserted is obscure, but in the eyes of the Liberal elite it had been inflicted 'by a lot of old women in the House of Lords'[49] and was 'forcibly illustrative of the mischievous manner in which business is done in [Lords] Committees at the end of a session'.[50]

As all this suggests, parliamentary committees could hand out pretty rough justice to municipal authorities. We have seen how Rochdale's 1872 Improvement Bill was denuded of its sewage clauses by successive Commons and Lords committees; indeed, for one terrifying moment the Lords Committee refused to proceed further with any of the clauses — eventually resuming consideration only 'as a matter of indulgence'.[51] We have also seen part of the process whereby Bolton's 1854 Bill received even nastier treatment. After the Home Secretary had removed the cemetery clauses the Commons committee expunged those empowering the corporation to purchase the gasworks, whilst its counterpart in the Lords devoured the clauses on water supply and smoke pollution. Meanwhile the combined attentions of both committees reduced proposals to increase corporate borrowing powers from the original £150,000 to £50,000. Finally, as also noted, Bolton lost nearly the whole of its proposed borough extension of 1877 in a hostile committee of the Commons.

Sometimes such horrendous things were done because a given Bill was ill designed or conflicted with national legislation. More frequently, legislative amputation was a response to local objectors, and the result of much more subjective motivations. Parliamentary committees often showed themselves remarkably tender-hearted to the claims of men of property outside the municipal limits. They were particularly sympathetic where landed property was involved. It was no accident that a Commons committee in 1872 should have refused Rochdale a sewage farm, given that the chief objector was the Earl of Derby.

We should remember that the membership of both Houses was drawn predominantly from the landed classes and that, into the 1880s, the representative system was heavily weighted in favour of rural and small-town areas. Private Bill committees normally showed the same bias. As a result, improvement legislation was probably sometimes mauled because committee members disliked not merely the Bill but towns in general. This seems a very possible explanation for the virtual failure of Bolton's attempt to expand in 1877. Most out-township opposition, as we saw, had been withdrawn by the time the Commons committee decided against amalgamation. That committee was wholly composed of county members and, as the *Bolton Weekly Journal* had noted earlier, 'it may be expected . . . to sympathise with rural rather than town interests'.[52]

Whatever motivated them, parliamentary committees were normally the point of final decision on the attempts of urban corporations to expand their powers, and the final arbiters of unresolved local disputes about those powers. This role made them the key to much that happened in nineteenth-century urban political systems. The expense involved in obtaining improvement legislation, and the nasty things that might happen to it, made municipal leaders anxious to conciliate both opposition and potential opposition — not just while the Bill was proceeding through Parliament but preferably long before it got there. Moreover, almost any opposition might become worth conciliating — even when, as we shall see in the next few chapters, it emanated from within the town and from some way down the socio-economic scale.

However, outside opposition was certainly the most formidable. If attempts at conciliation failed, then, as we have seen, corporate leadership might well simply abandon the legislative effort before it got under way. Certainly this seems to have lain behind the abandonment of Bolton's attempts to expand its water resources in 1871, and to extend its boundaries in 1864.

It is obvious from the panoply of powers that urban authorities like Rochdale, Bolton and Salford came to possess that they did not always receive parliamentary treatment as cavalier as that described above. Nevertheless, whatever their behaviour, the crucial point is that legislative committees were subject only to the most tenuous municipal influence. Faced with angry or indifferent outsiders, urban leaders were weak. They had few sanctions. With those adjacent to borough boundaries they might try inducement and persuasion. With those in London they could often only plead.

Notes

1 For a survey of other constraints on the autonomy of local decision — making, see R. J. Morris, 'Class, Power and the Parameters of Localism', paper presented SSRC Urban History — Politics Study Group, April 1981.
2 *SR*, 16 January 1897, p. 4.
3 *SWN*, 6 April 1861, p. 3.
4 Quoted *SWN*, 15 May, 1875.
5 'Ratepayer', *ibid*.
6 Alderman Thomas Davies, *SWN*, 9 June 1883, p. 3.
7 *SR*, 10 August 1901.
8 Alderman Thomas Agnew, *MG*, 10 November 1849, p. 9.
9 J. S. Ormerod, *MG*, 12 January 1837, p. 3.
10 *SWN*, 23 February 1861, p. 2.
11 *SWN*, 20 April 1861, p. 2.
12 Quoted *SWN*, 6 April 1861, p. 3.
13 Alderman Thompson, Manchester Council, *SWN*, 16 July 1887, p. 4.
14 Alderman Bromiley, *SWN*, 4 October 1870, p. 3.

15 Alderman Platt, *ibid*.
16 Ibid., p. 2.
17 Council statement, *SWN*, 5 September 1862, p. 3.
18 Council Parliamentary Committee report, *BC*, 13 May 1854, p. 6.
19 Quoted *RO*, January 1872, p. 7.
20 Mayor, *RO*, 3 February 1872, p. 6.
21 Commons Committee proceedings, reported *RO*, 27 April 1872, pp. 6-7.
22 Milnrow ratepayers' meeting, quoted 3 February 1872, p. 7.
23 Mayor, *RO*, 6 July 1872, p. 6.
24 *Ibid*.
25 Councillor R. Brierley, *RO*, 3 February 1872, p. 7.
26 *RO*, 14 April 1877, p. 5.
27 Ratepayers' meeting, *RO*, 13 January 1872, p. 8.
28 *BC*, 28 April 1877, p. 4.
29 Township meeting, *MG*, 24 November 1847, p. 4.
30 *BC*, 12 November 1864, p. 7.
31 'Blue book on Parliamentary Boundaries', quoted *BC*, 25 July 1868, p. 3.
32 *BWJ*, 10 October 1876, p. 9.
33 Parliamentary petition, *BC*, 3 March 1877, p. 7.
34 *BC*, 3 March 1877, p. 7.
35 *BC*, 16 December 1876, p. 7.
36 *BC*, 21 April 1877, pp. 2-3.
37 *BC*, 7 April 1877, p. 5.
38 *BWJ*, 7 April 1877, p. 5.
39 See opposition to Bolton's gas Bill, *BC*, 13 April 1872, p. 5.
40 *BC*, 19 November 1864, p. 8.
41 See also ratepayer associations and the Halliwell and Astley Bridge Local Boards, *BWJ*, 18 November 1871, p. 9.
42 Parliament's role in local authority life is largely unexplored. Attention has concentrated on governmental relations: see R. J. Lambert, 'Central-local relations in mid-Victorian England: the Local Government Act Office, 1853-71', *Victorian Studies*, VI (1962-3); E. P. Hennock, 'Central-local relations: a historical outline, 1800-1950', and C. A. Bellamy, 'Central-local relations, 1871-1919: the case of the Local Government Board, both papers to SSRC Urban History-Politics Study Group, March 1980. The growing literature on the Poor Law and on public health is also relevant. For significance of central-local relations in contemporary debate see W. C. Lubenow, *The Politics of Government Growth, 1833-48* (Newton Abbot, 1971).
43 *BC*, 13 May 1854, p. 6.
44 *BC*, 20 January 1877, p. 7.
45 See S. E. Finer, *Life and Times of Edwin Chadwick* (London, 1952), p. 433.
46 *BC*, 17 February 1855, p. 7.
47 *BC*, 18 August 1877, p. 7.
48 *RS*, 17 June 1854, p. 8.
49 R. Tweedale, *RS*, 2 September 1854, p. 8.
50 *RS*, 17 June 1854, p. 8.
51 Quoted *RO*, 29 June 1872, p. 4.
52 *BWJ*, 7 April 1877, p. 3.

6

Local authorities and the outside world

II. The world within the municipal borders

In the last two chapters we have argued that any idea of a municipal elite, however richly endowed with political resources, achieving its end with untroubled ease is much too simple. Such a picture cannot adequately describe the outcome of relationships within local authorities, and between them and the world beyond the municipal borders.

From now on we shall be concerned with local authorities' relations with the areas they were charged with administering. We have already seen from chapters 2 and 3 that a pure elitist model had much to commend it as a description of this sphere. It told us much about political recruitment and about the wide area of discreet politics. In examining active issue politics we shall come across further supporting evidence. Nevertheless we shall also argue that the full picture is again more complex — as regards both the configuration of power and the factors governing that configuration. In the Victorian industrial town political success was rarely easy, and was not determined by economic factors alone, contrary to what the pure elitist model might suggest.

There is no doubt that economic factors were highly important in determining who got what from issue politics. Economic substance greatly aided the municipal elites. It would be surprising if local leaders able to command so much dependency, both on their own account and through others of their kind, were not able to do well in the local political battle. Such resources were immensely useful in garnering signatures on petitions in favour of desired municipal projects, and very likely in persuading the population to accept municipal policies once applied. Meanwhile the networks of contacts built up in the economic and philanthropic worlds were likely to be valuable adjuncts to the achievement of municipal success. Furthermore, whatever their problems in obtaining improvement Bills, well-heeled leaders of local communities might be expected to have certain advantages in dealing

with well-heeled and hierarchically-minded parliamentarians, as compared
with more lowly souls seeking to oppose municipal aims.

In fact none of what follows will deny a substantial gradient of political
influence and advantage, tilted towards the elite and against those outside the
municipal circle and further down the social scale. Moreover the gradient was
also tilted in favour of the class from which local leaders were most
numerously drawn. As we shall see, the severest troubles experienced by
municipal elites often originated from individuals and groups on a comparable
economic level.

Nevertheless it will become clear that, though the gradient was steep, it
was not vertical. Furthermore, it was neither stable nor uniform in the three
towns. As chapters 8, 10 and 11 will show, other groups could influence the
style and content of local decisions — negatively and sometimes positively. In
the right circumstances even socially humble groups could have considerable
impact. They could do so particularly in the early decades of our period;
indeed, in Rochdale their influence was evident throughout it. Moreover it
will become evident that, whatever the social origins of politically trouble-
some groups, one of the commonest situations in urban government was
paralysis, often undesired paralysis.

Given these elements of pluralism and constraint, and given the variations
in them according to time and place, it seems probable that we need more
than the presence or absence in politics of economic substance to explain
them. This becomes clearer in view of the paradox that Rochdale's very
popular pattern of politics was presided over by the most economically and
socially resplendent municipal elite in any of the three towns. Local leaders in
Salford and Bolton, though still formidably endowed with economic and social
resources, were somewhat less impressive. Yet, as will become evident,
Bolton's (and even Salford's) politics were more oligarchic than Rochdale's,
even if equally prone to paralysis.

Economic factors, it is true, can still take us some way in explaining even
the paradox. As we saw in chapter 1, Rochdale's factories were rather smaller
on average than either Bolton or Salford's. Patrick Joyce has argued
persuasively that relations between employers and employees were more
egalitarian in small factories and more paternalistic in larger ones.[1] Although
Joyce is mainly concerned with constituency and electoral politics, it seems
reasonable to assume that Rochdale's more extensive, more autonomous and
ultimately more influential working-class population, and the more populistic
attitude of her leaders, can partly be attributed to such economic relationships.

Nevertheless economic factors can only get us so far. Rochdale's relatively
democratic politics, for example, affected all levels of local society and its elite

— including even the very largest manufacturers turned politicians. Moreover factory size cannot really explain the political fluctuations evident in all three towns. In particular, it cannot explain the precise coincidence of changes in Bolton and Salford towards narrower and more controllable political patterns with the date of incorporation in those towns.

In chapters 8, 10 and 11 we shall argue that to comprehend fully the varying ability, or inability, of municipal elites to achieve their ends we need to turn to four more immediate factors. Though these were related to economic substance and structure, they also operated independently of them, and in a mutually reinforcing way.

1. *The level of conflict within the elite*. Local leaders were not united but divided along lines of religion, geography (in Salford) and, most important, of party. As we shall see, these divisions varied in intensity according to time and place. They were more intense at the beginning than at the end of the period, and more intense in Rochdale throughout than in Bolton or Salford. In the right institutional circumstances, intense conflict could produce the sort of paralysis evident in Bolton and Salford before incorporation. It could also produce appeals for support to others further down the social scale. In Rochdale, and in Salford before 1844, such appeals drew the interests and demands of lowly groups into the political calculus. Alternatively, successful moves towards unity could pay handsome dividends to any elite — as was most dramatically evident with regard to Salford's incorporation in 1844. Such divisions were also related to:

2. *The nature of the institutional system*. The constraints upon local leaders varied according to the number of local government institutions, the number of access points to the political process that they provided and to whom this access was available. As we shall see, life was most difficult for the elite when institutions were numerous and under divided party control. Whether such difficulty was due mainly to individuals and groups on a comparable social level to the majority of the elite (as in Bolton), or whether it was also due to other groups further down the scale, depended on whether local institutions were open or closed. Access might be restricted to groups able to approach individual legislators discreetly, or open to any group able to fill a public meeting. The more of the latter that were available, and the more they were exploited by competing parties, the less predictable was politics likely to be, and the more bargains the controlling section of the elite had to strike in order to retain control. As we shall see when we come to Salford, the council's internal arrangements could also affect the possibility of achieving desired ends. Finally, there was one point of access common to all towns — the parliamentary improvement process. This will not be dealt with specifically in our treatment of the institutional systems, since its role was analysed

in chapter 5. Nevertheless we shall come across further illustrations of the extreme vulnerability of municipal elites — this time to pressures from *within* their boroughs — whenever they had to 'go to Parliament'.

3. *The attitudes of local leaders to popular opinion*. The extent to which outside opinion was taken into account in policy-making also varied according to municipal leaders' beliefs about the legitimacy of outside pressure. Like party conflict and the institutional system, these varied according to time and town. In Rochdale local leaders were populistic and often purported to see themselves as tribunes of 'the people', among whom they specifically included the working classes. In Bolton such attitudes, though not unknown (at least before incorporation), were much rarer. In Salford delegatory postures were common before incorporation but much less so thereafter, though they partially reappeared after the 1867 Reform Act. Attitudes were affected by the level of party conflict and the nature of the institutional system. Yet they also had their own effect, helping to determine, for example, how far town and township meetings became part of the institutional system.

4. *The level of popular mobilisation*. This varied in terms both of popular expectations about participation, and the spectrum of groups mobilised. In Rochdale, as we shall see, expectations were high and the spectrum was wide. In the context set by party competition, institutional opportunities and elite attitudes, many groups could influence municipal politics in some way. In Bolton and Salford the situation was different, and the pattern of influence varied accordingly. Meanwhile not everyone needed to mobilise. Some could rely on discreet approaches and, as we saw in chapter 3, those at the top of the economic scale could influence policy by 'reputation for power' alone. Sometimes even 'ratepayers' (and this economically minded category might include workingmen) could prove influential in this way. Generally, however, the more lowly the group the more was mobilisation a precondition of influence. The desire and ability to mobilise, as we shall see, was related to the nature of local society. Yet it could also be encouraged or discouraged by local leaders, and by the opportunities offered by the institutional system.

Notes

1 *Work, Society and Politics*, chapter 4.

7

Rochdale politics I

On the evidence so far, Rochdale provides the best test among the three towns of the power of a political elite composed of social and economic leaders operating in a situation favourable to its rule. As we saw in chapter 3, the town's government contained very large numbers of economic and social leaders, functioning before an absorbed and often economically dependent local audience. Given this array of resources, here if anywhere political action might be expected to prove as elitist as the theory legitimising business participation in local government suggested it ought to be: a municipal leadership such as this should have been able to achieve autonomously determined purposes with the minimum of fuss and reference to those affected in the world outside.

As a picture of who got what, such a model has considerable strength: the generalisations in chapter 3 about policy and social control apply as much to Rochdale as to Salford and Bolton. However, in many respects political life was more complex. This was so even in some of the aspects of discreet and private politics. In this chapter we shall examine the factors conditioning politics in the more conventional sense, and will argue that Rochdale possessed a conflictual pattern of party politics; a relatively open institutional system which (unlike Salford's and Bolton's) did not substantially close after incorporation; a populistic local elite, and a thoroughly mobilised population. As a result we shall argue here, and more extensively in chapter 8, that Rochdale's configuration of power was different from Bolton's or Salford's. Admittedly, as there, many of the troubles of the municipal leaders were caused by groups on the same economic level. Nevertheless many groups (including the working classes) could achieve appreciable political salience, and Rochdale's politics were markedly and consistently more pluralistic than those of Bolton and Salford.

The divided elite

Rochdale's local political elite was not united but continuously and often bitterly divided along overlapping lines of religion and party. The religious conflict was fought out between Nonconformists and churchmen. This battle centred upon Church rates but also spread into other issues and into other institutions besides those of the parish. Church rates were not peculiar to Rochdale, but they did cause particularly bitter and all-embracing contention there for several reasons. Nonconformity, being heavily influenced by the Weslyan Methodist Association, and having anyway a substantial majority of religious adherents among the population, was more aggressive and more influential than in Bolton or Salford.[1] The conflict with Anglicanism was also intensified by the wealth and central economic position of Rochdale's parish church. In 1839 the living was estimated to be worth £12,000, and the vicar from 1848, W. N. Molesworth, was undoubtedly one of the town's wealthiest men. The Church owned approximately one third of the land within the pre-1872 borough boundaries, and was thus ground landlord for large areas of the town centre.

This drew the Church into many key local issues. In some respects it was a rival authority to the Liberal and Nonconformist-dominated police commission and council. Certainly the vicar's decisions about the terms of lease-holding on the Glebelands, about what was to be built there and how, and about street levels were all of deep concern to the commissioners.[2] The Church also stood in the way of several important things that the dominant Liberal municipal elite wished to do. As a result, it had to be bargained with. Moreover, as we shall see in chapter 8, its own deep internal conflicts (particularly about ritualism) damagingly affected the elite's ability to achieve desired ends.

The divisions within the elite were further exacerbated by the heavy overlap between religious and party conflict. As we shall see, few churchmen were Liberals and few Nonconformists Tory, and the central institutions of religion and party tended to coincide in each case. Thus one conflict fed upon the other. Partly as a result, and much more than in Salford or Bolton, party cleavage was deep, unforgiving and continuous. As Derek Fraser has observed in nineteenth-century Leeds,[3] so in Rochdale the battle was waged at all levels of the local political system. In 1847 a government commissioner, presumably hardened in the ways of urban politicians, felt it worth telling his superiors that 'party feeling is carried on to a great extent here . . .'.[4] Long before and long after this comment, party dominated the electoral processes of the police and improvement commissioners, the council and the board of guardians. It deeply affected the deliberations of town, township and (owing to the overlap with religion) parish meetings. It influenced relations between the public utility companies and the local authority. Party, in fact, dominated consideration of every political issue — and did so more deeply and continuously than in either Salford or Bolton. It also penetrated much deeper into the deliberations of the police and improvement commissioners, the council and the board of guardians, moving beyond the customary joustings over the aldermanic bench into most policy issues. Periodically there were attempts at compromise. Sometimes, particularly in council elections, they were successful. Yet peace never broke out because of any genuine amicability between the two sections of the elite — as was the case in Salford after 1844 and more intermittently in Bolton. Rather, electoral compromise was simply a recognition by the ·Liberals that the Tories, for the moment, constituted no danger to their domination of the town; and a recognition by the Tories that they could temporarily get no further, or that, if they withdrew from the scene, they might later benefit from 'the large amount of odium' resulting from Liberal mistakes.[5]

Given these facts, it is unsurprising that the incursion of party politics into local affairs was largely taken for granted in Rochdale. Unlike many other places, there was little sense that the 'intrusion' of party into this area was 'improper'. Rather the reverse: in 1857 Alderman G. L. Ashworth, a leading Liberal, told 250 canvassers that he 'intended to make the council a political institution', and had 'no notion of his political existence being ignored because he had been appointed to a seat . . .'.[6] Somewhat further to the political left, Edward Taylor was equally cavalier, describing the council in 1860 as being 'as much a political body as any other form of government in the country'.[7] Unlike many local newspapers, the *Rochdale Observer* never championed political castration. In 1873 it asserted, 'Nothing can be gained by enunciating the dogma that politics have no place in these elections. When it is recollected the important political measures that have come before the Council, it is of the highest importance that the burgesses should be careful whom they elect.'[8]

As already suggested, there were always forces within each party pushing towards compromise, and Liberal political success tempted some Tories simply to give up. Yet such forces failed to produce lasting results. They failed because of the character of the two parties. Liberals and Tories were divided from each other by religion, business and social networks, and by political opinion. Each was also internally divided — on grounds of politics and social status. As will now be argued, internal and external differences reinforced each other, producing a mix which helped perpetuate party conflict.

The Liberals were almost exclusively Nonconformist. They contained most of the business elite, and manufacturing families were central to Rochdale

Liberalism. Names like Ashworth, Tweedale, Pagan, Bright, Tatham, Petrie
and Heape occur and recur among the ranks of active party leaders and
municipal personnel. These families were frequently linked by business and
marriage as well as religion. Only rarely were they linked in any of these ways
with the Tories.[9] Religion, political interest and sometimes marriage also
linked them to a crucial group of altogether less well-heeled individuals:
shopkeepers, small manufacturers and Co-op leaders — men like Edward
Taylor, John Dania, William Simpson, William Shepherd and, most crucially,
Thomas Livsey.

Although, in the context set by the town's open institutional system,
Rochdale Liberalism was always markedly more radical than its counterparts
in Salford and Bolton, Liberals were often quite deeply divided over the
degree of popular participation desirable in the political process. Here the
socio-economic gap tended to complement the political divide: most, though
not all, of the manufacturing elite took a more conservative view (for
example, heavily backing the more oligarchic schemes for incorporation in
1856[10]), whilst the radicals were primarily, though not exclusively, smaller
men.

Yet the two sections needed each other. The 'Whigs' needed the radicals
because of the latter's closer links with Rochdale's relatively autonomous and
politicised working class.[11] The radicals were stronger in Rochdale than in
Salford or Bolton, and proved it decisively in 1856 by winning the battle over
the representational basis of incorporation. The Whig-radical alliance,
though subject to considerable stress, was also markedly more resilient. The
conflicts of 1856 divided them temporarily, pushing the radicals into alliance
with the democratic wing of local Toryism, and causing them to drop a
bucketful of metaphors on their erstwhile allies: 'While [the Whigs] were
lavishing kisses upon our cheeks, they were prompted by the feelings of a
Judas, and the cloven foot has at length become unmasked.'[12] Yet the rift
merely served to emphasise mutual need. There could be no permanent
future for the radicals among the Tories. However, co-operation lasted long
enough to demonstrate how damaging to Whig political fortunes rupture
might prove in Rochdale's open political system — with a radically supported
Tory capturing the politically crucial post of assistant overseer in Castleton in
1857. Mostly the two sections remained united, and the alliance pushed the
Liberals as a whole to the left — a bias observable in the regular selection of
radical-leaning parliamentary candidates, in Poor Law administration and
certain aspects of council policy. In general, what the radical editor of the
Rochdale Observer said of the period before 1856 remained true for many
years thereafter: 'the Whigs saw it to be in their interests to meet the
democracy of the [radicals] half-way'.[13]

The character and internal dynamics of Rochdale Toryism also intensified party conflict. The Conservative minority of the local business elite were united by an almost exclusive attachment to the Church. They were also insulated from the Liberals by social network. Their elite of large manu-facturers, merchants and bankers were members of families who, unlike their Liberal counterparts, were either on their way out of the urban middle class into the lower ranks of the landed interest, or had already arrived there a generation or more previously. The Schofields, Jewisons and Nields, as first generation small estate owners, are examples of the first category; the Fentons, Royds, Ramsays and probably the Fishwicks fall into the second. Meanwhile, even more than the Liberals, and normally quite separately from them, the Conservatives were strongly linked by marriage.

The effects of Tory social autonomy were reinforced by the party's own internal dynamic. Like the Liberals, they had a populist tail of smaller men who, however distasteful their behaviour might sometimes appear to their social superiors, were crucial to the Tories' modest political fortunes. For the Conservatives, as for the Whigs, factory-based paternalism and dependency were not enough. As a result the populists, led most notably by Peter Johnson, beer-seller and election agent, came to dominate the electoral style of municipal Toryism, and lent it a competitiveness that its instinctively oligarchic elite might not otherwise have promoted. In the context set by the open local institutional system the Tories became ready to profit from any dissatisfactions accruing from the municipal policies of the dominant Liberal majority — whether emanating from Roman Catholics, small proprietors, small gas consumers or even working-class ratepayers.

However, as implied above, the results of such conflicts within the elite can be understood only in terms of the characteristics of Rochdale's institutional system. For such divisions both reinforced the open nature of that system, and were themselves exacerbated by the rewards for successful competitors that it provided.

The institutional system

Throughout most of our period Rochdale possessed an open institutional system containing a complex and overlapping array of authorities, elected or appointed at different times of the year, by different electorates or appointing bodies, and often presiding over different geographical areas. Connected with them were several institutionalised occasions for public discussion and consultation — meetings of town, township and parish. As a result, the system contained many points at which a wide variety of groups (in the circumstances created by the other factors discussed in this chapter) could gain access to, and influence over, the local political process. Although Rochdale's institutions were mostly Liberal-controlled, the system was sufficiently diffuse to make total control impossible. Until at least the mid-1850s the Tories continued to control the more oligarchic points of access like the county magistrates, and could thus wreak considerable havoc. Moreover they, or others, could always stage surprise attacks, gaining seats on the police commission or control over some of the more obscure but politically important offices like those of assistant overseer or elective auditor. Thus the Liberal elite always felt obliged to reinforce its position by appealing to, and conciliating, all those groups with access to the more popular parts of the system. This was particularly necessary given the tendency (which Derek Fraser has observed elsewhere[14]) for battles originating in one institution to spill over into others. The conflict over Church rates, for example, affected not merely Rochdale parish and church wardens but also the police commissioners, overseers and magistrates.[15]

We can divide our analysis into two periods.

1830-56

The main corporate body before incorporation in 1856 was the police commission. Though its character changed in a democratic direction, it was always somewhat oligarchic. As established in 1825, it consisted of any property owner or occupier, to the yearly ratable value of £35, who cared to register and wait three months. After 1844 this gave way to the theoretically more powerful Rochdale Improvement Commission, consisting of sixty members, with one-third elected annually from three wards by all £10 householders. Membership was still restricted to those paying rates at £35 or over. In 1854 this was lowered to £20 and voting opened to all owners and occupiers irrespective of length of residence. However, the democratic effect (by 1856, there were some 5,628 electors, compared with 1,036 in 1844) was heavily counteracted by a provision allowing wealthy individuals to cast up to six votes.

These formal oligarchic tendencies, however, did not stop the commissioners and their Liberal majority from behaving in populistic ways.[16] Indeed, they reinforced such behaviour because of the commissioners' need for popular support against the more oligarchic Tory-controlled parts of the system like the magistrates' bench. Partly as a result, in spite of the property weighting, and the prohibition on publicans as members, commissioners' selections and elections provided access to quite a wide variety of groups. In particular, several Chartists became members, including Thomas Livsey — leader of Rochdale's working-class radicals. Significantly the commissioners elected Livsey chief constable in 1852.

As this suggests, the last office is also important from our present viewpoint. The incumbent was elected annually by the commissioners and, like them, normally Liberal. He resembled an unprestigious mayor: he chaired commissioners' meetings, was the town's civic head, and led corporate delegations to Parliament. However, his main importance, in the present context, was twofold. First, he could call town meetings when petitioned to do so by groups of inhabitants, or commissioners. The power was discretionary, but when sympathetic he was a point of potential access to groups — including Chartists — quite a long way down the social scale. Second, a radical incumbent like Thomas Livsey could use the strategic position thus provided to increase access — by calling public meetings on request, and by getting democratising clauses inserted in improvement Bills.[17]

The significance of these functions, however, can only be properly understood by appreciating the role of town meetings — and public meetings generally — in Rochdale's political life. For, along with other exercises in participation, town meetings were a central feature of the local political process before and long after 1856.

They were used for two main purposes. First, they were often called, on petition to the chief constable, to discuss general issues of public concern (like factory regulation or parliamentary reform) which some group within, or outside, the elite wanted to see aired. Second, they were frequently asked to discuss, and sometimes effectively to decide upon, some local political issue. This might result from legal obligation. The 1844 and 1853 Improvement Acts, for example, obliged the commissioners to obtain explicit ratepayer sanction for any rate increase beyond 1s (and up to an absolute maximum of 2s) in the pound. Town meetings might equally be called because the dominant Liberal leadership, or some group within it, wanted public legitimation for its actions. Thus the police commissioners sought endorsement in their battle for control of the police against the Tory-dominated bench of county magistrates in the early 1840s. Town meetings were utilised frequently in the long radical-led battle against the full imposition of the New Poor Law; and they played a crucial part in the complex manoeuvrings between radicals, Liberals and Tories over incorporation.[18]

Whatever their origins, and particularly when the effect was enhanced by party conflict, such meetings provided points of effective access to the local political process for a wide variety of groups. Sometimes this meant publicity. Thus various chief constables agreed to call meetings 'chiefly of the working classes' to petition against the New Poor Law (the first, in January 1838); to petition the Queen 'to call in a government who will pass the Charter' (June 1842);[19] to elect Chartist Convention delegates (December 1842), and to hear

Richard Oastler and others declaiming against employers evading the Ten Hours Act (August 1849 and March 1850).

Equally frequently, town meetings allowed effective participation, and even final decision, in the local political process. There were few rules as to who was entitled to attend, and certainly none was ever enforced. Partly as a result these points of local decision-making could draw in people from a long way down the social scale. Moreover, as chapter 8 will show, variously congregated publics played a crucial part in major decisions from the late 1840s up to, and including, incorporation in 1856.

Besides the town meeting there were two other intensely public parts of the institutional system — parish and township meetings. The first were held annually in April, and drew upon an area much wider than that governed by the commissioners — embracing the whole of the partially municipalised townships of Wardleworth, Spotland and Castleton plus the autonomous ones of Wuerdle Wardle, Todmorden, Butterworth and Blatchinworth. The parish meeting was not as centrally concerned in the politics of Rochdale's local government as it was in Salford, because it was not involved in appointing the overseers, and because the churchwardens (whom it did appoint) had no Poor Law functions. Nevertheless, throughout the 1830s and 1840s, it was the centre of massive public attention. This was due to its role in levying the annual Church rate, and in appointing nine of the parish's ten churchwardens who assisted the vicar in collecting and administering the dues. It thus became the arena for the ferocious Church rates battle.

That this should become such a important issue is not surprising. The Parish Church was a central institution in Rochdale. Set on a cliff overlooking the centre, it dominated the town visually. It was immensely rich, partly as a result of being ground landlord for one third of the town. This was in a town and parish that contained a heavy Nonconformist majority.

From our present standpoint the parish meeting was important in three senses. First, and most obviously, it provided a significant point of access not merely for all sections of the middle classes but also for the many working people who seem to have found Church rates genuinely irksome. Not all parish meeting participants were in this position, and their support was probably either manipulated or bargained for. Nevertheless many, even among the working classes, felt the issue to be deeply important — and their participation helped produce an atmosphere that the *Manchester Guardian* felt was 'highly injurious to . . . good order'.[20] For such people the parish meeting and the poll which often followed gave authoritative access to a point where the decision on an issue crucial to them was being taken.

Second, for leaders on both sides, however impressive their socio-economic standing, the parish meeting was difficult to control. It took place in the churchyard. The open location and the rowdy atmosphere made it impossible to determine who had the legal right to participate. Outcomes were neither certain nor permanent, for the meetings were always open to surprise attack by one side or the other, and decisions about Church rates and church-wardens could always be overturned — by a subsequent poll, or at the meeting the following year. Furthermore it was impossible to prevent such occasions being turned to other purposes. Sometimes the crowd cheerfully turned their attention from Church rates to the Charter.[21] Meanwhile the churchwardens and sidesmen elected on the Nonconformist ticket often contained a proportion of Chartists.[22] In common with the town meeting, therefore, the parish meeting could provide access to publicity and office for those engaged in more autonomous lower-class protest.

Third, although Rochdale's Nonconformist/Liberal leaders eventually won effective abolition of compulsory Church rates, it probably left them with political debts to their followers that had to be paid off elsewhere — in support for more central lower-class causes, and benefits elsewhere in the institutional system.

Overall, parish meetings reinforced the tendency for competing sections of the local elite to appeal for support to those further down the social scale. Such trends were reinforced by township meetings. These took place annually in April (and occasionally at other times) in most townships of the parish, and after 1838 in those of the differently bordered Poor Law Union. Their functions, though mostly informal, were politically crucial. They nominated candidates for overseer to the county magistrates. They also often appointed a salaried assistant overseer. Overseer and assistant exercised functions which made them politically very important: they collected the poor rate, administered poor relief before the appearance of boards of guardians and, most sensitive of all, compiled the local and parliamentary electoral rolls.

Township meetings also authorised, and could determine, the level of the poor rate. They could decide to appoint a select vestry, and the governor and governess of the workhouse. The meeting might also nominate the town-ship's contribution to the parish constabulary.

From the viewpoint of local leadership, township, like parish, meetings were unpredictable, easy to pack, but difficult to control. Attendances often reached several hundred, and it was hard to determine who had the right to participate — particularly because decisions were taken on a show of hands. Where they were disputed, matters were taken to a township poll. Thus, as with parish meetings, a defeated group could always try for success at the second attempt. Unpredictability was increased by the fact that their various functions, and those of the officers whom they appointed, made the meetings very important to all sections of the community. For the competing local elites the noisy township deliberations about overseers' nominations had vital implications for the results of parliamentary elections — and there was therefore every reason to try to control them. This might sometimes be achieved by dragooning obedient factory hands. Yet wealthy local leaders had also to face the fact that the working classes and shopocracy had genuine interests of their own in what transpired. For them, township meetings were important points at which they might hope to influence Poor Law administration, the level of the poor rates or, more modestly, simply to gain access to some of the less prestigious offices in the local political system.[23]

Thus, although the Liberals (with the lion's share) and the Tories probably divided up most of the township spoils between them, the Liberals in particular had to let at least some radicals in. This was necessary if they were to retain the mass support that was so essential to them both here and in other popular parts of the system — or at least not lose it to the other side. The evidence about township proceedings in the pre-incorporation period is often rather scanty. Nevertheless it was perhaps through these sorts of channels that two Chartists came to be selected as overseers for Wardleworth.[24] The costs of not properly looking after one's supporters were probably revealed in April 1843, when the Spotland Liberals tried to restore the assistant overseer's salary to the level from which it had been reduced by the Tories in a surprise attack on the township meeting of the previous year. This time the Liberal motion was defeated 'by a combination of the Chartists and Tories'.[25] Meanwhile it may well have been an independently mounted radical attack on township proceedings in 1842 that obliged the county magistrates to contemplate a set of parish constables for Castleton that, in their fevered brains at least, comprised 'the names of some of the most violent Chartists in the Kingdom'.[26]

This final point should not be exaggerated. The evidence is of fluctuating quality, and on that occasion the magistrates applied an appalled veto to Castleton's nominations. It is nevertheless true that township meetings were unpredictable and open to anyone who turned up. Moreover one of the elite's principle remedies for the problems thus created was a generous dose of populism. The results, as implied above, can be seen in elite support for working-class-backed candidates to township office. However, the popular political debts incurred in the townships — as in the other open parts of the local institutional system — were probably also paid elsewhere. Among other places, they were paid in elections to the board of guardians.

At first sight the guardians seem an unlikely point of lower-class access and influence. Elections were designed to give property its due weight — with individuals casting up to six votes according to poor rate contribution. Yet in 1844, poking its head disapprovingly northwards, the *Manchester Guardian* was appalled to discover that those elected to Rochdale's board of guardians 'are nearly all of them Chartists'.[27] The verdict may have been coloured by the paper's tendency to lump all the varieties of radicalism into one horrifying category. Nevertheless, from its tentative inception in 1838, the board was and long remained under radical control; few of the basic principles of the New Poor Law were applied before the 1870s; and the board represented an important point of influence for the working classes, as for other lowly groups, in an area of policy that deeply affected them.[28]

Before, as after, 1856 the Liberal elite and their radical allies were able to control recruitment to most of the popular parts of the system. However, there were several oligarchic institutions which were not merely Tory-controlled but which gave that party access to patronage and policy. Their existence and politicisation greatly increased the local institutional system's tendency towards paralysis and confusion. Paradoxically, given their oligarchic character, they also further opened local politics to popular participation — because, in fighting these institutions, the Liberals had to intensify their appeal to those below.

The first and most important point of Tory access was the machinery of county administration — in particular the Rochdale branch of the county magistrates, and (after 1841) the county police. The magistrates had at least two functions drawing them into urban political conflict, and giving their Tory majority access to Rochdale's political processes. First, they had the legal right to appoint overseers for the parish. They could thus check the proceedings of the normally Liberal/radical–dominated township meetings. In most cases after the mid-1830s they simply assented to township nominations. However, through intermittent intervention of a more positive sort they inserted a reasonable sprinkling of Tory overseers, and thus ensured at least some Conservative influence on the composition of the electoral registers.

The magistrates' second politically sensitive function was that of petty law enforcement. In mid-1839 a battle for control in this area began between the Tory majority on the local bench and the Liberal minority. The two sections soon began meeting separately and actively competing for cases — sometimes actually burgling defendants from each other's courts. This led not merely to bizarre confusion but also to conflict with the police commissioners for control of the police function — police officers being the ones who brought cases before the magistrates and thus determined which section should hear them. After unsuccessfully attempting to take control of the commissioners, in November 1841 a group of local Tories, presumably acting on behalf of the majority section of the bench, successfully petitioned Lancashire's chief constable to introduce the county police into Rochdale. The commissioners thus lost control of the police function until their demise in 1856.

Meanwhile Tory predominance among the magistrates, and their eventual victory over the Liberal minority, ensured Tory pre-eminence in the general administration of justice. More specifically, it also gave them predominant influence (when they cared, and were united enough, to use it) over the enforcement of the licensing laws, the trial of political partisans for minor electoral offences and the enforcement of the town's nuisance regulations. In the last of these areas the improvement commissioners were complaining by 1850 that 'their orders were continually ... rendered nugatory by the Rochdale bench of magistrates'.[29] The magistrates were also able to preside over the fate of individuals refusing to pay Church rates, and over the associated legal battle in 1846 between the police commissioners and the vicar about the former's right to fix official notices to the church door.

The other points of Tory access were the private utility companies — particularly those supplying gas and water. Ostensibly politically neutral and concerned only with providing a service, they intermittently lent the Tories, who were always majority shareholders, the means of fighting the Liberal-dominated institutions of the town. In some respects, given their powers over all aspects of supply and maintenance, and their ability to apply to Parliament for local Acts, they constituted rival local authorities.[30] They were also formidable obstacles to powers that the police or improvement commissioners wished to take over. The companies were sources of custom which could be bestowed exclusively upon tradesmen who voted the right way in parliamentary and local elections.[31] Finally, as large conglomerations of property, they possessed multiple votes that the Tories were not averse to wielding when the heat was on — as in a contest for Butterworth township's assistant overseer in 1838, and in a Church rates poll in 1843.[32] All this in turn helped heighten resentment, particularly among the commissioners, and increased the tendency on both sides to compete for popular support.

1856-80

After 1856 the local institutional system changed in important respects. Unlike Salford and even Bolton, however, incorporation did not produce any substantial closing of local politics. Partly because of radical influence on the shape of incorporation, partly because of the factors under discussion in this chapter, the basic characteristics of the pre-1856 system remained — a multiplicity of access points that were difficult to control and could be used by a wide variety of groups.

The most obvious consequence of incorporation was the replacement of the improvement commissioners by the council. In one respect the situation was more closed against lowly groups than before. Though the franchise theoretically embraced all adult male ratepayers, the new requirement that a man must have resided in the borough for two years eight months resulted in the number of voters declining from 5,628 in the last year of the commissioners to 3,206 in the first council election. Most of those disenfranchised almost certainly came from the lowest and most migratory sections of the working classes.

Nevertheless, in most respects, the new council was not less democratic. Some of the loss in electors was due to the disappearance of plural voters. The burgesses were still more than double the parliamentary electorate, and thus almost certainly contained a working-class majority. Moreover by 1862 the burgesses had risen again to well over 5,000, all now individual voters and outnumbering the constituency electorate by over three to one, and representing around 65 per cent of all householders.

Meanwhile, as the radicals had predicted, the compensations for the new electoral residence requirement were considerable. The property qualification for municipal membership was reduced from £20 for commissioners to £15 for councillors (in most councils it was £30). This had no effect on the type of person recruited into municipal politics (in fact he was more likely to be wealthily proprietorial than before), but it did help ensure the continuance of Rochdale's predominantly populistic political style. Even more so did the fact that candidates still had to stand for election in three large wards (each with around 1,500 voters by 1859, and 2,200 by 1868) instead of in what most of the elite would have preferred — five or eight much smaller wards. As the radicals hoped, this probably prevented municipal wards from becoming cosy pocket boroughs by cancelling out the possible effects of factory influence.

In the circumstances created by continuing party conflict the system ensured that local politicians, however prestigious, had to lace their personal appeals with more tangible promises of performance. The 1856 settlement meant that council elections provided groups at all but the lowest, 'residual' levels with points of access to the political system. At least intermittently, elections were forums for the lively discussion of sensitive local issues, and for posing real alternatives on matters like the municipal purchase of Church lands, and the provision of parks and baths. The character of incorporation also helped ensure that social policies like these were embraced by the Liberal elite.

The democratic character of the new council should not be exaggerated. Issues were not always clearly posed, and elections, as noted in chapter 3, were quite frequently not contested. However, such witting or unwitting encouragement of oligarchy was mitigated by the popular character of the nomination process. Whether ultimately elected or simply returned unopposed, candidates were normally selected in ward nomination meetings that any ratepayer declaring himself to be a party voter could attend. Democratic fervour varied considerably, and it was sometimes plausibly claimed that the meetings did little more than obediently ratify nominations carefully 'cooked beforehand'.[33] The evidence is, anyway, difficult to interpret, owing to the party-political partiality of local newspaper sources. Even so, the various stages of nomination do often seem to have been genuinely open. Nomination meetings could draw large attendances; occasionally sitting councillors unwillingly disappeared;[34] there were sometimes more nominations than places available. Where this happened, particularly in the early years after incorporation, final selection seems to have been conducted with meticulous democratic care. In 1857, for example, a Liberal ward meeting in Castleton went through a process of multiple balloting to reduce the number of nominations from eight to four. Similar events took place in Wardleworth in 1858. In both cases the successful candidates were then submitted to 'public meetings' for final ratification.[35]

Moreover press reports also indicate that nomination meetings often vigorously discussed issues currently before the council. Thus, even where candidates were ultimately returned unopposed, the nomination process ensured some public discussion of municipal projects like the park or town hall, major municipal concerns like policies on gas prices or water supply, the level of rates or more specific ward grievances. Sitting councillors up for re-election, particularly if they were committee chairmen, often seemed to feel obliged to defend current policies. Many candidates, new or old, were obliged to identify their stance on major issues — and were sometimes nominated or refused nomination accordingly. Thus in 1865 Castleton's Liberal burgesses chose four candidates from six nominations, rejecting two sitting councillors. The merits of all had been discussed, 'those apparently being most popular who would vote for . . . the equalisation of the price of gas, the reduction in the police force and the purchase of the gas works'.[36]

Apart from the council, the other major local government institution until the 1870s was the board of guardians. Although voting was still weighted according to property, the annual guardians' elections continued to provide an important point of lower-class access to decision-making in an area closely affecting them. Partly as a result the board, under the radical chairmanship of Thomas Livsey, remained militantly and successfully opposed to the central principles of the New Poor Law until at least the late 1860s.[37]

Rochdale's school board was established in 1870. The entire body was elected in mid-November every three years, on a cumulative voting system. As seen in chapter 3, many among the elite regarded educational debate as dangerous and counter-productive.[38] They therefore tried hard to close this part of the local political system against popular participation — by producing agreed slates of candidates for unopposed return. In Rochdale the attempt was generally successful. Nevertheless, as in council elections, the process of nomination was more open. As we also saw in chapter 3, the means by which the list was produced had to be pluralistic, at least within certain limits, if the attempt at electoral compromise was to be successful.[39] Moreover, in the atmosphere created by religious and party division, the appearance of even a few unplanned candidates could throw the entire electoral process into a dangerously unpredictable state. In 1870 three candidates appeared in opposition to the official list and were all successful — two of them ending up among the first four. According to the *Rochdale Observer* their appearance enabled at least the Catholic and working-class sections of the electorate to replace those nominated for them by the elite.[40]

The points of exclusive Tory access to local politics (the public utilities and the county magistrates) declined after 1856, and their capacity for paralysis lessened. The improvement commissioners had already municipalised the gas company in 1844. The council ingested the water company in 1866, and the market company in 1872. These utilities had anyway become markedly less politicised some time before their disappearance. The county magistrates retained the important power of final appointment over the overseers in townships within the Poor Law Union. However, as a result of incorporation they lost their judicial functions to the council-nominated borough magistrates. Meanwhile the county police gave way to the new borough force controlled by the council's watch committee.

Nevertheless other parts of the local institutional system remained open to Tory attack. They could, of course, contest council and guardians' elections. In the 1870s they also began successfully contesting the obscure but potentially important office of elective auditor — using it as a platform from which to gain publicity for attacks on the spending policies of the council's dominant Liberal elite. Finally, the Conservatives, along with other lowlier groups, were able to intervene in the public meetings that still formed an important part of the local political system. For although a compromise on the Church rates issue in 1853 made parish meetings far less important, two other crucial points of direct democracy remained: town and township meetings.

In some respects after 1856 the town meeting became less important as a point of public access to decision-making. Until 1872 the council's powers were determined by the 1853 Improvement Act. This laid down that any rates increase beyond 1s in the pound required the ratepayers' consent. The clause never needed to be invoked after 1856, because Rochdale's various improvement schemes could be financed either within the maximum rate or, increasingly, out of profits from the thriving gas undertaking. The same Act also specified that the corporation could take an improvement Bill to Parliament provided a majority of the ratepayers had not objected within a month of council ratification. This was, to say the least, a decidedly passive form of consent — and one that allowed councillors to interpret the absence of objection as evidence that 'the public were perfectly satisfied with regard to the application to Parliament'.[41]

Partly as a result, public meetings fell into disuse for a while as points of policy determination, and as means of ratifying elite decisions. The trend was carried further by the 1872 Improvement Act, which not only increased the maximum allowable rate to 2s 6d in the pound but also laid no obligation on the council to consult the ratepayers formally if it wished to exceed the figure.

In spite of these changes town meetings remained an important though informal part of the local political system. As before 1856, they were often called, on petition to the mayor, to discuss issues of general public concern (particularly franchise reform). More pertinently from the viewpoint of local politics, they were a regular means of pressurising the council — playing some role, for example, in the ultimately successful campaign to establish a public park in the town centre.[42]

Finally, and most important, as a result of the 1873 Borough Funds Act Rochdale's council, along with those elsewhere, had to seek positive consent from a ratepayers' meeting before sending an improvement Bill to Parliament. This resurrected the town meeting as a legally constituted point of public policy decision — providing ratepayers at all levels with access to the political process. As we shall see in chapter 8 in the context provided by party conflict and mass arousal it had important effects on subsequent council behaviour.

Like town meetings, township meetings also remained important after 1856 and of potential interest to all groups. Each of the three townships within the Poor Law Union continued annually to nominate the overseer, and had the right to appoint and dismiss the salaried assistant overseer who increasingly took over the functions of electoral registration and rate collection from his now largely honorary superior. The two officers were obliged to bring poor and borough rates before the townships for approval. Although township powers here were largely formal (they could not refuse approval), the meetings did provide opportunities for the expression of poor ratepayers' grievances about the level of expenditure. Townships also had real powers of refusal when requested to grant a supplementary rate.[43] Finally, townships elected relief committees (as they had before 1856) to assist the guardians in giving local poor relief. Though strictly extra-legal, these committees were generally accepted by the guardians and came to exercise quite wide functions. In 1862 Rochdale's board refused recognition to a relief committee elected by a township meeting of mainly 'poor ratepayers' in Castleton. Yet even here the guardians were ultimately obliged to resume co-operation.[44] Through the medium of township meetings the working classes were thus given the means of influencing an area of policy which deeply affected them.

This fact, together with the high level of party interest of the electoral functions of the overseer, resulted in township meetings intermittently becoming the focus of considerable popular attention. Admittedly attendances could be modest; in Spotland meetings were actually abandoned for several years. Yet turn-outs of several hundred were still frequent, and crowds of much greater size could suddenly appear.[45]

As implied here, township meetings after 1856 remained unpredictable and difficult to control. Retiring officers could not depend upon being able to nominate their successors. The Liberals exercised predominant influence in township affairs, but they could never secure complete or permanent control. For example, in 1857, in the wake of the Liberal-radical split over incorporation and in retaliation for alleged Liberal tampering with radical voters, the radicals switched their support to Charles Cheetham, the Tory candidate for assistant overseer. This ensured his election. In 1868 Spotland township witnessed an exciting contest between thirteen candidates for the two posts of assistant overseer. After five successive ballots among the 1,500-2,000 present, the two Liberal candidates won. The most adjacent losers then demanded a poll. There followed an exciting seven-day election, conducted on the basis of what one observer called 'household and female suffrage'.[46] It eventually resulted in the return of one Tory (at the head of the poll) and one Liberal. Such unpredictability again reinforced the tendency, particularly of the Liberal elite, to broaden their appeal and to make concessions to those further down the social scale, both here and in other parts of the local institutional system.

Elite attitudes

The open institutional system thus encouraged parties to compete. High levels of conflict helped keep it open. To these ingredients must be added a third which again affected party competition and open politics, *and* was itself reinforced by them. This was the fact that local leaders were prepared to respond to the desires, and assumed desires, of the inhabitants with intense populism. The Liberals, particularly under the influence of their radical wing, were the main initiators of such attitudes. Yet, though the Tories initially seemed quite content with their image as defenders of wealth and property, they too eventually competed eagerly for the championship of the common man.

For a start, Rochdale's municipal politicians had a strong awareness of 'the people outside', and a strong feeling (not unnatural in such a visible local arena) that they were the subject of their absorbed attentions. Commissioners, guardians and councillors revealed this in what they said. Speeches — particularly just before an election — were often highly theatrical, with speakers (as their opponents sometimes irritably noted) posturing to impress those outside. There was a strong sense that corporate actions required careful public explanation lest they be misunderstood. Councillors and even aldermen commonly sought to strengthen arguments by pointing shaking fingers to 'certain lynx-eyed persons watching them ... [whose] little grievances would work at the next election'.[47] In 1868 Alderman G. L. Ashworth asked a question about municipal contracts, pronounced the relevant committee chairman's answer satisfactory, 'as expected', and then predicted that 'as it was going through the press it would do much good in disabusing the minds of many people in the town who were ... wishful to find fault ... '.[48] A few weeks earlier Ashworth had shown less council spirit in scampering to distance himself from the water committee's policy during a drought: 'he meant to stand clear before the public. The responsibility was so great that ... he would have no share in it'.[49] Similar concern about the watchers beyond the walls was evident among the guardians. As we shall see in chapter 8, these concerns reinforced anti-Poor Law attitudes.

Such sensitivity was not unknown in Bolton and Salford. What distinguished Rochdale was its greater frequency and the widespread feeling that it was legitimate. This partly accounts for the continuing place of town and township meetings in the political process — their use being quite as often a result of a radical–democratic tradition as of legal obligation. This same tradition produced a strong preference for public political processes — a preference that could sometimes lead to embarrassing difficulties. In 1859 the council tied itself into knots over whether the press should be excluded from its deliberations about the comparative merits of various sites for the new town hall. Nearly everyone felt that publicly identifying the sites would raise asking prices, but few wished positively to exclude the press and nobody was prepared to move a motion to that effect. The *Rochdale Observer*'s reporter was asked to withdraw voluntarily, but refused. After much embarrassed indecision, councillors embarked upon a somewhat red-faced public discussion of the sites.[50]

There was also markedly less resentment of outside pressure than was evident in Bolton and Salford by at least the late 1840s. Council and guardians' debates were often laced with references to rate-paying opinion. When pressure was applied, even aldermen could be found expressing pleasure at 'the ratepayers taking an interest in their own affairs'.[51] During the cotton famine of 1862 the guardians received a petition against their own labour test from some of those working under it — and were persuaded to suspend their proceedings whilst a messenger was sent to find and bring the petitioners to hear the subsequent debate.[52] In the same year public agitation for a park prompted the mayor to muse ambivalently about the council's proper attitude to outside pressure:

In consideration of the great feeling . . . at a public meeting, we are bound . . . to pay . . . respect to those wishes, though at the cost of some personal feeling, and must obey their behest so long as they do not demand the sacrifice of conscientious scruple.[53]

As the mayor implied, many councillors liked to see themselves as delegates or tribunes of the people, and the council as a mere reflector of public opinion. They were sometimes given to telling outside audiences 'to keep their eyes on the members of the Council . . . the inhabitants acquiesced in its deliberations too quietly'.[54] In 1857 John Pagan, an erstwhile supporter of the more oligarchic five-ward system of incorporation, told an audience of 'operative canvassers' that 'their next duty was to keep their councillors to their duty . . . they wanted baths and wash houses . . . and a public park; . . . why shouldn't a working man enjoy the sight of trees and flowers as well as the rich employer?'.[55] Councillors indeed liked to claim that policies were solely the result of public opinion. G. L. Ashworth, wealthy mill owner and one of the foremost Liberal leaders, was particularly given to such observations. On most issues, he professed to believe, 'we ought to leave it to the public to take the initiative',[56] and after the event was given to reflecting that projects had been 'engaged in not by the wish of the council merely, but in obedience to the will of the ratepayers'.[57]

Significantly, given what we are arguing about elite attitudes, such populistic postures were equally common on the more oligarchic improvement commission. Debates about gas prices invariably induced deliberations about consumers' wishes, small as well as large. In 1849 Thomas Livsey, the gas committee chairman, explained that 'the cottagers had not complained [about gas prices], but if they did so, he should then take up the question'.[58]

It is difficult to talk about elite attitudes without examining the role of Thomas Livsey, the man who both typified and affected them. He was the single most influential figure in Rochdale politics throughout the 1840s, '50s and early '60s, and his influence was felt long after his death in 1864.

The son of an extensive local blacksmith, Livsey was successively apprentice miller, blacksmith, ironfounder, cotton spinner and railway company agent. His consuming passion for politics ensured that these activities were never very successful. Nevertheless his business, family and marriage connections ensured a close relationship with the Liberal elite. Partly as a result, his political career was impressive. He was police and improvement commissioner, chief constable in 1852, churchwarden for many years, chairman of the board of guardians throughout most of the period until his death, and councillor and alderman continuously from 1856.

Yet what also explained his municipal success was his deep involvement in working-class politics. The nephew of a leading local radical, he liked to see himself as a disciple of 'Billy Cobbett' and was drawn into radical politics from an early age. He was a great mass orator and leading local Chartist (of the moral force school), who remained a convinced advocate of the Six Points to his death. He was also the leading local figure in the Ten Hours Movement, and in the remarkably successful local campaign against the implementation of the New Poor Law.

Livsey was thus leader of Rochdale's working-class radicals, and possessed spectacular influence with the local working class in general. In this respect he was at least as important as any of the Brights. When, in 1859, the 'non-electors' held a dinner to celebrate the return of Richard Cobden as MP, 'a portrait of John Bright [was] displayed on each side, and a portrait of Alderman Livsey [was] exhibited at each end of the room'.[59] In 1857 he returned from a trip to London to defend Rochdale's recent parliamentary election result against a Tory petition, to find himself greeted by a huge and apparently spontaneous demonstration of working-class affection. His funeral in 1864 was reportedly watched by a silent crowd of 40,000. Shortly afterwards an awestruck Richard Cobden observed:

during the last quarter of a century, there were no working men of Rochdale who, if they believed themselves aggrieved by those in authority, did not turn their footsteps instinctively towards the door of Mr Livsey ... if the grievance was a just one ... they found in him a self-sacrificing friend and protector.[60]

Yet Livsey was important for other reasons besides. Indeed, his popularity here rested partly upon his careful maintenance of contact with groups both important in themselves and likely to influence working people's perceptions. Thus he was a popular figure among the town's relatively small Catholic population, and (unusually for a Liberal politician) among the publicans. He was responsible for the removal of the prohibition upon the latter holding local political office. Meanwhile, once the Church rates battle was over, he seems to have repaired his bridges with the Vicar of Rochdale, W. N. Molesworth. Alone among Liberal leaders he supported the Church's case to have a part of the town cemetery set aside for Anglicans. His contacts seem to have been crucial in the early stages of the Corporate negotiations with the vicar to buy Church lands for a public park. So close had the relationship become between these erstwhile enemies that when Livsey died Molesworth had the parish church bells tolled in mourning.

In any case, Livsey's activities extended far beyond strictly working-class causes. He was involved in the Anti-Corn Law League, and led the Nonconformist battle against Church rates. He was also a valued and skilful negotiator in Parliament, and with government on behalf of regional causes like the campaign over the Liverpool town dues, and local ones like incorporation, improvement legislation and the municipalisation of utilities.

These skills and his popular political influence gave him a central position in Rochdale politics. He was the crucial intermediary between the Liberal elite and the working classes. The elite needed him, and admitted it — sometimes ruefully, sometimes generously. This is implicit in the corporation's almost unprecedented decision to attend his funeral as a body. It is also implicit in Cobden's statement quoted earlier. Embracing Livsey more gingerly, John Bright described him as 'a diamond, though not highly polished'.[61] W. A. Scott, a leading councillor, admitted to the commission of enquiry into Rochdale's incorporation that it was doubtful 'whether it would have been carried [in the town] had not Mr Livsey taken it up . . . [he] has great power over [the working classes] and it would depend entirely upon the course he and Mr Bright had adopted'.[62] In its two-page obituary Scott's paper paid even greater tribute to the deceased's political utility, declaring that Livsey was well known 'to Cabinet Ministers [and] to chimney sweeps . . . High Government officials spoke of him with the same respect as cotton operatives'.[63] All this gave Livsey not merely great political influence but also made him an effective channel for working-class influence on municipal decisions, and helped explain the continuing political clout of the radicals in their alliance with 'the Whigs'.

Political mobilisation

The impact of party competition, the open institutional system and elite attitudes upon politics was causally and consequentially linked to the level of political mobilisation. This was higher and spread consistently further down the social scale than in Salford or Bolton. As such, it greatly increased the potential prizes for successful populism and party conflict. It also reinforced the tendency of competing parties to exploit openings in the institutional system. Elite competition for group loyalty in turn helped reinforce mobilisation, particularly among those towards the bottom of the social scale, by conferring respectability and self-confidence.

Rochdale possessed a strong democratic tradition. This had two interconnected aspects: a widespread predisposition to participate in all aspects of local political life, and, a vigorous associational life. We will deal with each in turn.

Although somewhat variable, participation at the various points of public consultation and decision in the political process was generally substantial and enthusiastic. During the Church rates conflicts in the 1830s, '40s and '50s parish meetings invariably attracted hundreds, often thousands. Polls following disputed results drew even more. Those of July and August 1840, for example, were participated in by 8,000 and 12,000 voters respectively — with levels of excitement 'far exceeding . . . any contested election for borough or county'. When the second poll opened there arrived from Todmorden 'forty waggons . . . laden with voters of both sexes and all ages . . . accompanied by two bands of music besides several flags and banners waving in the air'.[64] Township meetings to elect overseers, etc., could draw up to 2,000 people, and polls (like that in Spotland in 1869 when virtually the whole electorate voted) as many as 9,000. As this last event suggests, such levels of participation (unlike Bolton and Salford) continued long after incorporation. Two meetings in the town centre to protest against the price of meat and milk in July–August 1872 were attended by up to 3,000. Other public occasions after 1856, like nomination and township meetings, were often impressively supported.

Oddly, council election turn-outs, though good by late twentieth-century standards (around 60–70 per cent in contested wards), were generally lower than in Bolton. However, this partly reflected the high numbers on the municipal electoral registers. In any town (before and to some extent after 1867) these were always potentially more extensive than their parliamentary counterparts because the rate-paying franchise was wider than the £10 householder. However, in neither Bolton nor Salford was the disparity as wide as in Rochdale, where from 1858 to 1867 municipal voters outnumbered their parliamentary counterparts by well over three to one. The figures look even more impressive when set against those for inhabitant householders. For example, in 1861 there were 5,019 municipal voters, representing 65 per cent of householders (7,579). By 1871 8,316 voters constituted 86 per cent of the same group (9,591) — the discrepancy between the two years probably being mainly explained by the inclusion of female householders in 1871.

Such levels of registration and participation partly resulted from party competition and the elite's efforts to galvanise its many dependants.[65] However, they were also generated from within: for Rochdale's population exhibited a more active and autonomous associational life, and at lower social levels, than did Bolton or Salford's.

Formal mobilisation of groups at the upper levels of local society was not particularly evident, and scarcely necessary. The chamber of commerce was not founded until 1866. Its late appearance, and the infrequency of its explicit municipal interventions, testify to the effectiveness of the discreeter forms of influence analysed in chapter 3.

However, other groups mobilised much earlier. As we have seen, one of the earliest and most fruitful sources of mobilisation was religion. Nonconformists and Anglicans were locked in battle until the mid-1850s over Church rates, and the conflict was partially resurrected around the education board in the '70s. Though a smaller group than in Bolton or Salford, Rochdale's Roman Catholics could also become passionately aroused — as happened for example in the mid-'60s over the costs of building a Catholic chapel in the town cemetery.[66] Such conflicts were evident elsewhere, but in Rochdale they seemed to arouse greater passion from far more people at all levels of society. Moreover the experience gained by the participants probably carried over when it came to organising themselves for other purposes.

Certainly the various forms of small proprietor were organised at an early stage. Licensed victuallers and beer-sellers had formed protective associations from at least the early 1850s — first separately and then, by 1870, jointly in the Wine and Beersellers' Association. As elsewhere, their interest in local politics was intermittent. Their functions were partly self-policing and friendly society. More than other groups, their attention was often focused on Parliament and government, to safguard their trade against temperance legislation. Nevertheless these associations were also concerned to defend their members at the magistrates' annual licensing sessions. Furthermore they intervened in the incorporation struggle to remove the prohibition on publicans being council members, and supported the successful radical campaign for the more democratic three-ward system.

Builders' and property owners' organisations appeared from at least the mid-'40s. Though intermittent and often poorly supported, their activity was frequently recurrent. Unlike the drink interest, their attention was almost exclusively centred on local government: indeed, the appearance of a property owners' association normally resulted direct from corporate activity like building regulations or rate increases. Property owners shaded inperceptibly into ratepayers' associations. Sometimes the latter were mere disguises for the former. Sometimes they spread their net more widely to include other sorts of proprietor and even working-class ratepayers — their spokesmen complaining about rates 'now too heavily imposed on the operatives, artisans and ratepayers at large'.[67] Whatever their catchment, the political mobilisation of ratepayers was intermittent but frequent.

Thus far, small proprietorial politics shows few qualitative differences from elsewhere. Indeed, Rochdale's property owners are less impressive politically than Salford's.[68] However, one group — the shopkeepers — were organised much more effectively. Originally formed in 1863 in protest against the mode of relief adopted during the cotton famine,[69] the Merchants' and Tradesmen's Association rose rapidly in strength and prestige. It broadened its activities (or at least the public image of them) to include 'any grievances affecting the general trade of the town and the public of Rochdale',[70] and began to express opinions about a wide range of issues, including railway accommodation, education, gas charges for small consumers and the maintenance of public footpaths. By 1868 its membership was nearly 300, and the Liberal elite were paying warm tributes to its 'enormous power'.[71] A more eccentric mark of its strength was the annual 'tradesmen's trip' which, by the mid-1870s, was receiving lengthy press coverage and regularly transporting around 3,000 joyous souls to the seaside.

The other group mobilised more formidably than in Bolton or Salford was the working class. Employers undoubtedly played an important part here. Certainly Liberal hegemony in Rochdale rested partly upon the sort of paternalistic factory culture described by Patrick Joyce in his picture of the Lancashire cotton area.[72] Indeed, the contemplation of such strings of dependency was a major reason why Liberal and Tory elites jointly supported schemes for a larger number of smaller wards in 1856, whilst the radicals opposed them. With small wards, it was felt, 'you would be placing in the hands of a few millowners the choice of the council'.[73]

However, there is also much to suggest more autonomous forms of mobilisation. Working-class participation in Chartism and, much more formidably, in the campaign against the imposition and operation of the New Poor Law throughout the 1840s and '50s[74] points in this direction. Furthermore mass participation in the Church rates campaign was too spontaneous to be ascribed merely to factory influence. It is also significant that most of Rochdale's working class supported the radical campaign on incorporation against schemes backed by the majority of large employers.[75] Working-class involvement in pressure on the council from ratepayers and small gas consumers suggests similar autonomy.

Part of the explanation for such behaviour lies in the smaller size of Rochdale's factories.[76] However, what also underpinned working class mobilisation, ensuring that it was maintained with substantial autonomy far beyond the demise of Chartism, and in spite of the steady rise in factory size, were the Rochdale Pioneers. Founded in 1844, their membership had reached 3,500 by 1860, over 7,000 by 1867 and 8,415 by 1875. Even excluding Pioneers' families, this last figure represents nearly one in five of the town's population. Indeed, the *Rochdale Times*, by no means a friendly observer, estimated in 1873 that, taking membership and commercial transactions into account, 'the society must constitute a one third part of the town'.[77] This leaves aside the break-away Provident Co-operative Society, with 1,808 members in 1872.

The Pioneers spanned the entire range of working-class purchasing. Apart from 'The Store', as the main establishment significantly became known on all sides, by 1866 the Pioneers owned ten groceries, nine butchers', three shoemakers', three cloggers', one draper's and one clothier's.[78] Such operations represented a considerable accumulation of capital. In 1861 it was estimated at around £40,000, and in 1870 at £94,000. The annual profits for 1872 were £33,640 and the turnover was £267,577.[79]

From the mid-'50s the Pioneers were also a manufacturing concern. By 1870 the corn mill was worth £95,000 and the Manufacturing Society, with its cotton factory at Mitchell Hey, £109,000.[80] There was also, by the early 1860s, a Co-operative Building Society linked with the Pioneers. In 1868 it was responsible for 103 of the 500 new cottages built in Rochdale.[81] In November 1871 the Pioneers formed a 'new building department' with 'power to buy, sell and mortgage land or buildings and advance money on security of the same'.[82]

The Co-op in fact spanned a wide range of working class needs and activities. Quite apart from retailing, building, manufacturing and employing, it was a major savings institution. It possessed a public hall seating 1,400, a library of over 9,000 books (by 1873) and eleven newsrooms. It also ran an extensive programme of educational and social activities for its members, as well as a sick and burial society.

The Pioneers were an important focus for working-class decision-making. Meetings were well attended and discussion was vigorous. A furious debate about purchasing policy in July 1868 drew 3,000 members and continued into the early hours of the morning.[83] Such activities were important in themselves — helping to promote a tradition of working-class self-management. They also provided important training for participation in the wider political system.

The Society's influence ranged below and beyond the ranks of the skilled working class. Its membership alone, together with that of the Provident Coop Society, suggests this. So too does the fact that in 1872 it was found to be building several tiny one-room cottages.[84] The Pioneers, in fact, were a central institution in Rochdale society — and recognised as such by the elite. Their activities received increasingly wide coverage in the local press, and 'the Store Hall' was often hired for major Liberal meetings. The Pioneers greatly added to the strength of radicalism in its alliance with the Liberals.[85] So important were they as a (mainly Liberal occupied) channel of influence to the working classes that the Conservatives formed their own Conservative Independent Co-operative Society in 1869.[86]

Overall, though clearly tied to capitalist society and accepting many of its values, the Pioneers' wealth and range of activities made their members partially independent of it, and provided a strong counter-influence to the factory. Moreover the co-operative version of those values, with its emphasis on mutuality, was not totally identical with the middle-class version. Certainly, as we saw in chapter 3, when they did enter the political arena their espousal of working-class self-help did not necessarily lead them to the same prescriptions as the elite.[87] In fact such collective political interventions were rare. Nevertheless the Pioneers were highly relevant politically and were one factor ensuring that, as we shall see, the Liberal relationship with the working classes was based on negotiation as well as deference.

Notes

1 See chapter 1; also Gowland, *op. cit.*, pp. 68-93.
2 See police commissioner's response to the Glebe Bill, 1845, *MG*, 15 January and 21 May 1845.
3 *Op. cit.*
4 Quoted *MG*, 10 March 1847, p. 8.
5 *Spectator*, 1 August 1844, p. 50. On Rochdale parties, see J. Vincent, *The Formation of the British Liberal Party 1857-68* (Harmondsworth 1966)
6 *RO*, 21 November 1857, p. 3.
7 *RO*, 27 October 1860, p. 2.
8 *RO*, 1 November 1873, p. 7.
9 There were some links in the philanthropic field, but far fewer than in Bolton or Salford.
10 See pp. 154f.
11 See pp. 132f.
12 *RO*, 10 May 1856, supplement.
13 *Ibid*.
14 *Op. cit.*
15 See p. 119.
16 See pp. 125f and chapter 8. Anyway, the restrictive clauses in 1844 and 1853 had been inserted at Tory behest.
17 See p. 143.
18 See chapter 8.
19 *MG*, 8 June 1842, p. 2.
20 *MG*, 5 August 1840, p. 3.
21 See, for example, *MG*, 17 April 1841, p. 2.
22 See, for example, *MG*, 2 April 1842, supplement.
23 See Fraser, *op. cit*, chapter 2, for the significance of Chartist participation here.
24 See *MG*, 6 April 1842, p. 2.
25 *MG*, 5 April 1843, p. 7.
26 Clement Royds, JP, *MG*, 19 November 1842, p. 3.

27 *MG*, 5 April 1844, p. 7.
28 See pp. 150-4.
29 *MG*, 23 February 1850, p. 10.
30 As, in a less partisan sense, did the railway companies.
31 See comment in *MG*, 4 August 1841, p. 2.
32 See *MG*, 18 April 1838, p. 2, and 26 April 1843, p. 3.
33 Letter, *RP*, 1 October 1870, p. 5.
34 See, for example, Castleton ward meeting, 1858, when all the retiring councillors were rejected, *RO*, 23 October 1858, p. 3.
35 See *RO*, 24 December 1857, p. 3, and 23 October 1858, p. 3.
36 *RO*, 28 October 1865, p. 4.
37 See pp. 150f.
38 See p. 46.
39 See p. 54.
40 *RO*, 26 November 1870, p. 4.
41 Edward Taylor, *RO*, 9 March 1872, p. 6.
42 See pp. 146f.
43 See Castleton ratepayers, *RO*, 10 January 1863, p. 4.
44 See *RO*, 22 March 1862, p. 5, and 19 April 1862, p. 4.
45 See below.
46 'Conservative workingman', *RP*, 17 April 1869, p. 4.
47 Alderman E. Taylor, *RO*, 4 March 1871, p. 7.
48 *RO*, 3 October 1868, p. 7.
49 *RO*, 5 September 1868, p. 8.
50 *RO*, 22 October 1859, p. 3.
51 Alderman J. S. Littlewood, to public meeting against selling corporation land to council members, *RO*, 17 February 1877, p. 6.
52 *RO*, 12 July 1862, p. 5.
53 G. L. Ashworth, *RO*, 6 December 1862, p. 2.
54 Councillor W. T. Shawcross to Rochdale Merchants' and Tradesmen's Association, *RO*, 15 January 1870, p. 5.
55 *RO*, 21 November 1857, p. 3.
56 *RO*, 6 August 1864, p. 4.
57 *RO*, 8 August 1868, p. 5.
58 *MG*, 23 June 1849, p. 10.
59 *RO*, 18 June 1859, p. 3.
60 Quoted Enid Summers, 'The Operation of the Poor Law in Rochdale' (Ms 1973, Rochdale Reference Library).
61 Letter, *RO*, 6 February 1864, p. 6.
62 Report, *RO*, 10 May 1856, p. 3.
63 *RO*, 30 January 1864, p. 4.
64 *MG*, 5 August 1840, p. 3.
65 It was also probably connected with the level at which compounding started in Rochdale. See Hennock, *Fit and Proper Persons*, p. 11.
66 See *RO*, 28 January 1865, p. 5.
67 J. F. Frankell, *RO*, 29 October 1870, p. 1.
68 See p. 215.
69 See p. 58.
70 Quoted *RO*, 11 March 1865, p. 5.

71 G. L. Ashworth, *RO*, 16 January 1869, p. 5.
72 *Work, Society and Politics*.
73 Peter Johnson, Tory radical beer-seller, *RO*, 10 May 1856, supplement.
74 See pp. 50-4.
75 See p. 155.
76 See p. 10.
77 *RT*, 5 July 1873, p. 6.
78 *RP*, 6 October 1866, p. 3.
79 See *RO*, 4 June 1870, p. 5, and 5 July 1873, p. 6.
80 A. Greenwood, *RO*, 4 June 1870, p. 5.
81 *RO*, 2 January 1869, p. 6.
82 Quoted *RO*, 6 November 1871, p. 5.
83 *RO*, 11 July 1868, p. 5.
84 Council meeting, *RO*, 6 April 1872, p. 6.
85 As a minor example see Edward Evans on the character of South ward in 1878: 'there was a strong batch of Radicals . . . especially in the Store Houses, and they read and thought a great deal', *RO*, 26 October 1878, p. 6.
86 For its activities see *RT*, 5 July 1873, p. 6.
87 See p. 000; also Crossick, *op. cit.*, and Tholfsen, *op. cit.*

8
Rochdale politics II

Our argument so far has been that Rochdale politics were subject to the mutually reinforcing effect of four factors: high levels of party conflict, an open institutional system, a populistic local elite and a relatively politicised local population. I now want to examine how this affected the configuration of power. Two arguments will be advanced: first, as in Bolton and Salford, the political process was susceptible to damaging confusion and constraint; second, the elite was highly 'political' and subject to influence from outside. While much of it emanated from those on the same economic level as the dominant Liberal section of the elite, politics were also influenced by groups much further down the social scale — and much more consistently than in Bolton or Salford.

Evidence for the first point is already implicit in the foregoing analysis of the institutional system. We saw that, given the effect of party politics, the numerous institutions having governmental functions before 1856 produced a situation in which conflict was endemic — conflict damaging to the Liberal elite's ability to achieve intended effects. The eccentric party-orchestrated manoeuvrings on the county magistrates' bench in the late 1830s and early '40s over the administration of justice point to this conclusion. So does the connected battle — which the Liberals also lost — for control of the police.[1] In the '40s the improvement commissioners became locked in a more successful, but equally dysfunctional, conflict with the Tory-controlled gas company over prices. It led to the town being unlighted through the winters of 1841-42 and 1842-43. As we shall see in regard to the 1855 Improvement Bill, town meetings also could have paralysing effects on the Liberal elite.

Though incorporation alleviated the situation, such characteristics did not completely disappear after 1856. The Church's position as ground landlord hamstrung the efforts to establish a park.[2] Even more damaging to the power of the Liberal elite was the notorious clause 96, inserted into the 1853 Improvement Act at the instigation of two Tory mill owners, which prevented the tipping of sewage into the Roche above a certain point. The only solution was to build an intercepting sewer to carry the material farther down. However, clause 97 compelled the corporation to maintain the river water at a constant level, whilst clause 98 guaranteed compensation to anyone sustaining injury by the abstraction of water. Councillors therefore felt themselves 'placed between two fires'.[3] Together with subsequent injuctions, the clauses paralysed efforts to make a permanent outlet for waterborne sewage until well after 1880.

Much of the foregoing suggests that political decisions, however stultified, were still the preserve of the elite, however divided. The suggestion is misleading: Rochdale's politics were highly susceptible to outside influence of many kinds.

For a start, the four factors discussed earlier produced an elite of the most 'political' kind, willing to compete for the support of almost any group. One expression of this was ostentatious sympathy. Few important meetings of the Tradesmen's Association, the Pioneers or the Licensed Victuallers and Beer-sellers were complete without a panoply of Liberal (and some Tory) leaders turning up to praise their activities and 'show that [they] cordially sympathised with . . . the existence of the Association'.[4] The Pioneers learnt of 'a bright halo' around their activities,[5] whilst the Tradesmen discovered that they were part of a triumvirate consisting of 'the Corporation, the Tradesmen's Association and the Chamber of Commerce, a threefold cord not easily broken . . .'.[6] Besides the Co-op, other working-class causes were effusively patronised. From the beginning of the 1850s the Liberal elite flocked to suffrage meetings, while throughout the period special non-electors' meetings were 'consulted', with careful ritual, about Liberal parliamentary candidates. (Quite apart from their role in parliamentary elections, many non-electors were municipal voters.) Liberal attitudes towards rate-payers' and property owners' activities were more hesitant, but even here they showed increasing reluctance to allow the Tories exclusive rights of exploitation.

Empathy was competitive: Tory and Liberal politicians appealed against each other for the support of those much further down the social scale. This lent a distinct lower-class orientation to much political debate. The Liberals appealed downwards in their conflicts with the Tory-dominated parts of the system before 1856. Thus the fights against the Church, the gas and water companies and the county magistrates were all portrayed as battles for the poor. There were boasts that 'but for the commissioners the poor would have been charged 10 shillings a year for [water in] the meanest cellar'[7], and claims that 'the Church had robbed the poor of £10 million a year; and its ministers . . . had leagued with their oppressors'.[8] The tendency was strong enough to be satirised in the press:

Commissioner Plump rose . . . having stated that he was there for the express purpose of seeing that aiqual justice was dealt out in the same ratio to the poor as to the rich . . . wished to know if the gas in the streets was turned on as high in those places where the poor resided, as it was in the residences of the . . . wealthy . . . he wished to have a distinct answer as the people were to a man looking up to him for justice and protection . . . [9]

Many Liberal actions after 1856 were painted in the same light. Working men were told that Tory-backed property owners were 'all pocket . . . your mental and physical improvement may go to the dogs for what they care'.[10] Building regulations were portrayed as 'merely' attempts 'to make the cottages of the working man . . . fit to live in'.[11]

Liberal orientations were intensified because the Conservatives, encouraged by their own populists, were also willing to appeal to the working classes — indeed, were eager to exploit any grievances resulting from Liberal policies. They were always prepared to capitalise on builders' dissatisfaction with corporate regulations, often generalising them into complaints that 'the better class of working men are almost stopped from building houses for themselves'.[12] They tried to outbid the Liberal elite for Catholic support — as, for example, in 1865, when a 'stinking' Liberal offer to build a Catholic chapel in the cemetery by public subscription produced a furious Catholic reaction, and a Tory demand that it be charged to the rates.[13] They constantly criticised Liberal extravagance. From municipalisation onwards Conservatives tried to exploit small consumers' dissatisfaction about gas prices, as early as 1844 demanding to know on behalf of the labouring classes why 'they are compelled to pay the same . . . as under the old Gas Company'.[14] As implied here, Tories were always willing to exploit working-class grievances — about the rates, the stopping of Sunday funerals, water shortages, the mode of poor relief or the refusal of Liberal employers to give time off to celebrate the return of the first working-class MPs.

Tories were often involved in organisations of the municipally disgruntled. Most ratepayers and property owners' associations soon acquired Conservatives on their committees. Meanwhile in 1871 there emerged a 'Rochdale Freehold Council' to protest at council neglect of 'the Freehold' — a working-class slum district. Conservative councillors rushed to embrace it. They fought a by-election on the issue, with their candidate promising to 'eradicate every evil which mitigated against the interests of the people of the neighbourhood'.[15] A month later, party leaders consolidated this bridgehead by founding a Conservative Co-operative Freehold Newsroom and Store as 'a boon to the working classes who reside at long distances from other Conservative stores . . .'.[16]

The Conservatives were thus as political as the Liberals — and seen to be so. Nothing better demonstrates the finely honed political sensitivities of both sections of the elite than this Liberal description of the Tories: 'a certain political faction intends at the next election to make political capital . . . by converging to the focus of their own party the scattered elements of discontent which will always . . . exist amongst us'.[17]

Such competitive sensitivity deeply affected policy-making. It guaranteed that the reaction of the corporate elite to manifestations of public opinion was always flexible. Since the constant features of Rochdale politics in the period are more impressive than the changes, we will treat the material on an issue rather than a temporal basis.

Sanitation and water supply

Flexibility was not necessary on every issue. Sanitation and water supply, for example, were areas about which 'the public' were only occasionally aroused. Decisions about sewage disposal, river pollution, the siting of reservoirs, etc., were highly technical and the outcome of a process involving key members of relevant committees plus a few corporate servants like the borough engineer. Even where there were disputes on such issues (and in Rochdale there were severe ones over sewage processing) they were non-party, did not therefore involve 'appeals outside' and were thus largely confined to the council circle. (The sewage clauses in the 1853 Act were a notable, but isolated, example.) Even the municipalisation of water supply took place in 1866 without party conflict, and was therefore a smooth and exclusively corporate operation. There were severe constraints on the elite's power in these areas. However, these generally came not from public opinion inside the borough but (as evident in chapters 4 and 5) from limited technical knowledge and from interests beyond borough boundaries which were affected by corporate plans.

Nevertheless, even on these issues, Rochdale's 'public' at all levels could become influentially involved. Thus council anticipation of future opinion may have been one motive behind the municipalisation of the water undertaking. G. L. Ashworth, the central figure in the decision, told fellow councillors (nearly all of whom were already converted and required no persuasion) that, in a few years, 'public feeling would go so strong [as to] . . . compel . . . this Corporation to purchase'.[18]

More certain influence was exerted over building regulation. Admittedly this elicited little effective reaction from displaced cellar dwellers. The 'residuum' were rarely regarded as legitimate political participants — and the very act of displacement probably ensured their non-appearance on the municipal register. Builders and property owners, however, were altogether more formidable. There are several examples of their influence (and probably more hidden from view). One occurred in 1879. After a long dispute with the property owners' association, the building committee, though empowered to make them obligatory, issued its regulations as 'recommendations to property owners'.[19]

The most dramatic examples of outside influence in these fields occurred over specific nuisances or expenses resulting from council policy. Here influence could be exercised not just through overt protest but also through the 'reputation for power' of those who might be outraged. The clearest example of how inhibiting such forces could be, particularly when backed by the minority party, began in March 1875 during a smallpox outbreak. Under pressure from the Local Government Board and the Rochdale guardians, councillors agreed to a health committee recommendation to purchase several cottages for an isolation hospital. The decision was taken in spite of Conservative protests that the move 'would be unpopular amongst the bulk of the working men in the town' owing to the popular impression (wrong, so the committee earnestly insisted) that patients would be compulsorily isolated. Persuaded by local doctors, the committee decided on a permanent hospital. In spite of two months' searching, it failed to find a site, and recommended the erection of a temporary building. After considerable indecision the council referred the decision back, and empowered the committee to take over some unspecified piece of corporation property for the purpose. A week later the committee reported that 'there would be great opposition [from] persons in the immediate neighbourhood' of all the possible sites.[20] It was still prepared to go ahead, but only if strengthened by specific authorisation. This proved too much for councillors' political willpower. Instead they implicitly agreed to the use of the old council rooms in the town centre. However, in June the 'decision' was reversed, and the health committee was told to look for a new site on the motion of a leading Liberal who had discovered 'with a shudder' that the rooms were 'only separated by a brick wall from one of [his] places of business'. That other factors were involved is indicated by the comment of a leading committee member who accused councillors of 'yielding to pressure outside . . . [Because] a protest from one body had been received a door had been opened for others'.[21]

Nothing further was heard about the hospital until January 1876, when it was said to be 'in abeyance'. The question puttered on for the next four years, accelerated occasionally by bouts of fever and delayed, like other projects, by a growing belief that the corporation had exhausted its borrowing powers. Connected with this were increasing fears of how 'the ratepayers' would react to increased expenditure — fears intensified by Conservative attempts at electoral exploitation. In March 1878 the health committee chairman explained that his committee had been 'slightly terrored from going to any great expense because there was an opinion in the council and outside that whatever [they] did was unnecessary. So long as that ... persisted, they had to walk very carefully ... '[22] In April the council agreed to purchase the old workhouse for a hospital, then changed its mind because the price was too high. Finally, in October, it agreed to rent the building after revealing explanations from the committee chairman and vice-chairman. The first said the purpose was partly 'educational', and timidly hoped 'the inhabitants [would come] to see that the immediate isolation of patients was to their advantage'. The second explained that the committee 'had been seeking a [permanent site] for some time. They had not been able to get an inch of land anywhere. There was always someone up in arms about it.'[23]

Improvement

In sanitation the influence of public opinion, where it existed, was largely negative and implicit. Awareness of present or probable public reaction inhibited the elite from taking otherwise intended actions. Influence of a sometimes more positive and certainly more dramatic sort can be seen in the overlapping field of improvement. Here the impact of popular arousal, in the contexts of an open political system, party conflict and elite populism, can be seen clearly.

We will first examine the improvement issue between 1848 and 1855. The question initially emerged late in 1848 as an argument in the Rochdale Improvement Commission about whether to adopt the Public Health Act. Commissioners were evenly divided, showing it by defeating a proposal to enquire into the possibility by twelve votes to ten. They reconsidered the issue in October 1849, and decided to bring it before a ratepayers' meeting. This was held in November, and was very crowded. After long discussion the participants unanimously resolved to establish a committee to decide which clauses of the Act Rochdale needed, and to bring them before a further public meeting 'for approval or disapproval'.[24]

The committee did very little, however, partly because of growing popular hostility to the Act, led by Thomas Livsey. Thus when the public meeting was held in December they presented no resolution. Several leading members of the elite, including the chief constable, supported adoption, but those claiming centralisation to be 'un-English' won the day — and the Act was defeated by 200 votes to 5.[25]

The improvement question then disappeared, at least from newspaper view, until October 1852, when, following a 'numerously and influentially signed' petition, the chief constable (now Thomas Livsey) called a public meeting to consider applying for an improvement Act. Whether outside pressure really initiated the move is uncertain. Livsey implied that the commissioners had their own reasons for going to Parliament (wanting increased powers over street sewering and paving[26]) but later 'admitted' that 'the ratepayers forced the necessity . . . upon them'.[27]

As first envisaged the Bill sought powers to provide baths, cemeteries and better drainage, and the meeting duly passed resolutions to that effect. It established a committee to investigate how the powers could best be obtained, and to induce the improvement commissioners to support them. However, the radicals tried to persuade the meeting to insert clauses democratising the franchise and lowering the property qualification of the commissioners. Many of the original promoters opposed this move, arguing that it would ensure parliamentary failure. They withdrew their objections after an ominous intervention from Thomas Livsey threatening 'his most strenuous opposition' (and presumably that of his mass following) to the Bill if such clauses were excluded. Livsey was appointed committee chairman.[28]

Two weeks later the committee called a second ratepayers' meeting. They reported that appropriate powers could be obtained via an improvement Bill and that parts of the Public Health Act could be embodied without centralisation. They therefore recommended a parliamentary application for all the proposed powers, including those democratising the commissioners. The meeting authorised the committee to formulate a Bill, and then to recall the ratepayers for a final decision. It left the committee to decide whether to include smoke and river pollution controls, after hearing about favourable representations 'from nearly every medical gentlemen in the town'.[29]

The third meeting was held in February 1853. It was 'large but not very full', 'very excited' and lasted over three hours. The Bill now included all the proposed powers and several others, including clauses extending the gas supply. Mostly participants were simply asked to endorse or reject formulated clauses. However, they were also given a choice between two sites for the new cemetery, presented to them by sections of a divided committee — and heavily backed the majority plan. On a radical motion the parliamentary deputation supporting the Bill included 'one or two non-electors'.[30]

'A powerful opposition' then arose — partly from interests threatened by the Bill (like the Vicar of Rochdale and various manufacturers), and partly from the Tory elite plus several disaffected wealthy Liberals who disliked the Bill's democratising clauses. In response, the new radical-dominated sponsors sought and obtained endorsement from yet another town meeting in mid-March.

In June the Bill began its parliamentary progress. Apart from several 'saving clauses' protecting objectors, and the insertion of the notorious clause

96,[31] most of the projected powers remained intact. In spite of the prestigious opposition the democratising clauses were also retained. However, they were counterweighted by a provision for plural voting according to property — and this was retained despite angry radical appeals to a further down meeting. On this issue the result was a draw.

It is fairly clear that, through the medium of the town meeting, the 'public' played a crucial part in the various stages of the foregoing decision. It was not precisely Athenian democracy, since the public's power was mostly the power to *ratify*. Yet anticipation of what the ratepayers would accept may well have affected what was presented to them. They could refuse ratification, and their meetings were certainly much more than managed occasions. This is suggested by the radicals' ability to take control in spite of opposition from Tory, and some Liberal, employers, and by the fact that the renegade Liberals always turned up to justify their actions.[32]

These points are suggested even more strongly by the eccentric proceedings surrounding the 1855 Improvement Bill. Here Liberal-radical attachment to government by town meeting resulted in paralysis. The sewering clauses of the 1853 Act had soon proved inoperable, owing to clause 96. After much agonising the improvement commissioners asked the ratepayers to endorse a parliamentary application to remedy the problem. The public meeting in February 1855 was given no direction. No resolutions were presented. Instead, leading commissioners simply explained the sanitary dilemma created by clause 96 and asked those present for their views on what should be done.

Then commenced an extraordinary, chaotic, sometimes riotous and ultimately paralysing exercise in popular democracy, lasting for four separated evenings and 'fourteen mortal hours'. Motions to apply to Parliament, to build floodgates and to postpone the issue for six months were all considered and rejected. Participants came from all social levels, and included several working men urging caution, 'as they would be called upon to pay the cost'. The exasperation of leading commissioners even reached Thomas Livsey. At the end of the third night, in a significant commentary both on the extent of the elite's populism and the effects of undirected popular participation, he commented:

After . . . three evenings, the first of which was a comedy, the second a farce, they had come to a pantomime . . . He would ask [them] if by their conduct they were not sacrificing their right of public meeting. The Commissioners had done everything . . . to conciliate the ratepayers. They could have sewered the town in spite of them, and at enormous expense.[33]

Matters eventually ground to a halt. On the final night the ratepayers were persuaded to endorse a parliamentary application to repeal clause 96.

However, the experience seems to have put the commissioners off altogether. No application emerged, and the idea was eventually drowned in the battle over incorporation — a decision in itself probably linked to this chaotic experience.

After incorporation the predilection for such spontaneous forms of public endorsement for parliamentary applications understandably declined in favour of more manageable forms of consultation like petitions. Partly as a result, the 1872 Improvement Act met relatively little opposition within the borough — though, as we saw in chapter 5, there was plenty from outside.

The 1872 Borough Funds Act, however, restored town meetings to their former place in decision-making — doing so sufficiently for such consultation to affect the 1876 Improvement Act dramatically. Here we see again the crucial opportunities presented to a politically mobilised group by the existence of a public entry point to the political process — particularly when grievances were subject to party political exploitation.

The Bill was initiated by the council, and published in November 1874. It aimed to augment borrowing powers for waterworks expansion, to increase powers over street levels and nuisances, and to purchase land for tramways. Opposition within the borough came almost entirely from property owners, and centred on the issue of private improvement rates. The fact that individuals had to pay for compulsory street improvements affecting their property had long been a grievance. Partly anticipating the corporation's attempt to expand its powers in this area, the property owners' association had been resurrected in September 1874, and was enthusiastically embraced by the Conservatives. Because of association pressure, the published version of the Bill already contained concessions — several clauses specifying the notice to be given by the corporation before compulsory improvements were carried out.[34] These, however, were regarded as totally unsatisfactory.

At the beginning of January 1875 the property owners met and condemned five of the clauses: clause 10, increasing Corporation charges for connecting a house to the main sewer; clause 14, empowering it to declare a newly paved and drained street a public highway whilst leaving house owners liable for subsequent street maintenance; clause 19, absolving the corporation from paying for any damage it did while undertaking private improvements; clause 26, specifying that street improvement expenses should have priority over any other expenditure undertaken by the house owners in that street; and clause 35, allowing the corporation to make byelaws in pursuance of the Act. After assurances from Liberal councillors present at the property owners' meeting that representations might well result in 'the objectionable clauses being removed', the association sent a deputation to the general purposes committee.[35]

The worry underlying such conciliatory offers — as publicly made clear by councillors and the town clerk — was that unreconciled opposition would necessitate a poll, and even parliamentary opposition. This would be expensive and might also mean losing the important water expansion clauses.

The association's meeting with the corporation produced an agreement which, the mayor claimed, had 'perfectly satified the property owners'. He was optimistic, to judge by the anger expressed at the statutory ratepayers' meeting the same evening. Consequently negotations continued there also. The town clerk declared the council's willingness to alter the Bill 'in Parliament, and before, to suit objections as they arise'. According to the *Rochdale Times*, 'the style' now 'became conversational'. A strange process of public negotation ensued between platform and audience, with the town clerk complaining about irregularity and making concessions at the same time. Clause 35 had already succumbed in the morning. Now clauses 10, 14 and 19, which had then been merely altered, were also withdrawn. Tory councillors supported the property owners throughout the meeting. At the end they took further advantage of the corporation's 'amiable disposition to defer to the ratepayers' by inducing changes in the clauses relating to water rates charged to outside consumers. At an earlier council meeting the Liberals had heavily defeated a Conservative proposal for a 12½ per cent rise in such rates instead of the Bill's projected 7½ per cent rise. Now, by persuading the meeting to endorse this demand, the Tories forced the corporation to accept it. As the Liberals had anticipated, there was determined opposition from local boards of health, but even this was apparently preferable to the prospect of further trouble from the meeting or from a subsequent poll.[36]

The park

Outside influence of a more ambiguous and more conflicting sort can be seen in the 1860s in the battle to establish a park. The corporation had first acquired the appropriate powers in the 1853 Improvement Act but, significantly, made no attempt to use them until enough gas profits had accumulated to partially fund the project. This minimised the risk of a politically dangerous rate increase.[37]

Negotations to purchase part of the Glebelands for the purpose were opened in 1859. They came to nothing and instead puttered hesitantly on for the next seven years, being concluded only in June 1866. The reasons for the long prevarication were twofold: the parish church's position as ground landlord, and the ambiguous state of public opinion.

One problem was uncertainty about who, in the Church, had the right to sell the land. This was made worse by a continuing twenty-five-year-old battle between the two main candidates, the Bishop of Manchester and the Vicar of Rochdale. The 1859 negotations had been conducted with the bishop, at his initiative. He offered the land at £200 an acre. Negotiations were rapidly discontinued after 'some correspondence' between the bishop and the vicar, in which the latter probably challenged the former's right to sell.[38] In spite of further overtures from the bishop (now asking £400 an acre) in 1861 the corporation took no further action until there was pressure from outside. In November 1862 there was a crowded public meeting in support of a park. It was organised by a group of notables, formally headed by John Bright, and demanded the purchase of a large chunk of Church land for the purpose.

By this time the council had concluded that the vicar was the appropriate vendor. It accordingly opened negotiations to buy or lease two tracts of Church land — one for the park and the other for a new town hall. Although the second site was eventually purchased, nothing was done about the first. The council began negotiations but rapidly backed down because 'the shadow of the Bishop . . . had crossed the scene . . .'.[39] He had refused to enter into the negotiations and then, even more alarmingly, in March 1864 directly challenged the vicar's right to sell without his concurrence. He suggested that Molesworth's price (£400 per acre) was below market value, now gluttonously estimated at £1,000 per acre. This enabled the Tories and the Liberal 'economists' on the council to argue, and the more timorous spirits among its pro-park majority to believe, that if the council purchased the site at the vicar's price there might be litigation — with the bishop, the Ecclesiastical Commissioners, or both. As G. L. Ashworth, an erstwhile park supporter, explained, 'our position is one of great delicacy and . . . may in the future be one of great difficulty'.[40] Despite several agonised debates, one lasting over four hours, the council remained paralysed.

Timidity was intensified by an extravagantly insulting public debate between the two ecclesiastics, with the Tories enthusiastically taking the bishop's side. This was merely the latest round in a twenty-five-year war over jurisdiction and doctrine. Some Liberals also suggested that the bishop had 'a son-in-law' in mind as future vicar of Rochdale. Were the land sold now, this relative 'would never receive one penny from the transaction'.[41] Either way, the Church's position in Rochdale ensured that an essentially private battle inhibited municipal action for seven years. Eventually, in March 1865, the council agreed to purchase a small section of the land, but only after the Ecclesiastical Commissioners had been drawn into the negotiations. It purchased the rest only when the Rochdale Vicarage Act finally settled the legal situation, making the Commissioners formal owners.[42]

The Church's quarrels, however, were clearly not the only inhibiting factor — particularly given that the council had received two independent legal opinions confirming the vicar's right to sell without the bishop's consent.[43] The second problem was the elite's uncertainty about the state of public, including working-class, opinion. Although the campaign's promoters organised an enthusiastic town meeting in October 1862, followed by a petition in May 1863, they seemed unable to sustain the momentum. In spite of the council's prevarication no further meetings were organised until December 1864. The issue was used in council elections, but electoral compromises prevented the emergence of any clear mandate. Thomas Livsey's death in January 1863, moreover, probably made working-class mobilisation more difficult.

Meanwhile, on the other side, the Tories and some Liberals were organising popular support for inaction and economy in the form of a ratepayers' association. Unlike Bolton, Rochdale's council seems to have been poorly furnished with financial expertise: there was always uncertainty about how much remained of the borrowing powers granted in 1853, and unwillingness to borrow more. This was particularly evident during the cotton famine, in spite of the generous borrowing and repayment facilities available under the 1863 Public Works Act. Meanwhile the cost of the corporation's other major project, the town hall, was steadily escalating. Thus, in the absence of any sufficiently clear evidence of the park's continuing popularity, the council's waverers were prey to anxiety about what the ratepayers would tolerate. On this as on other issues, public opinion was still central in the minds of leading Liberals; but here it was also ambiguous. Even the *Rochdale Observer*, edited by Councillor W. A. Scott a leading park supporter, felt impelled to urge caution until after the 1864 council elections. Then 'if the burgesses really want a park let them speak out'. In the same issue G. L. Ashworth could be found reporting 'great apathy' to his council colleagues and urging that 'as it is a question in which the public are so much . . . concerned, . . . we ought to leave it to them to take the initiative'.[44]

Gas policy

In much of the foregoing 'the public' appears as an influential but primarily negative factor. In gas policy the influence of public opinion (including working-class opinion) was more positive. This stemmed partly from the fact that, unlike sanitation, gas was an area of almost continuous public concern and party conflict. It resulted also from the way gas had been municipalised in 1844, and thus emerged from the logic of the elite's own populism. As we shall see, outside opinion affected two areas: supply and prices.

Municipalisation was probably motivated primarily by the desire of local manufacturers for greater efficiency in a service upon which they were heavily dependent. However, given Tory control of the gas company and the Liberal elite's need to strengthen its credibility in Parliament, municipalisation had to be a popular cause. Thomas Livsey's central role in the campaign made this even more likely. Thus it was portrayed as a crusade to improve service and cheapen prices to all inhabitants, particularly the working classes. The trend was intensified by the attempts of the company and its Tory supporters to defend themselves by competing with the Liberals for public esteem. During the Bill's parliamentary progress both sides thus fought a propaganda battle in the streets, defending and denouncing the company's treatment of 'the labouring classes'.[45]

Once the company had been municipalised the controlling Liberal majorities of the commissioners and the council had to fulfil the expectations thus aroused — particularly because the 1844 Act itself specified that gas had to be supplied to anyone who applied, and because the Tories were always ready to exploit any disappointment. Thomas Livsey significantly became first gas committee chairman, and pursued a policy of universal gas supply. By 1850 consumers had risen by 904 to 1,476; by 1854 they had reached 2,650 and six years later there were 8,557 inside and outside the borough; six out of every seven houses in the borough were gas-lit. The committee's rhetoric matched its record — 'every poor man could now have his humble domestic hearth lit at small expense'.[46]

This policy, itself partly the result of popular appeasement, led to opportunities for further lower-class influence over detailed aspects of gas administration. Most of Rochdale's many consumers were, after all, municipal voters. As was constantly shown in council discussions, their assumed opinions became a central factor in the calculations of local politicians — the more so because gas, unlike many areas of sanitation, for example, was a perennial topic of public agitation, election debate and party conflict.

This affected policy. Worries about public reaction set an informal limit on gas profits of around 10 per cent.[47] In 1861 Livsey, still gas committee chairman, tuned his political antennae to the public wavelength and predicted that people would not 'long be satisfied to give 4s per 1,000 cubic feet for their gas if the Corporation continued to receive such large profits'.[48] When profits exceeded 10 per cent, prices were almost automatically reduced. Price rises on the other hand, however much necessitated by falling revenues, were undertaken more cautiously. In 1874 the council persuaded the gas committee to postpone proposing a rise for three months following words of tremulous disdain from the deputy mayor: 'He himself paid very little concern to those things, but he thought ... they ought to consult the feelings of the great body of the ratepayers who, not being so well informed as the chairman of the Gas Committee, would view the increase with considerable indignation'.[49]

Here there may well have been considerable consensus between large and small consumers. Elsewhere their interests bitterly diverged, putting conflicting pressures on the council. When this happened the result was a significant draw. Thus, although the discount to large consumers was not abandoned (as some radicals wished), it was steadily reduced as small consumers increased, falling from 1s 4d per 1,000 cubic feet in 1844 to only 3d by 1880. Similarly meter inspection charges (cheap from the first to encourage consumption, but always 'a considerable percentage of small consumption'[50]) were reduced in 1866 and abolished in 1878.

These measures were taken in spite of bitter objections, from council champions of large consumers, about being made to 'produce all the gas profits'.[51] With constant Tory attempts to exploit small consumer grievances electorally, the council majority seemed equally impressed by evidence of 'great clamour . . . against discounts',[52] or by claims that meter charges were hated 'by every . . . small and middle-class consumer'.[53] This was particularly so when discontent was given unnerving form by 'public indignation meetings' or pressure from the tradesmen's association.

In the issues thus far the working classes have sometimes figured quite influentially but largely in company with other groups. On two issues — the Poor Law and incorporation — they were more centrally and more positively salient.

The Poor Law

As regards the Poor Law, Rochdale's political elite was consistently radical — markedly more so than Salford or Bolton's. Though guardians were elected to appoint a Registrar of Births, Marriages and Deaths in February 1837, they pursued a militantly anti-Poor Law policy from the start. Defying the *Manchester Guardian*'s confident prediction of defeat, they successfully resisted the Law's imposition until 1847. After its formal introduction by the county magistrates the board continued opposition by other means. Like most northern Unions,[54] it never applied the workhouse test, almost invariably gave out-relief to the able-bodied and, until at least the late '60s, refused to impose a labour test on any but 'vagrant' applicants. Relief was never centralised but administered, as in the past, on a township basis by local groups of guardians in concert with township-appointed relief committees. Moreover, in spite of strong Poor Law Board pressure, the guardians refused to begin building a Union workhouse until 1871, well after most urban Unions had succumbed.

Meanwhile the spirit of Poor Law administration seems to have remained more and longer at variance with the deterrent principles of 1834 than in Salford, Bolton and probably many other northern Unions. Though undoubtedly grimy, the small township workhouses were run in a relatively relaxed way. To leading guardians they were 'almshouses'[55] and not workhouses at all. Until the mid-'50s inmates were allowed to come and go more or less at will. Indeed, Sunday was a day on which most left to visit friends or go drinking. For many years inmates were even allowed their own furniture and crockery. Some workhouse masters referred to them as 'the family'.[56]

The elite's rhetoric gives the same impression. In 1862 G. L. Ashworth predicted that using the labour test for anyone but vagrants would merely reproduce what was allegedly happening in neighbouring towns and 'men would discover that, far from the Poor Law being a fund to which they could look in ... emergency, it was becoming a source of ... tyranny and degradation'.[57] A year later Thomas Livsey opposed publishing the names of relief applicants, reflecting that he had 'always reminded respectable persons, ... compelled to apply for relief that they were only receiving aid from the fund to which they had contributed'.[58] In 1865 Ashworth even hoped 'to see the time when ... relief will be so arranged that the respectable ... but necessitous poor will feel that [asking] for what is their right is not attended with ... degradation'.[59] Though not every guardian was so generous, and things changed in the 1870s, such emphasis was virtually absent from Bolton and Salford.

How far working-class influence was responsible is difficult to establish. Partly, such attitudes were generated from within the elite itself. Historians have emphasised the early unanimity of northern opposition to the Poor Law. Even the hardest-nosed manufacturer perceived the irrelevance of the workhouse test as a remedy for cyclical unemployment, and all realised that centralisation meant loss of local control.

However, the fact that Rochdale's opposition was carried further, persisted longer and was led by a more unanimous elite than Bolton or Salford's, suggests that other factors were involved. Several circumstances make it probable that elite sensitivity to working-class opinion was an important determinant. For one thing, this was an area where Rochdale's working classes were intensely mobilised — and mobilised far longer than in the other two towns. As late as 1852 feelings about the labour test drew 'one of the most numerous meetings ever held in Rochdale',[60] whilst a meeting on this subject ten years later could still attract 'a large and enthusiastic audience'.[61] The elite certainly acted as if working-class support was crucial. Indeed, we see here Liberal leadership at its most populistic. The guardians took great care to ensure that each manoeuvre against the Poor Law Commission was legitimised by a town meeting. At least eight had been called by 1845 — nearly all by the authorities themselves — and more were to follow.

Surveying politics, particularly up to 1856, one can reasonably see elite support for working-class opposition to the Poor Law as part of an implicit bargain. Though the Tories were never strongly represented in the Poor Law machinery, they stood ready to exploit any Liberal failing. Moreover Liberal leaders needed working-class support not just to add weight to their own grievances against the Law but also in their struggles elsewhere in the system. Thus Liberal enthusiasm here was probably partly implicit payment for working-class support against the Tory magistrates, the public utilities and the Church, as well as in the battle for constituency control.

Such a bargain seems the more likely given Thomas Livsey's central role in the campaign. He was board chairman almost continuously until his death in 1863, and was the campaign's main tactician. It was on this more than any other issue that he gained his role as working-class tribune. Liberals and Nonconformists saw his support as crucial to their other campaigns about Church rates and incorporation.[62] Thus their support for this most central of Livsey's causes was unlikely to falter, particularly in view of his willingness to mobilise his working-class constituency against some of the more faint-hearted guardians.

Rochdale's Poor Law machinery contained several points where working-class pressures could be more directly applied. The relief committees, elected by township meetings to assist the giving of local relief, and often composed of 'poor ratepayers', were probably one such. The guardians never seem to have felt inclined to refuse co-operation, and the committee's presence probably helped ensure that anti-Poor Law attitudes were normative.

This was certainly the case with guardians' elections and petitions. Just how potent the latter could prove in securing communal solidarity is indicated by a petition to the Home Secretary against the imposition of the New Poor Law in 1844. The organisers decided to take all names: those against the Law, 'those . . . favourable . . . [and] those . . . neutral'.[63] Partly as a result, 11,415 declared their opposition, only fifty refused to sign and only fifteen found the courage to support the new law. Here solidarity was mobilised by the authorities themselves. Yet it could also be potently exerted against board actions, as in 1860, when petitions from all three urban townships in the Union persuaded the guardians to rescind, by a large majority, a previous decision to close one of the local workhouses. Those organising the pressure believed that closure would lead to a Union workhouse, would be unconducive 'to the comfort of the aged poor', and that 'the board were guardians of the poor, not of the rich who found the money'.[64]

However, the force of petitions can be understood only in terms of their implicit message about the guardians' electoral prospects — and it was around the annual elections that working-class pressure most successfully centred. This was due not just to the influence of poor voters (necessarily limited because of the electoral weighting given to property) but also to pressures from non-electors.

In the early years pressure of this sort reinforced the campaign against introduction of the New Poor Law. In August 1845 eighteen candidates were nominated as guardians. All but three refused to stand. Opponents of the Law threatened to carry effigies of the trio through the streets to be 'shot at and burned' and circulated 'inflammatory papers' against them. Livsey suggested that they 'be ridiculed wherever they were met'.[65] The results are somewhat obscure, but certainly one was induced to resign, whilst the names of the other two do not appear again in connection with the guardians.

Such influences — particularly when reinforced by party competition — continued to ensure the normativeness of anti-Poor Law attitudes long after its formal introduction. In 1851, just before the board elections, some Spotland guardians visited Bury workhouse to inspect that Union's separation system. Livsey accused them of wanting to introduce the rigours of separation and 'less eligibility' into Rochdale. The miscreants (both Tories) vigorously denied it, asserting their opposition to the Law and claiming they only wished to separate unmarried paupers.[66] However, the accusations were repeated in the town by placards claiming that some guardians 'wanted the Bastilles'. This produced a significant piece of theatre at the next board meeting. The accused demanded that anyone wanting the Law should 'hold up their hands'. When, predictably, no one did the guardians ostentatiously resolved that the placard was 'totally false' and that its perpetrators, if identified, should be soundly punished by receiving a copy of the resolution.[67] In spite of such contortions one of the suspected backsliders lost his seat in the subsequent elections. Perhaps significantly, three months later the board unanimously rejected a Poor Law inspector's request that they should build a Union workhouse.

Outside pressure again became salient in March 1862 when the guardians refused to join the council in sending a deputation to London demanding relaxation of the Poor Law during the cotton famine. There followed a large and angry town meeting, agilely attended by leading members of the council. It condemned both guardians and Poor Law board after a fiery speech from Thomas Livsey (temporarily not a guardian) advising the working classes to remove 'the renegades' at the next guardians' elections.[68] Subsequently two Tories lost their seats in contests that 'turned on . . . the truckling of some Guardians to the Poor Law Board',[69] and Livsey briefly returned. After further manoeuvres showing continuing concern about 'what would go forth to the public' the guardians were persuaded to unanimously petition the Poor Law Board to suspend out-relief regulations. They also resolved to change the limited labour test applied by the Spotland guardians to unemployed applicants (another major cause of dispute) into work paid above the basic relief level.[70]

Incorporation

Working-class influence, albeit allied to that of sections of small property, is equally evident in the incorporation battle. Here a thoroughly mobilised lower class, using entry points provided by the open institutional system, was confronted by a (for once) united elite. Populism was still important, but primarily as a background factor, conditioning popular expectations and determining that the elite would seek incorporation by public rather than private political means. This, in turn, opened up channels for lower-class influence.

The decisive initiative for incorporation came from within the municipal elite. In June 1855 the improvement commissioners established a committee to inquire into the benefits of incorporation in similar towns elsewhere. Incorporation was attractive as a way of escaping the jurisdiction of the county police. It also conferred the right to appoint borough magistrates, thus increasing municipal control over the enforcement of nuisance regulations. A corporation, it was also believed, would command more respect than the commissioners in and outside Rochdale — a point that persuaded Thomas Livsey to give the movement his crucial support.

The committee reported favourably, and then — true to populistic tradition — called a town meeting in mid-September to consider the issue. Doing so imposed certain necessities on the incorporators. No record of the proceedings has survived. However, judging by subsequent radical claims,[71] the promoters, in order to gain popular support, spilled much rhetoric about the democratising effects of incorporation. This seems to have raised popular expectations.

The meeting endorsed incorporation in principle, and elected a committee to organise a petition and formulate a specific scheme. The first task proved easy enough. Incorporation had all-party support, and within three months a massively supported petition was sent to London. The trouble arose over the second. The committee's Whig-Tory majority drew up alternative plans for five and eight wards. Both entailed a £30 property qualification for councillors (effectively excluding most small shopkeepers) and small wards open to heavy employer influence — rather than large wards where such influences would arguably cancel each other out.

Led by Thomas Livsey, the committee's radical minority demanded that the chief constable call a further town meeting to consider this 'betrayal'. When he refused (presumably trying to keep the process under elite control) they called one themselves in February 1856. Significantly the committee's majority felt obliged to turn up and defend themselves in what proved to be a noisy four-hour marathon. After much radical invective against the 'traitors', those assembled censured the committee and 'asked' that it produce and support a plan for three large wards. Livsey warned the ratepayers to be on their guard or they 'would be sold'.[72]

The advice proved sensible. The committee produced a three-ward plan, but then simply sent all the plans to London without comment. Meanwhile its majority began canvassing the large ratepayers in favour of the five and eight-ward solutions. The radicals responded with another crowded town meeting in late February 1856. Though the incorporation committee refused to attend officially, most of its members again appeared, and proceeded to denounce each other violently. The radicals got much the better reception. The meeting almost unanimously condemned the committee's majority, backed the three-ward plan and elected its own committee (composed mainly of small manufacturers, shopkeepers and working men) to organise a petition.

There ensued a vigorous campaign by both sides — with the five- and eight-warders allegedly mobilising the large employers to dragoon factory workers to sign their petitions. Meanwhile the radicals had the crucial support of the town's sole newspaper (the newly launched *Rochdale Observer*), and the beer-sellers under their Tory-radical leader, Peter Johnson. Long legally excluded from the improvement commission, the same group again faced effective exclusion if the £30 qualification, common to both the five- and eight-ward schemes, was adopted. The beer-sellers were important not just in themselves but as a significant countervailing and consolidating influence over working-class opinion, alternative to that wielded by the great Whig and Tory manufacturers.

By the time the government commission of enquiry convened on 23 April the three-ward petition had been signed by much the larger number of ratepayers (2,750, against a total of 700 for the alternatives) but represented a markedly smaller accretion of property (£21,000 compared with £31,000). On these figures the class division between the two sides is striking, the average three-ward petitioner being worth £7 12s in ratable value as against £44 for supporters of the other solutions. Nearly all Rochdale's large proprietors were ranged on the latter side, whilst the lower-class character of the three-warders is emphasised by the uncontroverted claim that most of those assessed at over £15, with the exception of the beer-sellers, signed in favour of the larger numbers of wards.[73]

The commissioners' hearings lasted three weeks, taking huge quantities of testimony from both sides. The five- and eight-warders argued that greater efficiency, independence of party and honesty would result from small-ward representation. The radicals argued for three wards on grounds of democracy and the neutralisation of factory influence. However, their most telling argument, never really refuted by the other side, was probably the shortage of council candidates under a £30 qualification. Their claim that only 200 would be available was probably an underestimate. Nevertheless even the five-warders could rustle up only 558 — well below the 958 qualified at £15 and above.[74]

Neither side expected the three-ward victory announced in July 1856. Even radicals admitted that they had only entertained 'faint hopes'.[75] Parliament did not often provide access to men of little property. Allowing for hyperbole, the victors were probably correct in their assessment of the battle lines and the relative effectiveness of the pressures exerted: 'Nearly the whole of the wealth of the town was banded against the operative classes and the shopkeepers, but right has triumphed.'[76]

Influence must always be measured within its political context. This 'victory for working men' was achieved in a situation that was favourable in some respects. The provision for an alternative £15 qualification in the Municipal Corporations Act was intended for small towns, and Rochdale, with 40,000 inhabitants, was on the outer margins of being so classifiable. The three-warders' argument about the paucity of council candidates at £30 was a telling one. Moreover, as seen in chapter 2, the £15 qualification did not prevent the council from being dominated by the elite.

Nevertheless it was a victory, illustrating again how unpredictable this national dimension of the local political system could be. The battle had centred on a cause (the right to participate) that probably had great symbolic importance to many working men. Furthermore the victory ensured that the elite would need to continue its populistic and conciliatory ways; and that working men and small shopkeepers would continue to possess more political salience than elsewhere. This was immediately signalled by the beaming arrival at the three-warders' celebratory 'monster tea-party' of Jacob Bright, (an eight-warder until the beginning of the enquiry), and G. L. Ashworth, who had stayed neutral but now discovered three-ward sympathies 'all along'.[77]

It is evident that, in spite of Rochdale's immensely well endowed political elite, municipal politics were complex and, in some important respects, pluralistic. If we turn to Bolton we shall find a less pluralistic though equally complex situation.

Notes

1 See p. 119.
2 See pp. 146f.
3 *RO*, 30 April 1870, p. 5. See also pp. 000-000.
4 G. L. Ashworth to Merchants' and Tradesmen's Association, *RO*, 12 January 1867, p. 4.
5 G. L. Ashworth, *RO*, 28 May 1870, p. 5.
6 Rev. Parkinson, *RO*, 11 January 1868, p. 5.
7 Geo. Proctor, *MG*, 8 May 1847.
8 Thomas Livsey to vestry meeting, *MG*, 2 April 1842, supplement.
9 *Spectator*, December 1846, p. 3.
10 Letter, *RO*, 13 October 1860, p. 2.
11 J. Cookson, 19 October 1872, p. 5.
12 Joseph Ireland, election address, *RT*, 24 October 1874, p. 1.
13 See *RO*, 7 January 1865 f.
14 Letter, *Spectator*, 1 December 1844, p. 9.
15 James Swift, *RT*, 20 January 1872, p. 6.
16 *RT*, 10 February 1872, p. 5.
17 Letter, *RO*, 13 October 1860, p. 2.
18 *RO*, 3 March 1866, p. 6.
19 *RO*, 5 April 1879, p. 6.
20 *RO*, 15 May 1875, p. 6.
21 J. S. Hudson, *RO*, 5 June 1875, p. 7.
22 Alderman E. Taylor, *RO*, 9 March 1878, p. 6.
23 Aldermen Taylor and Schofield, *RO*, 7 October 1878, p. 6.
24 *MG*, 3 November 1849, p. 7.
25 *MG*, 22 December 1849, p. 7.
26 *MG*, 6 October 1852, p. 7.
27 *RS*, 19 August 1854, p. 8.
28 *MG*, 6 October 1852, p. 7.
29 *MG*, 23 October 1852, p. 10.
30 *MG*, 12 February 1853, p. 9.
31 See p. 101.
32 See speech by J. Hoyle, *MG*, 7 September 1853, p. 7.
33 *RS*, 17 February 1855, p. 8.
34 *RT*, 2 January 1875, p. 1.
35 *RT*, 9 January 1875, p. 4.
36 The increase was eventually fixed at 10 per cent.
37 See Thomas Livsey, *RO*, 3 September 1859, p. 3.
38 Thomas Livsey, *RO*, 8 October 1859, p. 3.
39 Editorial, *RO*, 16 April 1864, p. 4.
40 *RP*, 26 December 1863, p. 5.
41 E. Taylor, *RO*, 16 April 1864, p. 7.
42 See *RO*, 3 March 1866, p. 5, and 25 May 1866, p. 3.
43 See *RO*, 7 May 1864, p. 5.
44 *RO*, 6 August 1864, p. 4.
45 See *MG*, 24 April 1844, p. 7, and G. Chadwick in *MG*, 9 December 1844, p. 7.

46 Thomas Livsey, *RO*, 5 May 1860, p. 3. See also figures, *RO*, 15 September 1866, p. 4.

47 On limitation see *RO*, 8 May 1880, p. 7.

48 *RO*, 4 May 1861, p. 3.

49 *RO*, 10 January 1874, p. 6.

50 Gas/Committee Minutes, *RO*, 7 December 1878, p. 6.

51 W. Robinson, *RO*, 14 July 1866, p. 3.

52 Councillor R. Jewison, *RO*, 6 July 1861, p. 2.

53 Councillor J. Handley, *RO*, 18 August 1866, p. 4.

54 See Derek Fraser (ed.), *The New Poor Law* (London, 1976).

55 See Thomas Livsey to Poor Law Board, 1858, quoted in Miss M. R. Lahee, *Life and Times of the Late Alderman T. Livsey* (Manchester, 1865), p. 42; also Rhodes Boyson, 'The New Poor Law in north-east Lancashire, 1835-71', *Lancashire and Cheshire Antiquarian Society Transactions*, LXX (1960).

56 For Rochdale's workhouse administration see Rhodes Boyson, *op. cit*. See also remarkable 'Weekly Diary' of Spotland Workhouse Masters, 1836-45 (Ms, Rochdale Library).

57 *RO*, 28 June 1862, p. 5.

58 *RO*, 29 August 1863, p. 5.

59 *RO*, 18 February 1865, p. 5.

60 *MG*, 27 October 1852, p. 7.

61 *RO*, 1 March 1862, p. 4.

62 See p. 129.

63 *MG*, 23 October 1844, p. 7.

64 Quoted *RO*, 7 April 1860, pp. 2-3.

65 *MG*, 10 September 1845, p. 6, and 17 September 1845, p. 6.

66 See *MG*, 2 April 1851, p. 7.

67 *MG*, 9 April 1851, p. 7.

68 *RO*, 1 March 1862, p. 4.

69 *RO*, 12 April 1862, p. 5.

70 *RO*, 12 July 1862, p. 5.

71 See E. Taylor, *RO*, 3 May 1856, p. 4.

72 *MG*, 15 February 1856, p. 4, and 16 February 1856, p. 6.

73 See *RO*, 10 May 1856, p. 4.

74 See *ibid*., p. 3, and 25 April 1856, p. 3.

75 Editorial, *RO*, 5 July 1856, p. 4.

76 Advertisement, *ibid*., p. 1.

77 *RO*, 12 July 1856, p. 4.

9
Bolton politics I

As we have seen, Bolton's local government leaders were broadly similar in character to Rochdale's but differed in important respects. On the one hand they clearly constituted a social and economic elite: they were ostentatiously philanthropic, and contained substantial numbers of large proprietors, plus significant proportions of well-heeled professionals and shopkeepers. These municipal politicians seem doubly impressive, given that Bolton's factories were larger on average than Rochdale's.[1] On the other hand, manufacturing and mercantile men, particularly the greatest of them, seem not to have participated in municipal politics on the same scale, or for the same lengths of time, as their Rochdale counterparts.[2] On the whole, therefore, simply viewing the resources available to local leaders in achieving desired ends, one might expect them to find life harder and subject to greater pluralism.

In fact the real picture is again more complex, and this seems to be related to the rather different character of the interacting variables outlined in chapter 6. As we shall see, compared with Rochdale, party conflict, though important, was less intense and more intermittent; the institutional system, though chaotic, was less open; populism came less naturally to the elite; political mobilisation, though often intense, was less traditionally sanctioned and extended less frequently to the bottom of the social scale. As chapter 10 will show, the overall result was a political situation wherein paralysis was frequent, power often difficult to exercise and the municipal elite certainly influenced by the world outside. On the other hand, such influence was less evident and more intermittent than in Rochdale, and less likely to emanate from groups without substantial property.

The divided elite

In chapter 7 we saw that religion and party were both politically crucial sources of division within Rochdale's elite. Religious tension was certainly present in Bolton, sometimes quite intensely, but it never raised such passion. Not did it become polarised into the sort of furious and uncomplicated conflict between Anglicans and Nonconformists that annually drew hundreds and thousands of angry people to Rochdale's parish churchyard to do battle over the election of churchwardens. The church rates controversy was far less bitter and aroused fewer people. Although there were angry 'scenes' in and around the school board in the late '70s, the pressures against any 'continuous state of unwholesome foment amongst us'[3] on the educational question were normally successful.

The reasons for this relatively quiescent state of affairs are probably complex. The strong Anglican representation among the population was certainly one.[4] Bolton's Nonconformists were less likely to feel the self-confident outrage at contributing to the Established Church that was evident amongst their hugely majoritarian counterparts to the east. Anyway, Bolton's parish church was economically and geographically far less dominating than the elegant ecclesiastical ground landlord that flaunted itself before Rochdale's Nonconformists from its cliff in the town centre. As we saw in chapter 1, Bolton's Nonconformist sects were also composed differently and more moderately, compared with Rochdale's. Finally the town's religious divisions were complicated by the fact that around one in seven of the population was Roman Catholic.

This relative absence of religious bitterness among Bolton's elite probably affected the other more politically central source of division — that of party. Two points must be emphasised here: first, party was an important determinant of the way in which members of the elite reacted to each other and thus also to their followers; second, it was far less all-embracing than in Rochdale.

Party conflict was always important. Liberals and Tories were more evenly matched than in Rochdale and thus, in some respects, more competitive. Certainly party deeply influenced recruitment to all local governmental institutions: for long periods, it dominated elections to the Little Bolton trustees, the guardians, the townships and the council; it also heavily affected the more oligarchic deliberations of the two court leets, the county magistrates and the Great Bolton trustees — deliberations about who were to be selected as boroughreeves, constables, overseers, highway surveyors and new trustees. Moreover conflict did not subside after Bolton's incorporation in 1838 as it did after Salford's in 1844.[5]

Party also deeply affected relations between the town's governmental institutions. In particular, as in Rochdale, it produced strong hostility between the Tory-dominated and more oligarchic parts of the local political system (such as the Great Bolton trustees and the public utility companies), and the normally Liberal-controlled, and more democratic, parts (such as the township meetings, the Little Bolton trustees and the council). Particularly in the early decades of our period this hostility, as we shall see, was continuous and often paralysing.

Conflict was sometimes bitter and ruthless. In January 1840 Peter Naisby, a radical, painted a most unpleasing picture of Tory workhouse administration several years previously. Overseers, he alleged, were known 'to gorge themselves nearly every week' on 'sundry turkeys, ducks and green peas' and then, 'in the face of the workhouse inmates, were seen to throw up the contents of their stomachs in the yard, and . . . return to the governors' residence to refill them'.[6] Naisby's opponents described him more entomologically as 'a filth fly'.[7] In the same period arguments on the board of guardians sometimes caused 'gentlemen to leave the room' and produced language that local newspapers 'were unable to print'.[8]

Periodically, party battles were carried to considerable lengths. As we saw in chapter 3, particularly before 1850 such conflict always threatened to invade philanthropy and to produce 'a complete defeat of the object . . . in view'.[9] In the municipal sphere, posts tended to change hands whenever there was a change in party control — the council merely following a tradition long since established, so it was alleged, by the Tories, under whom 'there was not a single officer in the town from the highest down to the common bellman but was either an orangeman or a blackface'.[10] Meanwhile the minority party's aldermanic seats were invariably fair game even when the majority's advantage was overwhelming.[11]

Policy consideration too was sometimes deeply affected by party conflict. Incorporation in 1838 provides the most notable example. This Liberal move was not merely contested by the Tories, but the very existence of the new corporation was subject to a four-year legal challenge. A more general example of the same trend was the recurrent pattern whereby the minority party attacked the improvement 'record' of the majority on grounds of economy.

Though often important and never completely absent from local politics, the intensity of party conflict fluctuated considerably. It was a continuous fact of life at many levels before 1850, but much more intermittently thereafter. Indeed, it became largely peripheral to council elections between 1852 and 1867, dramatically increasing again only when the Reform Act made municipal elections seem worth fighting in order to limber up for the now more challenging constituency spoils. This spell of intense rivalry, moreover, lasted only until 1877.

Even at its most intense, party was never as all-embracing as in Rochdale. There was a pronounced feeling, particularly among the upper levels of the

elite, that its 'incursion' into local politics was illegitimate. Though deter-
minedly Conservative, the town's most influential newspaper, the *Bolton
Chronicle*, was a consistent exponent of this view. It constantly ascribed what
it saw as the decline in the talent, prestige and proprietorial weight of council
members to the 'busy electioneering cliques' of little men, and frequently
advocated that men of property and standing should unite non-politically to
sweep such rubbish from the municipal scene.[12] The *Chronicle*'s diatribes
sometimes slipped into covert appeals for more Tory councillors. Nevertheless its views coincided with a substantial degree of popular opinion. The
success of occasional efforts by members of the elite to insert equally well-
heeled individuals into the council on overtly non-partisan tickets provides
evidence for this view.[13] Similarly, periodic accusations by partisans that it
was their opponents who had introduced party into municipal affairs argues
that non-partisanship had sufficient popular normativeness to demand at least
lip service.

Partly as a result, party affected legislative decision-making only intermittently. There were long periods of political peace on the board of
guardians. As early as 1843 the Liberal *Bolton Free Press* can be found
consoling itself for an overwhelming Conservative electoral victory on the
council with the thought that, from a policy viewpoint, it probably did not
matter which party was in control.[14] Unlike Rochdale, but like Salford, there
were strong feelings that, though mayoral and aldermanic elections were 'a
party question . . ., in matters of [council] business it was different'.[15] Thus
neither party tried to monopolise committee chairmanships,[16] and partisan
appointment to paid municipal offices, though frequent, was not invariable.[17]
Though there were policy conflicts, they only sometimes involved party.
Even in 1852, after a long period of electoral contention, the *Bolton
Chronicle* could note that the markets committee included 'persons of all
shades of politics and their proceedings in general have been . . .
unanimous'.[18]

Even in elections the urge towards 'amicable arrangement', especially
among the top elite, was strong. It was particularly pronounced on the school
board but also evident in guardian and council contests — especially in the
1850s, '60s and late '70s. The tendency was more evident than in Rochdale:
Moreover, though it was often based, as there, upon calculation of electoral
choice, it stemmed more frequently from underlying feelings of consensus
among the elite. In 1874 the Liberal *Bolton Weekly Journal* surveyed the
wards and found no 'keen desire to displace the party in power', and then
agreed that 'it is perhaps as well that [the Conservatives] should be permitted
to steer the ship for some time longer'.[19]

This was partly because local electoral battles were much more exclusively the result of constituency needs. Such calculations were present in Rochdale but rarely enunciated, and the local arena was always seen as worth contesting in its own right. In Bolton, particularly after the 1867 Reform Act, constituency calculations behind local intervention were constantly proclaimed: they represented 'still higher motives',[20] or 'higher and nobler ground than ... municipal affairs'.[21] Such priorities ensured that local elections would be at least periodically contested, but they also meant that when constituency needs became less pressing, then the intensity of local conflict declined.

At a deeper level this less conflictual pattern is related to the whole basis of party. Party division was much less reinforced than it was in Rochdale by other factors. Tories and Liberals were never divided to the same extent by religion. The Church rates controversy was never sufficiently intense to reinforce polarisation. Though Nonconformists were generally Liberal, there was a marked tendency for religion to straddle party lines. Thus the council of 1860/1 included ten Anglican Liberals and one Wesleyan Conservative.[22]

To a limited extent Liberals and Tories were connected by business[23] and marriage.[24] More important, the Liberals were not cut off from the land as they were in Rochdale. Over the years their ranks included, for example, Peter Ainsworth, the owner of the ancient country house of Smithhills Hall, related by marriage to the Earl of Mountmorris; John and Richard Harwood, both mayors of Bolton and the sons of a Heaton farmer; Thomas Thomasson, the grandson of a wealthy yeoman farmer and a long-term resident of the Scottish highlands.

Still more important, party never seriously affected philanthropic activity — partly because of determined efforts (significant in themselves) to prevent it doing so. A survey of the sponsors of all the major social and charitable institutions and movements throughout our period consistently reveals a strong intermixture of Tory and Liberal partisans. This was so even in the period of relatively intense conflict before 1850. Only during the bitter four-year dispute over incorporation was there any appreciable polarisation (with the Queen's birthday being celebrated in separate banquets), but even here social amenities were rapidly restored.

As in Rochdale, however, political relations also partly reflected internal party dynamics: particularly the character of the Whig-radical alliance represented by Liberalism. An alliance there certainly was and, particularly in the 1830s, the Whigs gave every indication of needing the radicals in their battles over the corn laws, and in their conflicts with the Tory-dominated parts of the local governmental system. In return, as in Rochdale, they were prepared to offer remarkably fervent support for causes like Chartism.[25] Nevertheless the alliance was always strained; increasingly so in the '40s,

when there were complaints that 'they were continually divided'.[26] Thereafter radical influence declined. The changing nature of the institutional
system meant that Whig need for the radicals diminished. They were never
again able to impose the sort of leftward bias that was continuously evident in
Rochdale, and could not prevent Whig–Tory accommodation.

Thus party conflict, though important, was less intense than in Rochdale.
Partly as a result, the competing sections of the elite were less populistic, less
politically opportunistic and ultimately less sensitive to outside pressures.
However, this contrasting situation can be understood only in the context of
the interaction between the intensity of conflict and the operation of the local
institutional system.

The institutional system

Bolton's political system was similar to Rochdale's but again differed in
important respects. Partly as a result, the difficulties experienced by the elite
were also very different. For reasons that will become obvious, it seems
appropriate to divide the period not in 1838, when Bolton became
incorporated, but in 1850, when the two sets of trustees disappeared and the
council became the central policy-making body.

1830-50

In this period the governmental system was, like Rochdale's, composed of
numerous institutions uneasily sharing powers, only partially sharing borders
and often fighting about both. Two points are important in what follows.
First, these institutions provided many points of access to decision-making.
Those using them had the capacity to paralyse each other and, indeed, large
parts of the system. Thus power, as in Rochdale, was always difficult to
exercise. Second, far more than in Rochdale, these access points primarily
simply provided competing sections of the elite with opportunities to stultify
each other. This was because more of the institutions were closed and
oligarchic. There were points of public access, and these could be important
— certainly important enough to tempt competing sections of the elite to
appeal against each other down the social scale. Nevertheless the opportunities open to lowly groups for direct access to decision-making were fewer
and less authoritative than in Rochdale.

Many of Bolton's governing institutions were closed and/or oligarchic. The
clearest example was the Great Bolton trustees — the main regulatory body
for the larger and more southerly of the two townships that constituted the
town. It was totally self-perpetuating. In 1830 this largely Tory body of £30
householders and above consented, informally and under pressure, to a mild

form of popular selection (upon a vacancy, a township meeting was to supply four names for the trustees to choose their new member from). However, within three years, finding the trickle of recruits too radical for their taste, they had unilaterally discontinued the arrangement — thereafter electing themselves 'without . . . interference'.[27] The trustees were also totally secretive, unwilling to confide news of their doings to the press or even their own minute book.

Operating quite independently with similar, though probably more adequate, powers were the almost exclusively Liberal Little Bolton trustees. Theoretically they were a more open body than their neighbouring counterparts. Their thirty members required a slightly lower property qualification,[28] and a third were elected yearly by a meeting of ratepayers of only seven months' standing or more. However, democracy was counterbalanced by a provision conferring up to six votes on great proprietors. Nevertheless, in Bolton as elsewhere, such ratepayers' gatherings were susceptible to guerilla attack. This the Liberals discovered in October 1838 when, in retaliation against the establishment of the new corporation, twenty-two Tories 'took the meeting by surprise',[29] produced 120 votes and inserted ten Conservative trustees. However, such unpredictability was counterbalanced by Bolton's relatively weak traditions of popular participation. Normally election meetings were thinly attended, and Liberal lists often appear to have been adopted without much discussion of persons or policies. Not surprisingly, the trustees were almost as secretive about their proceedings as those in Great Bolton.

Moreover, even if Little Bolton's trustees were relatively open, other institutions were emphatically closed. This was particularly true of the chief officers of the townships — the two sets of boroughreeves and constables. Whereas Rochdale's chief constable was chosen by the elected improvement commission, Bolton's invariably Conservative officials were selected by the Great and Little Bolton court leets. The latter bodies consisted of citizens picked mysteriously by the four lords of the manor.[30] The chief officers' powers were hazy but sometimes important. The boroughreeves chaired trustees' meetings, and had power (which they generally refused to use) to call township meetings. The constables controlled the police, and played a crucial role in Tory resistance to the corporation's attempts to absorb this function after 1838.

Equally closed, but sharing authority with the more formally governmental trustees, were the private gas and water companies. As in Rochdale, and like the railway companies, they had powers of compulsory purchase, could determine who was to be supplied, could decide prices within generous limits, could apply independently to Parliament for an extension of their powers, and could oppose Bills submitted by the two groups of trustees if they felt there were clauses interfering with their privileges. Their directors were 'chosen' by the often proxy votes of their shareholders, were responsible only to them and were effectively self-perpetuating. However, the worst sin of 'these over-bearing monopolies'[31] in Liberal eyes was that they were Tory-controlled and often highly partisan. Thus they were in almost perpetual conflict with the Liberal-controlled Little Bolton trustees, and later with the council, parti-cularly in its Liberal phases. They were capable of paralysing the govern-mental actions of the Liberal section of the elite, and were always a source of implicit of explicit constraint upon the authorities, whatever their party colour. Moreover (unlike their Rochdale counterparts), these companies would not go away — the water company survived until 1846, and the gas company until 1870.

The final closed institution was the Bolton division of the county magistrates. As in Rochdale, the magistrates were Tory-dominated and had an important role in the political system. Besides certain regulatory functions, they appointed the highway surveyors and, more important, the four overseers of the poor for each township. Normally they chose them from larger lists submitted by Liberal-dominated township meetings. However, because of the overseers' electoral functions, they periodically intervened to insert their own Tory nominees. Moreover, in the years immediately after 1838, the magistrates' Tory majority was further tempted to interfere because of the new corporation's attempt to use the poor rates (which the overseers collected) as a source of alternative finance while they were under Tory legal challenge. The result was that, in 1839, Great Bolton was landed with two competing groups of overseers appointed by the Tory and Liberal sections of the magistrates.

From the late 1830s these already conflicting institutions were joined, but crucially not superseded, by two others. The first was the board of guardians, which took over most of the overseers' Poor Law functions. As elsewhere, they were elected on a property-weighted franchise. In Rochdale this did not prevent guardians' elections from providing a point of access for working-class groups. In Bolton, however, the board was much more insulated from lowly influence, perhaps because the Union was more heavily dominated by rural townships, perhaps because of the weaker traditions of political mobilisation in the Bolton area as a whole. Rural overrepresentation on the board was enough to ensure an almost perpetual Tory majority, and con-siderable conflict between urban and rural guardians.

The second body was the council, introduced after a long battle in 1838. It was more open than the Great Bolton trustees, since it was directly elected. However, its democratic superiority to the Little Bolton trustees was more contestable. Admittedly the franchise was based on one ratepayer one vote, compared with the trustees' property weighting. However, like those in other towns incorporated under the 1835 Act, individuals had to have paid poor rates continuously for nearly three years, and not recently to have received them, before being eligible for the burgess roll. These provisions penalised potential working-class voters heavily (particularly at times of greatest need) and compared poorly with the more relaxed conditions governing voting for the trustees.

Furthermore Bolton's council was a distinctly less open body then Rochdale's. Councillors had to be £30 householders, compared with £15 in Rochdale. This provision probably had less effect on the nature of political recruitment (the proportions of large proprietors being smaller than in Rochdale) than on the style of politics: there was less need to appease those further down the scale. Another politically crucial fact about Bolton's council in this early period was that the two parties shared control. The Liberals had a majority up to 1844, while the Tories had one between 1844 and 1852.

With the appearance of the council, the confused collection of governing bodies was complete. Because the various institutions were controlled by different parties, the older ones did not willingly disappear, nor surrender their powers to the new corporation. There was too great a stake in the continuance of institutions which gave the parties access to power. In fact the situation was doubly complex because the trustees of Little and Great Bolton were each controlled by a different party. Thus when a Liberal council wanted to absorb the trusts it found itself opposed in Great Bolton; when the Tories took control they found their imperialistic aims thwarted in Little Bolton. Moreover uncertainly was intensified because the legal validity of Bolton's charter was subject to Tory challenge until August 1842.

In this way party conflict came to reinforce institutional chaos, and there ensued, after 1838, a prolonged period of semi-paralysis in which neither section of the elite could do much beyond stultifying the other. The exercise of positive power by anyone became extremely difficult. On the one hand, the council existed, under Liberal control but with few powers and only hazily legitimate sources of finance. On the other, the trustees, boroughreeves and constables had governing powers, but not the drive or political legitimacy to use them effectively.[32] Bolton's institutions thus provided both sections of the elite with opportunities for mutual paralysis. However, there were also points in the pre-1850 system where more lowly participants could gain access to the political process.

Some we have already partially covered. Subject to the limitations noted earlier, elections to the guardians, council and even occasionally the Little Bolton trustees provided opportunities for groups some way down the social scale to influence recruitment and policy. Thus James Flitcroft, a radical, was elected to the board of guardians in 1848 despite a concerted attempt to control recruitment, through compromise, between the Whigs and Tories of Great and Little Bolton. Several 'Chartist' candidates (some albeit of dubious pedigree) were returned to the council in 1839. All had been nominated, after a fierce Liberal factional battle, at 'a meeting of burgesses'. A similar meeting in Exchange ward in 1842 chose Joseph Wood as Liberal candidate in preference to retiring councillor Henry Macoun, on the grounds that Wood was more radical.

Meanwhile the pattern was quickly established whereby the minority party campaigned on an 'economy' platform against the alleged extravagance of the governing majority, and the majority then somewhat sheepishly defended its activist 'record'. It emerged as soon as parties began contesting council elections after 1842, and ensured that choices of a sort were presented to the electorate. Moreover, even though the economisers diminished electoral influence by moving in an activist direction once in power (as the Conservatives did after 1845), such battles did provide electors with the chance to register a verdict on the record of the party in power. Certainly the *Bolton Chronicle* saw the Conservative victory of 1846, after a year in power, in this way:

The opinion of the burgesses has been . . . unequivocally expressed. They have spoken clear in favour of . . . the measures of which Conservative councillors were the known supporters . . . [the election] establishes . . . that the feeling of the borough is in favour of local improvement.[33]

There were also points of more direct public participation. By far the most important and frequently used were the township vestry meetings of Great and Little Bolton. These had a 'customary' or 'moral' right[34] to nominate ten persons for the office of overseer, and ten for that of highway surveyor. From these the magistrates were expected to pick four overseers and two surveyors (normally the first names on the lists). The vestries also had the right to pass the constables' accounts, and could thus become a platform for the expression of poor ratepayers' dissatisfaction about local expenditure and the operation of the police.[35]

Vestry rights were somewhat hazy: the magistrates did not have to accept township nominations (though they often did), and could, in certain circumstances, reinstate rejected accounts.[36] In the last resort, wealthy ratepayers could circumvent vestry decisions by a Stourges Bourne poll, wherein voting was weighted according to property. Nevertheless, as in Rochdale, township vestries were potentially important. Their functions in regard to highway surveyors' and constables' accounts made them a centre for Liberal battles against the more oligarchic Tory-controlled parts of the institutional system. Because of the overseers' role in collecting poor rates, and the corporation's attempt to raise a borough rate under this guise between 1838 and 1842, the vestries were drawn into the conflict over the validity of incorporation. After the Conservatives took control of the council in 1844, the Little Bolton vestry also became the centre of Liberal-inspired resistance to the absorption of the trustees, and effectively made the decision to refuse consent to the proposed amalgamation of 1846.[37] Finally, the overseers compiled the electoral register, and were thus of crucial importance to both parties.

The Liberals in particular therefore needed to control the vestries. Normally they did so, but only by dint of radical support. In return (and in return for support for the anti-corn law campaign), they were obliged to flirt gingerly with more central working-class causes like Chartism.[38] Such necessities were the more pressing because vestries shaded imperceptibly into public township meetings called to discuss broader issues like the New Poor Law.

They became more pressing still because of the difficulty of controlling vestry meetings. The latter were sometimes crowded, with attendances up to 300. As in Rochdale, rules about attendance were hazy and rarely enforced. Not surprisingly, therefore, they sometimes got out of hand. More than one supplemented its original purpose by passing motions supporting the Charter, or by other 'vexatious conduct'.[39]

In May 1839 the Liberals convened a meeting to condemn the county magistrates for rejecting the township's nominations for overseers. Having obediently expressed no confidence in the magistrates, the Chartist majority, despite Liberal pleas, proceeded to demand the removal of the offending JPs from the bench. From this they progressed to more general denunciation of the parliamentary conduct of one of the magistrates — Bolton's Liberal MP, Peter Ainsworth.[40]

However, such points of popular access were less numerous, less important and probably embraced fewer people than in Rochdale. Township meetings — and public meetings generally — were less frequent, less well attended and less authoritative. They were never used, as they were in Salford, as means of effectively appointing the boroughreeve and constables. Nor were they used, as in Rochdale, as points of final ratification or rejection of parliamentary applications for improvement legislation. Town — as distinct from township — meetings practically never took place. Because the Church rates controversy was of relatively minor importance, parish meetings were also less frequent, less visible and mobilised fewer people than in Rochdale.

1850-80

The Improvement Act of 1850 brought important changes in the institutional system. After 1850 the opportunities for political access to groups outside the section of the elite that currently controlled the council lessened considerably. Consequently the strong tendency towards paralysis, observable before 1850, also weakened. Whatever difficulties the elite faced in achieving its ends, they were less likely to be generated by institutional rivalry.

The two trusts and the court leets and their appointees (the boroughreeve and constables) either ceased to exist or disappeared into obscurity. Their improvement, rate-levying and police functions were all absorbed by the corporation. Township meetings — and public meetings generally — tended to fall into disuse. With the disappearance of the old authorities, vestry rights over the highway surveyors and constables' accounts were automatically absorbed by the council. The latter had even tried taking over the nomination of overseers in 1841. Though the attempt seems to have failed, the vestries (unlike Rochdale) seem to have been summoned only rarely after 1850 — with current overseers simply nominating their successors,[41] and the guardians appointing the assistant overseers. In any case, the right of final appointment for the overseers now rested not with the county but with the borough magistrates, and their recruitment was heavily influenced by the council's majority party. Overall, the council therefore gained in legitimacy, and became the sole multi-purpose institution of local government.

Nevertheless it was not a totally closed system. There were still important points of access not controlled by the corporate majority section of the elite, and some that gave opportunities to groups below those from which the council was predominantly recruited. The board of guardians remained an almost exclusively Tory preserve, and one moreover subject to quite different non-urban influences from those affecting the council. Though the two did not come into frequent contact, there were occasional clashes over shared public health functions.

The remaining private utility — the gas company — was a more formidable source of difficulty. Its directors were still predominantly Tory. Though their policies were decreasingly influenced by party politics after 1850, it is significant that the company successfully resisted the Liberal-controlled council's attempts at municipalisation, and that it yielded its private virtue only to the seductive wiles of a Tory majority in 1870. Until then the company remained in some respects a rival centre of initiative and authority. As we shall see in chapter 10, it was a formidable opponent and a constant source of constraint on council actions.[42]

Petitioning provided wider opportunities of political access. So too did elections. As before 1850, periods of party conflict (up to 1852 and 1867-76) tended to present the electorate with at least some sort of choice between pledges of economy (in whose alleged benefits even working-class ratepayers might hope to bask) and rather sheepishly defended 'records' of municipal activism. Elections also provided opportunities for public discussion of more specific decisions currently before the council — some of special interest even to working-class electors. Contests after 1867 gave rise to vigorous debate between candidates, and some questioning from electors, about issues like increases in the police force, the cost of the new waterworks and town hall, the sale of refreshments in the park on Sundays, reductions in the wages of corporation workmen and the attempted council ban on working-class pig-keeping. Some (though by no means all) candidates were persuaded to identify their stance. Rather more sitting councillors were drawn into defending conduct and explaining council policies.

How far elections thus became a channel of influence between electors and elected is more doubtful. The variable nature of party conflict in Bolton and the drive towards compromise meant that electoral choices were only spasmodically available. In any case, the effectiveness of any choice between economy and activism was marred, after as before 1850, by the tendency of the economical minority to change emphasis once it became the majority. Nevertheless the out-party's exploitation of ratepayers' grievances may well have imposed at least implicit constraints on corporate behaviour, whoever won the election. The *Bolton Chronicle*'s advice to the Conservative majority in the light of the 1872 elections hints at this possibility. The cry of economy, it argued, had been less electorally potent than the Liberals had hoped, and there was no need for radical retrenchment. Nevertheless the results 'should not be without [their] effect on the party in power . . . they should not be unmindful that a vigilant oversight of the public purse will constitute one of their best claims on the continued confidence of the public.'[43] More generally, the possibility of electoral debate probably imposed the limited awareness of the wider world that, we shall argue in the next section, councillors possessed.

Electoral nomination also provided more direct chances of political access — to groups at least down to the level of small property owners. At various times — especially after the increase in party conflict in 1867 — temperance men, drink sellers, landlords, Roman Catholics and butchers (otherwise known as 'Knights of the Cleaver'!) all forced one or both parties to adopt chosen representatives as candidates. Alternatively they threatened destructive independent candidatures long enough for competing parties to give concrete pledges of sympathy in terms of council action.

A more unexpected point of access for some groups was the borough magistrates. The annual licensing sessions became a regular point of pressure for conflicting temperance and drink-selling groups. The magistrates' normal response seems to have been political compromise — one that left the number of licences more or less constant.

Opportunities like those described above were important. In some respects, moreover (as in Rochdale and Salford), they actually mutiplied and widened towards the end of our period. The arrival of the school board in 1870 increased the number of local governmental institutions to three, thus representing a partial return to the multi-institutional situation prior to 1850. Though determined compromise among the elite normally prevented electoral contests, the board, with its cumulative voting system, was susceptible to surprise attack. In 1879 working-class candidates broke through the arrangements made by the religious groups and forced the public discussion of issues central to working-class interests. Moreover, by encouraging supporters to give all their votes to a single candidate, they successfully forced one of their number to the head of the poll.[44]

The inclusion of compounders in 1859 and female householders in 1868 considerably widened the municipal franchise to include appreciably more of the working class. The ballot after 1872 potentially increased freedom of electoral choice.[45] Lastly, the 1873 Borough Funds Act, for the first time in Bolton, elevated town meetings to become the final point of decision on parliamentary applications for improvement legislation. As in Rochdale and Salford, this additional and very open point of political access was to have an important effect on the exercise of power.

Nevertheless Bolton's institutional system was less open after 1850 than it had been before, and less open than it was in Rochdale throughout our period. The points of direct public participation available before 1850 largely disappeared and, until 1873, were always less authoritative than in Rochdale. Moreover, even after the inclusion of compounders, there were fewer municipal voters per head of the population (around one in 9·25 in 1861, compared with one in 7·6 in Rochdale; and one in seven in 1871 against one in 5·3.) This may reflect different patterns of residence and mobility. Alternatively, it may reflect manipulations of the registration system by the parties — the sort of practices referred to by the *Bolton Chronicle* in 1874: 'it has been the rule of both parties to make objections almost exclusively to those persons who can ill afford to bear the loss of a day's wages in order to attend the revision court to sustain their right to be on the register'.[46] Either way, the difference in political disadvantage between the two towns was most likely to affect the working classes.

In fact the points of political access that Bolton's institutions provided were available primarily to rival sections of the elite. To a lesser extent they were available to those within the wider ring of property, however modestly. The fewest and least effective opportunities were available to those without property. While Rochdale might show a similar gradient of political opportunity, it was markedly less steep.

However, the character and consequences of the institutional system can be understood only in the context of the other factors under review. We have already suggestd a relationship between the degree of access available and the intensity of party conflict. We can now turn to the attitudes of leadership.

Elite attitudes

The attitudes of Bolton's leaders, Liberal as well as Tory, towards the popular world beyond the legislative walls were markedly more ambivalent and variable than Rochdale's. On the one hand, local legislators were certainly aware of that world. Some revealed a belief that their actions were subject to interested and critical scrutiny. Even guardians, in the early, more conflictual phase of the boards' existence, could show nervousness. Visiting relief applicants in their homes, it was suggested in 1839, 'would have a natural tendency to create an invidious distinction between those who visited . . . and those who did not. The former would be held up . . . as very benevolent; while the latter would be accused of hard-heartedness.'[47]

Some used the alleged state of public opinion as support for what they wanted to do, claiming that their ideas were 'decidedly popular out of doors',[48] or that even 'the straitened ratepayers in Dog-row . . . would be in favour . . .'.[49] There was quite a strong tendency to suggest that opinion, either now, or as it might be aroused in the future, would irresistibly demand, or more frequently constrain, action. In 1849 Councillor Ainsworth predicted that if the trusts were absorbed they 'would find the ratepayers very much in arms against them'.[50] In 1859 J. R. Wolfenden advised his colleagues against paving the river Croal because 'public opinion was scarcely ripe for it'.[51] S. G. Chadwick advised the opposite, because, though 'people cared very little' now, 'if a case of cholera were to happen, . . . they [councillors] . . . would all be jumping around with alacrity'.[52] In 1868 Samuel Rawsthorn supported an expansion of the police on the grounds that 'he should be afraid to go before his constituents' unless he did.[53]

These prognostications were not made just to support desired courses of action. Some councillors seemed genuinely to fear misunderstanding 'out of doors'. They advised that 'it was of the very greatest importance that these impressions should be removed',[54] or suggested that 'it was desirable to have the support of the public generally'[55] if particular policies were to be successful.

Such worries were particularly likely during periods of intense party conflict. This is suggested by a revealing council debate in October 1867, just before the elections that signalled the renewal of Conservative interest in winning a majority. The remarks of one councillor about the extravagance involved in the building of a new reservoir prompted long speeches from several colleagues. One feared that, if his statements were 'allowed to go uncontradicted, they would tend to arouse a feeling in the minds of the ratepayers that we . . . are totally unfit for the office we hold'. Another did 'not want to go before the public inviting them to say we are a lot of block-heads; we are in sufficiently bad odour already'. After three such fearful and self-justifying perorations J. A. Haslam spoke 'only briefly', on the grounds that 'I have not to appear before my constituency, as other gentlemen have, and therefore there is no occasion for me to make myself attractive to the public' — implying that some future electoral necessity might draw the oratory even from him.[56]

As this suggests, some legislators were given to striking postures for the benefit of 'the people outside' — again particularly in the atmosphere of intense party conflict. More than one debate just before the elections 'rang with electioneering speeches and party cheers'.[57]

Nevertheless Bolton was different from Rochdale. Perception of outside opinion was expressed much less frequently — particularly among the guardians — and awareness never reached the point, often evident in Rochdale, where local legislators seemed to feel that the entire body of ratepayers had them continuously under its gimlet eye.

Attitudes towards outside 'agitation' were also more varied. Some regarded it as perfectly legitimate, believing that 'the voice of the people . . . sways us . . . influences . . . changes our notions'.[58] However, many others disapproved. In 1856 Henry Ashworth, a Liberal, told his fellow guardians, 'if the ratepayers were to dictate to them after sending them as their representatives, they had better . . . do the work themselves. (Hear, hear.)'[59] In 1864 Councillor W. Cannon claimed that his support for a public park 'was not at all influenced by any agitation that had taken place out of doors . . . he deprecated that pressure . . . [and] should not consider himself a representative man or delegate . . .'.[60] Many disliked public meetings, proclaiming that they 'would never alter me', or arguing that 'the proper course was to approach this Council not by public meeting but by memorial . . . it was disrespectful . . . to proceed in that way . . . an attempt to override the opinions of the Council and stifle free discussion'.[61]

As this suggests, hostility to specific examples of pressure sometimes extended to distaste for public participation in general, at least of any direct kind. At an early stage, after the need to use them had passed, Liberals registered their dislike of public meetings. In 1841 several suggested that the council's attempt to take over the nomination of overseers was because 'if a public meeting had been called, it would have been of a tumultuous character and not ended satisfactorily'.[62]

Even those supporting specific outside pressure often did so in terms suggesting that attitudes varied according to its quality, according to whether it came from ratepayers or non-ratepayers or, more important, whether men of substance were included among the supplicants. Such attitudes were far more common, at least publicly (and public statements are significant in the context of attitudes to public pressure), than they were in Rochdale. Petitions from the lowly were dismissed because 'I don't think they have much responsibility attached to them',[63] whilst others, time and again, were hailed as worth consideration because they included 'the names of [all] the firms of any importance in the neighbourhood'.[64] Even petitions calling for public meetings were deemed to have a better chance if 'respectably and influentially signed by large, as well as small, ratepayers'.[65]

Given the foregoing, it is unsurprising that open political processes were often frowned upon. This helps explain the secrecy of the trustees before 1850. One incident illustrates the elite's general ambivalence towards the world outside. It implies that councillors sometimes behaved differently under the public gaze, but also that, for this reason, many were hostile to public processes. In 1875 Councillor Bromley started publicising general purposes committee proceedings on the grounds that 'things would not be proposed, or pressed forward . . . if the public knew who advocated them, and on what grounds . . .'. He was furiously assailed by colleagues who thought his actions 'very dishonourable' and 'suicidal to the best interests of the town'.[66]

These differences in attitudes between Bolton and Rochdale were partly related to Bolton's less open political system and to its more intermittent (and less radical-influenced) pattern of party conflict. However, elite attitudes were also related, as we shall now see, to Bolton's rather different traditions and levels of political mobilisation.

Political mobilisation

Bolton's public, and the various groups into which it was divided, were by no means passive, and periodically became highly mobilised. A meeting on the plight of the hand-loom weavers in 1837 drew 2,000.[67] The formation of a Reform Ratepayers' Association in 1847 to nominate councillors, guardians and overseers was admitted even by a hostile source to have been attended by 500.[68] In 1837, at the start of the Poor Law conflict, a meeting to nominate guardians for Great and Little Bolton had drawn a similarly sized crowd.[69] Council elections also generally seem to have attracted high levels of participation, with ward turn-outs commonly reaching 80 or 90 per cent.

Nevertheless participation was less intense and less continuous than in Rochdale — even in the early, more politically exciting, decades. There were fewer occasions when mass attendance was actively invited. In any case, Bolton's less conflictual pattern of religious division meant that parish meetings never had the generally mobilising effect at all levels of society that they probably had in Rochdale. Perhaps partly as a result, there was markedly lower mass participation even on those occasions which encouraged it. Meetings to elect the Little Bolton trustees were microscopically attended until the late 1830s, and even then rarely drew more than a hundred. Vestry meetings were equally thinly attended. Even what was perceived as 'a very large meeting' in 1835 amounted to no more than 200 — unimpressive by Rochdale standards.[70] Forty years later, 'a very good attendance' of 150 turned up to a town meeting to deliberate about the Improvement Bill of 1876.[71]

As this implies, democratic expectations were relatively low. It perhaps partly explains why town and township meetings had a less important place in the institutional system than in Rochdale's or even Salford's. In 1831 the Vicar of Bolton agreed that the town should elect one of the two church-wardens. Yet by 1836 he could claim without contradiction that 'the rate-payers had neglected to follow up the custom' for the last three years.[72] There never seems to have been much pressure — as there successfully was even in Salford — to have the boroughreeve and constables effectively elected by the two townships in spite of the fact that undisturbed court leet nomination delivered a monopoly of these offices to the Tories. Nor was the pressure against the closed nature of the Great Bolton trustees exactly militant or irresistible. In 1830 the Liberals and radicals asked only for an informal arrangement whereby township meetings should be allowed to nominate three candidates for every one vacancy occurring. They eventually settled on the trustees' offer of four for every one, and produced little visible protest when the trustees unilaterally returned to self-perpetuation in 1834. Equally symptomatic of the relative feebleness of democratic tradition was the fact that the new Liberal-controlled council in 1839 decided to appoint its first aldermanic bench from the ranks of those defeated in the recent elections, and that radical protests were limited to calling the decision 'a mistake which he hoped they would all forgive'.[73]

Bolton's weaker tradition of participation was connected with the character of group mobilisation. In many of its aspects Bolton's political group life was quite as active as Rochdale's. The drink-selling interest was, if anything, more formidable, being almost continuously mobilised from 1834, and claiming a membership of 150 by 1853[74] and a voting strength of 258 by 1863.[75]

Though, as in Rochdale, the drink-sellers' main concerns lay in Parliament, they also had local interests. Their self-regulating activities were partly designed to prevent local governmental supervision; they were periodically 'clamorous for representatives' in council elections,[76] and sometimes agitated against specific clauses in improvement Bills. More important, they mobilised themselves for the bitter annual joustings with Bolton's equally formidable temperance movement at the licensing sessions of the borough and county magistrates. As in Rochdale, the group's political salience was increased by municipal leaders' perceptions of its links with the working classes.[77]

Over the years there was an intermittent variety of other small property organisations — with provision dealers, butchers, market hall tenants, cottage owners and ratepayers all appearing and disappearing on the associational scene, and becoming involved in municipal politics. Their mobilisation was probably partly fuelled by a sense of small proprietorial disadvantage measured against men of greater substance. This was more evident in Bolton than in Rochdale. Beer-sellers complained of unfair surveillance, comparing themselves with the rich, who 'could let men get drunk in their houses and then drive them home in a carriage'.[78] Cottage owners spat their resentment of 'peddling [municipal] committees ... constantly inflicting their contemptible enactments upon us, whilst other offenders of a wealthier class ... go scot free'.[79] Others voiced suspicions that attempts to municipalise the gasworks were motivated by large consumers expecting to get 'their gas at a shilling per thousand whilst tradesmen, shopkeepers, beersellers and other smaller consumers would have to pay the highest price the Corporation could charge'.[80]

Of the other mobilised groups, the Catholics were by far the most important. With a seventh of the population Roman Catholic, the claims of the Catholic Defence Association to 'a just representation on the Town Council'[81] could hardly be ignored. In fact the association's importance probably lay quite as much in what local politicians assumed it might do if aroused as in what it did when it was.

Although some groups, like publicans, were only intermittently interested in municipal affairs, others resulted directly from them. The council was thus an agent of mobilisation. The formidable Bolton Medical Society arose from a council dispute with local doctors over the issuing of death certificates under the 1875 Public Health Act. Property owners' organisations were responses to building regulation, while the Butchers' Association resulted from the municipal regulation of slaughterhouses. From the mid-'50s the corporation found itself having to adjudicate between the often conflicting interests of large and small market tenants, auctioneers and outside shopkeepers because of its decision to establish a market hall.

Group life was thus often lively, increasingly complex and, as we shall see, politically important. Nevertheless traditions of participation were weaker than in Rochdale; partly as a result, mobilisation was less extensive. Property owner organisation fluctuated in both towns but seems to have been particularly patchy in Bolton despite the council's long campaign against cellar dwellings. A Property Owners' Protection Association and an Association for the Protection of Cottage Property both existed in 1858: the first rapidly disappeared and never publicly surfaced again, whilst the second petered out after a year, was reformed in 1865, only to subside once more. Though shopkeepers' groups appeared in various specialist guises over the years, there was no permanent all-embracing organisation as there so powerfully was in Rochdale.[82] Consumers of corporation services were never as politically salient as in Rochdale, partly because the gas undertaking was not municipalised until 1870. Finally, ratepayers' associations, so recurrent elsewhere, seem to have surfaced only occasionally.

The most important gap in Bolton's group life was the working classes. Chartism was highly visible in the late '30s and '40s, and sufficiently salient to require careful appeasement from the elite. However, so far certainly as local politics were concerned, there seems to have been little other consistent working-class mobilisation. Church rates were a far less all consuming issue than in Rochdale. The New Poor Law, though it aroused much initial working-class anger, never drew them into the political arena in the continuing way it did there. Indeed, as early as 1837, Bolton radicals were complaining of working-class apathy on the issue.[83]

Moreover once Chartism declined nothing really assumed its mantle. Working men were certainly drawn into the Liberal Party and into the Operative Conservative Association. They were also aroused over specific items of council policy like the stopping of Sunday burials in 1865 (1,500 attending a protest meeting organised by the trade unions and friendly societies) and the campaign to open the park on Sunday mornings in 1867. In 1866 a Workingmen's Pig-keeping Protection Association was formed 'to secure to the working-man . . . the privileges of his forefathers . . . the privilege of keeping . . . pigs' in response to a council decision to curb this widespread practice.[84] Working-class organisations also decisively intervened in the 1879 school board election over the enforcement of compulsory attendance.

As we shall see, such intervention could be crucial. But there was nothing to match the Rochdale Pioneers. The Bolton Co-operative Society was not founded until 1859 (fifteen years after the Pioneers). In 1866 it had 1,800 members (one in forty-eight of the municipal population) and 5,417 in 1877 (one in seventeen). Though the figures represent impressive growth, they compare poorly with the Pioneers, whose members constituted one in eleven of Rochdale's municipal population in 1860, and nearly one in five in 1875. Moreover the Bolton society's commercial activities were confined to retailing, and even its wider cultural ones never spanned its members' social lives to anything like the extent achieved to Rochdale.[85] Bolton's Co-op was never as visible in the press. Overall, only at the very end of our period does it seem likely that the Co-op could have even begun to provide the working class with the partial, but significant, level of social and cultural autonomy enjoyed much earlier in Rochdale. Meanwhile, no more in Bolton than in Rochdale, do the trade unions seem to have represented more than a very spasmodic municipal force.[86] In general there was little to suggest to the elite that specifically working-class opinions might be worth considering or being politically wary of.

Notes

1 See p. 10.
2 See pp. 16f.
3 Canon Powell, *BC*, 6 December 1879, p. 5.
4 See p. 10.
5 See p. 213.
6 *BFP*, 18 January 1840, p. 3.
7 *BC*, 12 June 1841, p. 3.
8 *BC*, 15 August 1840, p. 3.
9 Robert Heywood, *BC*, 22 February 1840, p. 3.
10 Quoted *BC*, 7 April 1838, p. 3.
11 See, for example, 1847 and 1874 aldermanic elections.
12 *BC*, 13 October 1855, p. 4. See also 5 November 1859, p. 5, and 9 November 1861, p. 4.
13 See, for example, victory of E. Barlow and R. Wallwork in West ward, 1858, *BC*, 6 November 1858, p. 4.
14 *BFP*, 4 November 1843, p. 4.
15 Councillor Ramwell, *BC*, 16 July 1867, p. 7.
16 After the Conservative victory of 1869 the Liberals were still left with five of their thirteen committee chairmanships.
17 See appointment of J. R. Wolfenden, a Liberal, as borough treasurer by the Conservatives in 1845.
18 *BC*, 11 September 1852, p. 6.
19 *BWJ*, 17 October 1874, p. 4.
20 Councillor Briggs, *BC*, 12 October 1878, p. 5.
21 Editorial, *BC*, 18 October 1879, p. 7.
22 There were also ten Anglican Tories, eight Wesleyan Liberals, ten Liberals of other Nonconformist denominations and two Catholic Liberals.
23 See, for example, the substantial Tory-Liberal cotton spinning parternship of Cannon & Haslam.

24 In 1864 the Tories supported the Liberal Richard Stockdale for mayor, allegedly because he was related by marriage to their own W. W. Cannon; *BC*, 12 November 1864, p. 4.

25 See p. 182.

26 James Flitcroft, *BFP*, 16 June 1845, p. 3.

27 John Bolling, *BC*, 30 September 1843, p. 4.

28 They were required to be £30 householders (as in Great Bolton) or possess £600 (compared with £1,000 in Great Bolton).

29 Subsequent comment from C. J. Dorbyshire, *BC*, 21 March 1840, p. 3.

30 The Earls of Derby and Bradford; Samuel Freeconton and the Lever family.

31 Letter, *BFP*, 17 June 1843, p. 3.

32 See pp. 187f.

33 *BC*, 7 November 1846, p. 5.

34 Solicitor for Liberals before magistrates, *BFP*, 30 March 1839, p. 4.

35 See *BC*, 19 July 1828, p. 4, and 29 October 1836, pp. 2-3.

36 *BC*, 18 May 1839, p. 3.

37 See p. 191.

38 See p. 182.

39 Robert Heywood, *BFP*, 12 August 1837, p. 4.

40 *BC*, 28 May 1839, p. 5.

41 This was different from Rochdale, where townships remained relatively vigorous — partly because of strong participatory traditions and party conflict; partly because township boundaries did not coincide so precisely with those of the borough as they did in Bolton.

42 See pp. 198f.

43 *BC*, 2 November 1872, p. 5.

44 See p. 55.

45 Note Patrick Joyce's argument about its effect in practice. *Work, Society and Politics. op. cit.*

46 *BC*, 19 September 1874, p. 4.

47 G. Woodhouse, *BFP*, 7 December 1839, p. 3.

48 Councillor Smalley, *BC*, 24 November 1860, p. 7.

49 Councillor Smalley, *BC*, 2 November 1861, p. 7.

50 *BC*, 20 October 1849, p. 6.

51 *BC*, 18 June 1859, p. 7.

52 *BC*, 26 November 1859, p. 6.

53 *BC*, 18 January 1868, p. 7.

54 Councillor E. Barlow, *BC*, 2 February 1861, p. 4.

55 Mayor, *BC*, 5 May 1866, p. 7.

56 *BC*, 19 October 1867, p. 7.

57 *BWJ*, 16 October 1875, p. 9.

58 Councillor Brown, *BC*, 13 July 1867, p. 4.

59 *BC*, 12 January 1856, p. 7.

60 *BC*, 18 June 1864, p. 6.

61 Councillor Marsden and Mayor Ferguson, *BC*, 6 July 1867, p. 8.

62 Councillor Winder, *BFP*, 27 March 1841, p. 3.

63 Councillor Makant, *BC*, 15 August 1863, p. 7.

64 Alderman Ferguson, *BC*, 19 September 1863, p. 7.

65 Councillor Smalley, *BC*, 24 November 1860, p. 7.

66 *BC*, 17 April 1875, p. 7.
67 *BC*, 24 June 1837, p. 3.
68 *BC*, 16 October 1847, p. 5.
69 *BC*, 29 March 1838, p. 4.
70 *BC*, 26 September 1835, p. 3.
71 *BC*, 7 October 1876, p. 5.
72 *BC*, 9 April 1836, p. 3.
73 John Nicholson to Derby Ward burgesses, *BC*, 9 February 1839, p. 3.
74 Licensed Victuallers and Beersellers' Society, *BC*, 6 August 1853, p. 7.
75 *BC*, 8 and 15 August 1863, p. 4.
65 *BC*, 17 October 1874, p. 4.
77 See council debate, *BFP*, 31 August 1839, p. 3.
78 Licensed Victuallers and Beersellers' AGM, *BC*, 5 August 1854, p. 5.
79 Letter, *BWJ*, 20 September 1873, p. 3.
80 Councillor D. W. Latham, *BC*, 16 March 1861, p. 7.
81 Quoted *BWJ*, 14 September 1872, p. 3.
82 See p. 132.
83 See G. Brandreth, *BC*, 10 June 1837, p. 4.
84 *BC*, 20 September 1866, p. 1.
85 Material taken from A. W. Peaples, *Great and Little Bolton Cooperative Society, 1859-1909* (Bolton, *c*. 1910)
86 This was despite the fact that trade union membership in Bolton was comparatively high. See H. A. Turner, *Trade Union Growth, Structure and Policy* (London, 1962).

10
Bolton politics II

In the last chapter we argued that, compared with Rochdale, Bolton's elite were divided but less bitterly so; the institutional system was less open, though equally fragmented; local leaders regarded outside pressure as less legitimate; and that Bolton had a shallower tradition of political mobilisation. Here we examine the impact of this situation on the wielding of power.

In some respects Bolton's elite look as politically sensitive as Rochdale's. Particularly before 1850, competing local leaders were prepared to seek support further down the social scale. Early in the period many of the wealthiest of them appeared on Ten Hours Movement platforms,[1] or gave support to working-class protests over the New Poor Law. Well-heeled Liberals lent public sympathy to the early stages of Chartism — providing meeting places, appearing on Chartist platforms and even specifically endorsing all Six Points.[2] In a politically emotional moment one young Liberal manufacturer was even alleged to have declared that Chartists 'had done well . . . to destroy property; he should not care if his own mill were . . . in a blaze'.[3]

The motives for such populism were mixed. As in Rochdale the various needs for lower-class support on the part of the Anti-Corn Law League and its opponents, parliamentary contestants, and those engaged in more parochial conflicts were inseparably bound together. The last of these was certainly important. The *Bolton Chronicle* saw it as lying behind Liberal support for Chartism: 'These worthies would willingly have excused themselves . . . but were threatened to be abandoned by the radical operatives in the Corporation elections'.[4]

However, because party competition was less intense, and the local institutional system less open, the need for mass support in local conflicts was less urgent. Consequently, Bolton's leaders never acquired the finely honed political sensitivities of their Rochdale counterparts. Liberal relations with Chartists were always strained, particularly as the latter moved leftwards from mid-1839. There was far less political concern in Bolton, particularly after

1850, about 'the non-electors'. They were rarely called together to endorse parliamentary candidates. The activities of working-class organisations were less fully reported in the press, and only rarely patronised by local politicians. Indeed, long after a working-class majority had appeared on both municipal and parliamentary rolls, it was still politically feasible to defend a wage decrease for corporation workmen by claiming that 'if the men were to leave they could get ... new hands on Monday morning'.[5] Overall, the elite's political antennae rarely picked up anyone below 'the most respectable artisans in the borough'. Indeed, the collective activities even of shopkeepers, publicans and other small proprietors often went unpatronised by Liberal and Conservative notables.

Nevertheless, though they saw less need to curry favour from the lower levels of society, Bolton's leaders still found difficulty in achieving intended effects. In the rest of this chapter we shall argue that the political process, particularly before 1850, was chronically subject to paralysis, and productive of situations in which nobody (however substantial) could effectively act. However, two crucial points will be made: (1) this paralysis resulted mainly from the activity of either the rival section of the elite to that currently in the majority, or those outside the immediate political circle but on a comparable economic level; (2) where governmental activity impinged on the wider population the latter was less likely than in Rochdale to be able to induce the need to conciliate. Overall, there was a steeper gradient of influence and political advantage.

We can illustrate these themes by looking first at two areas where, in Rochdale, we witnessed effective lower-class intervention — the Poor Law and incorporation.

The Poor Law

Bolton's Poor Law policies were, throughout, markedly different from Rochdale's. In the early years, it is true, both sections of the leadership were certainly hostile to the law. The board of guardians procrastinated about instructions from the Poor Law Commission, and sanctioned regular appeals to Parliament for repeal or amendment. In the longer term the full rigours of 'less eligibility' were no more applied in Bolton than elsewhere in the industrial north, the workhouse test never being practicable for even a substantial minority of able-bodied paupers, and out-relief always being the norm.

However, the short-term opposition of the elite to the Poor Law Commission was always more limited and more moderate. Far more than in Rochdale, it increasingly centred on those aspects of the Law's administration which the urban middle classes found most objectionable — particularly centralisation and the over-representation of rural districts in the Bolton Union.[6] Boards of guardians were elected regularly from February 1837, and raised few objections to meeting Assistant Commissioners concerned to implement the Act. So far at least as its formal outlines were concerned, local leaders generally emphasised that 'it is the law of the land, and the law must be obeyed'.[7] and that it was more practical to elect guardians who would administer relief humanely than to indulge in confrontation.

These last sentiments were not unrealistic. However, from around 1842 there also emerged significant elements of co-operation and even acceptance in Bolton leaders' responses to the Commission and its directives. In September 1842 the Conservative *Bolton Chronicle* surveyed the record of the Conservative-dominated board thus far and complained of 'a great deal of undue forbearance'.[8] Nine months earlier William Bolling, a leading Tory manufacturer and guardian, had announced himself 'favourable to the Law in some respects, not in others'.[9] Just what those former respects were, so far as Bolling and many other guardians were concerned, was revealed in years to come. In the early 1850s, unlike those in Rochdale, Bolton guardians co-operated with the Poor Law Board order directing that out-relief be given in kind, having heard without protestation the Poor Law inspector's explanation that relief 'was not a sick fund from which all who contributed had a right to claim . . . It . . . was a compulsory rate to save the destitute from starvation . . .'[10]

As the board's silence here implies, there was considerable sympathy in Bolton with the broad notion of less eligibility. Though the workhouse test could never be applied, deterrence came to affect the spirit in which both indoor and outdoor relief were given. Thus the guardians refused to provide either food or bedding in the tramps' ward of their workhouses. They constantly scrutinised workhouse diets lest generosity slip in. As early as 1848, and without opposition, they sanctioned the regular publication and distribution of the names of all relief applicants as a means of enlisting 'public knowledge' in the search for fraudulent claims. Though this practice was adopted by the Spotland township, there was always too much opposition for it to become general policy in Rochdale. From an early stage, most Bolton guardians proved sympathetic to the imposition of some form of labour test for able-bodied applicants. As early as 1840 the workhouse committee was considering reforming the work done in the house partly because 'it would have a tendency to lessen the wish to go in . . .'.[11] In the 1840s and 1850s stone-breaking and oakum-picking were periodically reported as being performed in the workhouses by able-bodied inmates, along with appreciable numbers of those on out-relief.[12] In 1848 the first of several workshop alterations in Bolton Workhouse was commenced so as to 'provide a proper classification for able-bodied paupers' and thus satisfy the Poor Law Commission 'as to the state of classification'.[13] Throughout the 1840's many country districts within the Union were employing out-relief applicants on the highways,[14] and the workhouse committee several times expressed itself favourable to 'some general plan . . . to provide employment for applicants for relief'.[15] In the late 1850s, rather in the spirit of persuading condemned men to dig their own graves, Bolton's guardians also used pauper labour in the early stages of building the new workhouse.

In fact work was never found for more than a minority of those on out-relief. However, the problems and objections were not ones of principle but of practicality — the inability to discover enough tasks, and the inefficiency of pauper labour.[16] Furthermore, the desire to use a labour test was a major factor behind the decision to build a Union workhouse in 1856.

The decision was significant in itself, and provides a major contrast with Rochdale, whose guardians consented to build one only in 1871, and never discussed the possibility before the late 1860s. In Bolton it was first raised and lengthily discussed in May 1847. Though heavily voted down, copious debate was resumed by the guardians at regular intervals. Opposition steadily diminished, until final consent was given for a workhouse for 1,000 by twenty-three votes to eighteen in January 1856.

The justification was partly humane. The two old workhouses were fairly appalling places, and the project reflected the appreciation by some members of the elite of the more enlightened aspects of the New Poor Law — the duty to provide separate facilities for children, old people and for 'the . . . liberal treatment' of the insane.[17] Nevertheless the desire to provide 'a legitimate test' of willingness to work was also central. This too could be enlightened. For some elements of local opinion, work needed to be 'of a remunerative character instead of the present system of . . . compulsory idleness and useless revolting . . . task work'.[18] The new workhouse had twenty acres of agricultural land where 'reproductive [paid] labour for the able-bodied' could take place, as well as 'a labour test for the idle and dissolute'.[19] Yet, as this suggests, the institution was intended to provide 'a complete test' for all able-bodied recipients, whether on outdoor or indoor relief, with the frequently quoted harsh insistence that 'he that will not work neither shall he eat'.[20] It was assumed that 'a larger proportion [of the working class] than hitherto would in future be compelled to seek shelter within its walls', thus preventing 'the idle and dissolute from so readily imposing themselves on their fellow men'.[21]

Bolton's Poor Law policies, then, were different from Rochdale's both in content and in spirit. What was also different was that the guardians proceeded without reference to public opinion, particularly lower-class opinion, which was certainly hostile to the Poor Law. In 1842 18,000 (nearly all the adult male population) petitioned for its alteration. Working-class opinion was almost certainly equally hostile to the new workhouse; so too, on economy grounds, was rate-paying opinion. In most towns 'the Bastilles' symbolised the Act's hated central principles, and the *Bolton Chronicle*, basically friendly to the project, admitted that 'the erection of a workhouse cannot be looked upon favourably by the working classes'.[22] One guardian thought they might physically attack it.[23] On the one occasion when the issue was presented squarely to the Great Bolton ratepayers, in the 1854 elections, five anti-workhouse guardians were returned.

Yet the state of outside opinion was scarcely mentioned during any of the guardians' deliberations — certainly never in discussions of the labour test, and only occasionally in those about the workhouse. Moreover it is a significant commentary on their indifference — particularly compared with Rochdale's guardians — that they felt able to discuss a workhouse as early as 1847, and that two of the debates (1854 and 1856), and the final decision itself, occurred shortly before the annual elections.

This illustrates the elite's general indifference to outside opinion that we noted in chapter 9. Yet it also indicates how this attitude was related to the other factors outlined there. The drive towards unity among Bolton's local leaders was particularly pronounced among the guardians — both in their deliberations and in their elections. 'Amicable arrangements' meant that it was rare for more than three or four of the Union's twenty-six townships to be electorally contested. Deliberately or inadvertently, this in turn helped insulate the board from outside opinion by making certain that policy issues were rarely presented to the ratepayers. It also meant that the two sections of the guardians had less need to appeal for outside support, and thus incurred fewer political debts. Overall, even more effectively than weighted voting, compromise ensured that the electoral entry point was largely closed against the lower levels of the population.

Occasionally popular opinion broke through and caused trouble even for a united elite. In 1847 a Great Bolton township meeting was called at the initiative of 'the heavy ratepayers' to consider the report of a special committee enquiring into 'the high expenditure of parochial funds' and into the township's sufferings in the rural-dominated Union. Owing to what Liberals and Tories agreed was 'the infamous behaviour' of radical 'marplots', the meeting never really discussed the report. Instead, having installed a radical chairman, it spent six chaotic hours over two evenings discussing a variety of issues, including workhouse administration. The result was that the committee's 'arrangements were upset; they were floored and knew not what to do'.[24]

Such interventions were rare. As we saw in chapter 9, popular entry points to Poor Law administration were more limited than in Rochdale. Moreover, on this occasion, the 'heavy' ratepayers were presented with a nuisance which they eventually largely circumvented by seeking popular endorsement for the approaches to the Poor Law board by a more controllable petition that was to 'lie for signature' at the newspaper offices. Generally, Poor Law policies were pursued peacefully and in the company of friends.

Incorporation and its aftermath

Incorporation in Rochdale involved considerable lower-class participation and influence. This was not the case in Bolton. The movement emerged in the late 1830s from two things: first, the dissatisfaction of the Liberal section of the elite with the existing system; second, the desire of a Manchester-based group, connected with and Anti-Corn Law League, to test the use of the Municipal Corporations Act as a means of achieving modern, and Liberal-dominated, local government in towns not automatically incorporated when the Act first came into force. Included among this group was John Ashworth, joint proprietor of the massive family enterprises on the outskirts of Bolton. Bolton and Manchester were chosen as test cases. Ashworth persuaded a group of local Liberal notables to initiate a petition to the overseers to call a joint public meeting of the two Bolton townships.[25]

It took place in January 1838. Though clearly a crucial point of decision (in that, had it proved hostile, the campaign would have been damagingly denied mass ratification at the outset), it was the only opportunity for direct public discussion during the entire campaign. Thus Bolton's incorporation was an altogether less public and consultative process than Rochdale's was later to prove. The meeting's role was also restricted to ratifying plans for incorporation drawn up by the organisers. Nevertheless it was crowded, and enthusiastically endorsed the proposition. It also elected a committee of Liberal notables, together with a sprinkling of radicals, to organise a parliamentary petition.

Tory opposition was rather slow to emerge. It was scarcely visible at the public meeting, and did not begin organising counter-petitions until at least a week later. Moreover its cause was not helped when a public meeting it organised to persuade the inhabitants of Little Bolton to opt out of incorporation was attended by only six Tory leaders, and taken over by what the *Bolton Chronicle* acidly described as 'a large crowd of clappers and gooers ordered by the Liberals'.[26]

Nevertheless vigorously competitive petition-gathering and propaganda continued through February and, in the opposition's case, into March. Both sides probably used the deference that their position as major employers lent them among Bolton's working population.[27] However, persuasion was also important. The Liberal case was based upon the alleged inefficiency, corruption, secrecy and popular irresponsibility of the old system. Conservatives countered by arguing imaginatively that the old system was publicly accountable, since the court leet was composed of local inhabitants, the Little Bolton trustees were popularly elected and police accounts were ratified by vestry meetings. The old system was cheap. A corporation would not merely be expensive but would also rob the inhabitants of control over their own affairs and, in Little Bolton's case, would narrow the franchise.

By mid-March both sides were claiming majority support. Some time around the 19th, Major Jebb, the government Commissioner, arrived in Bolton to examine the authenticity of the two petitions. The *Bolton Chronicle* reported that 'All Progresses Well' for the anti-corporators, and confidently awaited the public enquiry apparently promised by the Liberals.[28]

In fact nothing further publicly transpired until the charter was suddenly granted five months later in mid-August. The circumstances were mysterious. The *Bolton Chronicle* alleged that the charter had really been granted on 5 March,[29] around fourteen days before the government Commissioner began his enquiries, and whilst the anti-corporators were still agitating. This induced the Tory suspicion that the whole thing had been 'fixed' by the Whig government and the Liberal incorporators. In fact, once women and non-ratepayers had been expunged from both petitions, the incorporators had a majority in both popular and property terms. According to Major Jebb's final report, 3,213 males worth £40,530 were in favour, whereas only 1,886, worth £33,681, were opposed. Nevertheless the process by which the self-proclaimed 'little clique' of Liberal notables[30] had achieved their ends was somewhat suspicious, decidedly secretive and markedly less popular than the incorporation campaign in Rochdale eighteen years later.

The Liberals had got what they wanted. Yet this simply marked the beginning of a long period of difficulty and near-paralysis, induced mainly by the other section of the elite operating from vantage points which the old, and still persisting, system gave them.

The Conservatives ignored the council elections and immediately mounted a legal challenge to the new corporation. The Liberal council decided, in November 1838, to try and absorb the powers of the trusts, but rapidly withdrew their parliamentary application when it was challenged by the Little Bolton trustees (which the Tories now heavily influenced after a surprise electoral challenge) and the Great Bolton trustees. Attempts to take control of the police force from the two sets of boroughreeves and constables were similarly unsuccessful, these worthies 'refusing to recognise any Mayor of

Bolton or any Superintendent of Police'.[31] The battle spread to the vestry, where the Liberals tried to use their influence to deny finance to the old police (again unsuccessfully, because funds were restored by the county magistrates), and to use the Liberal overseers to collect money for their own modest rival force via the poor rate. This last move was also partly stultified, since several substantial Tory manufacturers refused payment. Partly in an attempt to settle the legality of the charter quickly 'through a friendly law suit',[32] the Liberals sued the renegades. There was no amicable outcome, and the original legal challenge, mounted in 1838, dragged on, delayed further by having to queue for legal consideration behind similar challenges to the incorporation of Birmingham and Manchester. Even the offer of twelve unopposed council election returns in 1841 failed to tempt the Tories from their chosen path.[33]

The issue was finally settled by parliamentary intervention via the Borough Incorporation Act in September 1842. The Liberals thus eventually won. However, they did so by conflict largely contained within the elite itself and involving the mass of the population only intermittently. They had used the vestry, and this had meant incurring limited debts to Chartist followers. But that was all.

Moreover Liberal victory had been achieved only with great difficulty. It was also partial. The two sets of trustees still remained. Since they refused to surrender their powers, and the Municipal Corporations Act conferred very few, the corporation, even when legally validated, had little to do.

It was partly to escape from this situation that, in April 1843, the corporation began a new battle which eventually produced the Water and Consolidation Bill. This originated from its decision to oppose the water company's private Bill to increase the company's capital by 25 per cent. The council decided to use the occasion to get profits limited to 10 per cent, and to establish a fairer system of water rates which fell less heavily upon the small consumer. By late May the corporation's parliamentary deputation was able to report some success in its negotiations with the company. The Bill now contained the required profits limit. Moreover a clause originally empowering the company to let its works to anyone it chose was now restricted to the corporation alone. Furthermore the company's proposed powers of distraint upon property for recovery of unpaid rates had been expunged.[34]

Nevertheless, as the deputation noted, the 25 per cent increase in nominal capital would probably result in the company increasing its rates simply to realise the 10 per cent profit. The deputation therefore recommended continued opposition to the Bill (in fact it was passed without further alteration) and a corporate parliamentary application to municipalise the company. There was a further recommendation. In recent months the Great

Bolton trustees, in association with local philanthropists, had been building reservoirs to supply the people with water. Partly as a result, and partly because the Liberals suspected that company directors and trustees were virtually synonymous, the deputation suggested taking over the trustees' powers, including their water supply functions. With little dissent the council gave preliminary consent to the proposals.

Though more closed than Rochdale's, Bolton's institutional system prior to 1850 was sufficiently open and party competition sufficiently intense (particularly with the Conservative decision to return to the corporate fray in 1842) to necessitate carrying the battle to the public. This probably involved making implicit concessions to procure mass support. Such motivations partly explain the initial emphasis on obtaining water and reducing rates for the poor. Certainly, by June 1843, there were signs of a public campaign against the company heavily laced with populism:

there are 3,231 of you assessed to the poor rate, many . . . are in cellars assessed at a shilling a week not assessed [*sic*] and all . . . are liable to be charged for . . . water from the . . . Water Company the sum of 10 shillings which is the same . . . as those who live in a house of £10 per annum . . . if you . . . don't . . . petition . . . Parliament, the same charge will continue to be made on you.[35]

It was sufficiently successful for the council, by the time it took the final decision to go ahead with its Bill in October, to be able to claim that it was acting at the behest of a petition from 400 electors.

For all the public bombast, however, the company's 'reputation for power' was formidable enough for the original municipalisation proposal to be omitted from the final version of the Bill. By October the corporation simply proposed absorbing the powers of both sets of trustees, including expanded versions of Great Bolton's water supply functions.[36]

Tory opposition to the proposals, as to incorporation, was slow to emerge. However, as it did, it became more formidable and (like the corporation campaign) more populist. On 1 November the Great Bolton trustees damagingly announced their opposition to absorption. Added to the certainty of water company opposition, it ensured that the parliamentary application would be expensive. Tory hostility intensified in the council elections, many candidates alleging that the take-over of the trustees would 'rob the poor of water', and criticising the corporation for not obtaining the ratepayers' consent.[37] This brought the voters marginally into the decision-making process, and the capture of eight council seats enabled the Tories to claim public support.

Nevertheless, in keeping with our general argument here, by far the most damaging blow to Liberal aspirations was dealt not by the ratepayers but by

Conservative legal attack on the corporation's still shaky financial powers. In December they obtained counsel's opinion that any payment of the Bill's parliamentary expenses from the Borough Fund would be illegal. Though the Liberals were initially contemptuous and asserted that, even if the opinion were correct, the money could be obtained by public subscription, the move eventually proved fatal.[38] In February 1844 the council rescinded its original resolution to pay expenses from the fund and instituted a public subscription. Thereafter the Bill disappeared from public view. Nothing more was heard until some rueful but significant comments from a leading Liberal in the 1844 council elections: 'seeing the probability of an expensive and prolonged contest they abandoned the application for the time being'.[39]

Liberal aims were thus frustrated. Yet the Tories were in no better position. It is true that a further dispute with the company, when they came to power in 1846, was amicably resolved by the corporation successfully negotiating to lease the waterworks with an option to purchase. It is also true that Tory control of the council resulted in the Great Bolton trustees becoming more amicable to absorption. However, the Liberals still controlled the Little Bolton trustees and were able to veto any further increase in council powers, just as the Tories had done from Great Bolton in years before. Thus the change in party control solved one set of problems only to raise equally paralysing ones elsewhere. The result was that the Tory corporation soon came to believe it had little 'to do but manage about twenty policemen'.[40]

The nature of the problem was illustrated in August 1846 when the council decided to apply for an improvement Bill that, in its final form, included the ratification of the water take-over, an expansion of water powers, the acquisition of improvement powers, the municipalisation of the gas company and the absorption of the Great and Little Bolton trustees.[41] In response to the last proposal, the Tory trustees of Great Bolton proved amenable enough, but the Liberal Little Bolton trustees insisted on submitting the question to a township meeting. This produced one of Bolton's relatively rare decisive, and apparently open, instances of public participation. The meeting lasted over two evenings, and received no overt recommendation from the trustees. Though attendance (around 100) was modest by Rochdale standards, the debate was lively and included individuals at all social levels. Eventually the Liberals' desire to preserve their political vantage point was melded with small ratepayers' fears of having to pay for Great Bolton's insolvency, and resulted in absorption being heavily rejected.

Initial Tory responses were contemptuous. Several vigorously defended their proposal in the 1846 council elections. Yet the alleged popular 'endorsement' that resulted was rapidly counterweighted by the Liberals repeating the earlier Tory challenge to the corporation's legal right to pay the parliamentary expenses of the Bill. Little Bolton's opposition ensured that those expenses would be large, and most Tories became convinced that Parliament would never give the council powers over only half the borough. These considerations seem to have been decisive. In mid-November the Tories agreed to abandon all of the Bill apart from the water and improvement clauses, on the telling justification that 'peace and quietness might be maintained'. They bowed 'to the minority [who] . . . were heavy ratepayers, though the majority of ratepayers . . . were favourable'.[42] The remaining clauses went through Parliament with relatively little trouble.

The main part of the project had thus failed, once again, on the vetoes of the minority section of the elite. The Act somewhat increased council powers. Nevertheless, contemplating a threatened cholera epidemic three years later, the Tories still understandably felt that

the Corporation, by the interference of other bodies, is deprived of its natural functions. Just where its powers should come promptly . . . into effect, it is without the means of enforcing anything.[43]

Positive action by either section of the elite was paralysed. As the *Bolton Chronicle* commented,

with the whole posse of Councillors, Trustees and Guardians . . . the . . . inhabitants are nearly as inadequately tended as if left to their own resources. A divided authority weakens power, shifts responsibility and leaves that which can only partly be done by each not done at all.[44]

In 1849 there was a further attempt at absorbing the trusts. It was partly prompted, as the above quotations suggest, by revelations of corporate impotence in the face of a threat to public health. Paralysis was made the more appalling to local leaders by discoveries about the unregulated state of the town's low lodging houses, wherein resided dirt and indecent abandon in the form of people of both sexes sleeping communally, 'all shirts and chemises taken off'.[45]

However, it is a significant illustration of the paralysis imposed by party conflict and institutional proliferation that it required the threat of outside intervention to effect change. The revelations above emanated from a Poor Law inspector. The remedy he suggested was Bolton's subjection to the Public Health Act. In pressing for the trusts' absorption the Tory majority could thus argue that, if the corporation did not take charge in the two townships, the General Board of Health would. They could also argue that insanitary situations at present tolerated would be illegal under the Public Health Act whereas, if Bolton got its own Act, 'the relevant stipulations might easily be modified to the great advantage of the borough'.[46]

The initial decision to attempt absorption was ratified by a large council

majority in mid-August 1849, and the detailed aims of the Bill were debated
in October. Besides amalgamating the trustees, the projected Bill now
included powers to erect a new market, to extend the water undertaking and
take over the gas company. It was proposed to incorporate a wide range of
sanitary functions from existing national legislation. Most of the powers were
to be obtained either by a local improvement Act or, if that proved
impossible, by adopting the Public Health Act.

The apparent willingness to consider the Public Health Act seems odd.
Leading Tory speeches indicate that there was no desire to encourage central
control. Probably it resulted partly from desperation at the failure of previous
amalgamation attempts (becoming a sanitation board under the Act seemed
to provide a way out of paralysis). Partly it was probably motivated by a desire
to embarrass the Liberals. It certainly divided them. Some opposed absorbing
the trusts, whilst others significantly suggested that even local Tory rule was
better than central control.[47]

The October meeting decided to press ahead with a parliamentary
application. Negotiations, already tentatively opened with the General Board
of Health by the council's improvement committee, were now intensified and
produced a compromise whereby the sanitary powers of the Public Health
Act were incorporated into Bolton's Bill. Edwin Chadwick, for the board,
insisted that Bolton could not thereby escape supervision, and the Act's
supervisory clauses were indeed embodied in the Bill. Nevertheless the
improvement committee undoubtedly (and justifiably) hoped to avoid the
worst centralised nightmares in this way.

The draft Bill was submitted to the House of Commons in January 1850,
and the opposing sections of the elite began mobilising opinion. The Tories
organised large majority petitions in favour from both townships, whilst the
Liberals gathered a substantial one from the ratepayers of Little Bolton, and
from the semi-rural Haulgh area of that township. Petitions also came from
the Earl of Bradford (one of the lords of the manor), from two railway
companies, the Bridgewater trustees, and a variety of private individuals
inside and outside the borough.[48]

As so often in such cases, the corporation reacted by appeasement. The
improvement committee had already carefully consulted 'many influential
and very heavy ratepayers' before finally deciding on the site for the new
market.[49] In March, among other alterations, it consented to weaken the
proposed smoke regulation after objections from several manufacturer
councillors. More important, it inserted a clause strengthening an existing
provision guaranteeing that any improvement applying only to one township
should be paid for from the rates of that township alone, thus successfully
neutralising the fears of many Little Bolton ratepayers.

The main outlines of the Bill were left intact during its progress through the two Houses of Parliament. Nevertheless significant amendments in detail were imposed or conceded even here. The borough rate was limited to 2s 6d in the pound (the corporation had wanted 3s 6d). Cottage owners' pressure won a five-year moratorium on the operation of clauses prohibiting cellar dwellings. Compensation was guaranteed to the lords of the manor where their rights were impinged upon by corporate operations. A clause prohibiting the pawning of articles and placing the onus of responsibility upon pawnbrokers was removed. So too was one closing refreshment places on Sunday, because it was 'rather invidious against a powerful interest in the borough' (the licensed victuallers) and because, if amended to exclude pubs, it would still affect temperance hotels and thus offend that interest.[50] The Bill was given the royal assent in July 1850.

The Conservatives had got most of what they wanted. However, it is clear that, even with strong external pressure (in the form of the Public Health Board) on their side, they had to make significant concessions to achieve their ends. A simple elitist picture does not fit Bolton's political process as evidenced by the progress of this Bill. At this (parliamentary) point of high vulnerability for any corporation, even small propertied groups could achieve some influence. Nevertheless influence did not extend as far down the social scale as in Rochdale. Moreover, as with other examples of Bolton's political process before 1850, the main problems arose from the minority section of the elite, and from well-heeled groups and individuals outside the immediate political circle. Finally, though both sides hailed 'the public' and its 'interest' in their support, there was little direct public participation of the sort frequently seen in Rochdale, and little was invited apart from controllable forms like petition-gathering. Certainly there was nothing to parallel the popularly originated paralysis that we saw over Rochdale's proposed improvement Bill of 1855.

Improvement and sanitation after 1850

Some of the same features are observable in the period after 1850. The simplification of the institutional system resulting from the disappearance of the trusts, together with the more intermittent character of party conflict, made life easier for whichever section of the elite controlled the council. The latter now had a full panoply of powers and, if it chose to do so, was better able to use or (subject always to the risky parliamentary process) extend them. Nevertheless there were still considerable difficulties and, where these arose, they were primarily caused by groups on a comparable economic level to the majority section of the elite — those best able to use the more discreet political opportunities the system still provided. Opportunities for those further down, though available, were fewer than in Rochdale.

The best indication of the possibilities now open to local leaders is the 1864 Improvement Act. This major expansion of council powers arose partly from projects put forward by the corporation during the cotton famine, and sanctioned by the government under the 1863 Public Works Act. Apart from consolidating existing powers, the Improvement Bill empowered the corporation to expand the waterworks, provide public parks, build a town hall and increase borrowing powers. It was concocted from council committee suggestions, and sent to Parliament without any form of public consultation in January 1864. What objections there were came almost entirely from interests outside the borough boundaries, and these were negotiated away with minor concessions between the Bill's Commons committee stage and the third reading. It went through the Lords unscathed and received the royal assent in July 1864.

Examples of greater difficulty, and its origins, emerge if we turn first to the general area of sanitary policy — much of which involved the enforcement of regulations laid down in the 1850 Improvement Act. As in Rochdale, the corporation was able to act — or remain inactive — in many areas of sanitation without arousing concern among any section of the public. But there were important aspects of policy which did arouse opposition. Where this happened, it was most effective from those at the higher economic levels.

The smoke pollution clause in the 1850 Act was never properly enforced, owing to the hostility, real or assumed, of large manufacturers. Clauses empowering the corporation to cleanse the river Croal had an equally thin time. As the result of industrial and human effluent the river was 'an open sewer'. Various plans were formulated by the sanitary and other committees and considered by the council. They ranged from modestly cleansing the river to paving its bed, covering it over and constructing an intercepting sewer. Yet paving and cleansing were not sanctioned even on a modest scale until August 1862, and nothing was done about an intercepting sewer until 1868. Equally significant, these works were only undertaken after central government intervention. Paving was undertaken when the Public Works Act made money available on easy terms, whilst the intercepting sewer was sanctioned only after forcible intervention by the Home Office.[51]

There were varied motives for prevarication. Partly it resulted from autonomous choice. Sanitation is an area where it is particularly difficult to identify a unified intention on the part of the elite. Thus it is equally difficult to gauge the achievement of intended effects. Even the majority section of the elite was divided into sanitary activists and economists, and the latter were urging delay partly from honest economical conviction, consideration of personal vested interest or the sincere if imbecile belief that 'there was no more healthy borough in the kingdom'.[52]

However, delay also resulted from more political considerations: from contemplation or anticipation of vetoes wielded from the outside world — sometimes from 'the ratepayers', but primarily from groups or individuals near the top of local society. In 1858 the *Bolton Chronicle* identified corporate inaction over the Croal as due to 'multiplied vested rights'.[53] Councillors sometimes identified the obstacles more specifically. Committees reported the refusal of property owners along the river bank to bear any portion of the cost. Attempts at paving 'had been discouraged' by, and more ambitious schemes for sewage diversion 'would meet with opposition' from, 'parties interested in the river waters'.[54] These included weir owners, house owners who had cut personal sewers to the river and, most important, manufacturers who had diverted water for industrial use. In 1869 the spokesman for one prevaricating sub-committee paid revealing tribute to the strength of such forces, explaining that his committee's 'whole aim' over the past two years had been 'to prevent law suits from injured parties whose mills would lose water as the result of interception'.[55]

The treatment of wealthy river users and abusers contrasts significantly with the council's dealings with less well-padded vested interests. Landlords seem to have been cavalierly treated by comparison with their counterparts in Rochdale and Salford, and with more substantial men in Bolton.

Elite attitudes towards house owners are best revealed in policy towards cellar dwellings. Bolton contained many such habitations, 1,600 cellars being used as dwellings in 1855, occupied by some 6,000 people (approximately a twelfth of the population).[56] The owners, with a few exceptions, were small men, sometimes only a few steps above the working class whose needs they inadequately served. The 1850 Improvement Act had adopted the Public Health Act clauses severely regulating cellar dwellings. These gave the corporation power to close them, or insist upon alterations.

The five-year moratorium negotiated with cellar owners in 1850 terminated in August 1855. The corporation then embarked on a measured but determined policy of closure, particularly after Fergus Ferguson became sanitary committee chairman in November 1858. 928 cellars had been inspected and 406 closed by the time of his succession. By 1866 closures had risen to 1,321 and only 428 (all of them altered) were still being used as dwellings.

The policy elicited considerable opposition. As we saw in chapter 9, a succession of property associations were formed to approach councillors or intervene in elections. Yet, though closures were enforced without compensation (the council having no power to award it), the opposition seems to have had little effect. Certainly there were periods of deceleration, and the closure policy was always 'careful'. But, to judge from the timing of delay and the comments of councillors involved, such hesitation resulted more from humanitarian concern for the plight of those displaced, and the realisation that comparably cheap accommodation was not available above ground, than from any political tenderness towards the cellar owners. In 1856 the sanitary committee chairman said that the cellar question was 'very difficult to deal with' because, if the Act were properly enforced, 'it must occasion a large amount of hardship'.[57] In 1858 even as determined a figure as Fergus Ferguson conceded that closure must proceed gradually, 'to give time for the building of cottages to accommodate those removed'.[58] Closure virtually ceased in 1862-63 because of the cotton famine, and ground to a more permanent halt in the late 1860s when it was discovered that the population was increasing much faster than the housing stock.[59] Significantly this was also a time when cellar owners were politically quiescent.

The argument cannot be pushed too far. Cellar owners undoubtedly had some influence. They were responsible for the original moratorium in 1850, and one delay was partly occasioned by a lawsuit brought against the corporation by the cottage owners in 1858. They had substantial support from some councillors, and in 1858 obtained favourable pledges from most council election candidates. Moreover, whatever the cellar dwelling policy, the byelaws on property above ground were often not enforced.[60]

Yet the cottage owners' legal challenge and electoral intervention were immediately succeeded by the appearance of the reforming Fergus Ferguson as sanitary committee chairman. Non-enforcement of cottage regulations was partly due to corporate perception of the housing shortage. Overall, though constraints on council action were considerable, they were more often environmental and humanitarian than political.

The impression of a steeper gradient of influence between the great and the lowly than was evident in Rochdale is reinforced if we look at questions of nuisance due to corporate sanitary operations. In Rochdale we saw that councillors' contemplation, or anticipation, of public anger effectively prevented the establishment of an isolation hospital in the town centre in the 1870s. No precisely identical issue arose in Bolton. Perhaps the best comparison is with Wellington Yard, established for the necessary but disgusting purpose of depositing night soil, in a working class area of Derby Ward. Though operations began without apparent opposition, aromas soon began to pervade the district. They were the subject of increasing local protest from the late 1850s, reaching a suffocated crescendo in the late '70s, when the yard became a regular election issue. The council majority responded by inaction, supporting the scavenging committee's constant assertion that no alternative site was available. Among the yard's supporters were two Derby Ward councillors. One even claimed that he could smell nothing, asserting ambiguously that 'people who lived ... near the Yard were in better health than the ordinary classes of the community'.[61] Only in 1879 did the committee produce the somewhat double-edged 'solution' of enlarging the yard so as to house 'a sanitary destructor'.[62]

Relations with the gas company

As we have seen, the 1850 Improvement Act simplified both the local institutional system and the elite's ability to operate successfully within it. Yet there was still one area — relations with the gas company — where institutional separation combined with party conflict to cause great difficulty for at least the Liberal section whenever it had a council majority (as was the case between 1853 and 1868). Though corporate influence over the company was increased by the fact that several councillors were large shareholders, the utility remained a major source of constraint.

This was demonstrated when the council attempted municipalisation in the 1854 Improvement Bill but had to accept the removal of the relevant clauses when the company applied for its own Bill to enlarge its works. The only concession was a minor, and subsequently unenforced, alteration in prices.

Relations thereafter were characterised by 'continuous bickerings, unpleasantness and law proceedings',[63] centred primarily on prices and street lighting. In November 1860 the corporation was prompted once again to a parliamentary application for powers to establish its own works and (given company consent) municipalise the existing ones. The application drew strong pressure for compromise, particularly from a wealthy group of gas shareholders, some of them Liberal councillors. The corporation was eager to negotiate, but the company refused.

It is typical of the political reflexes of even the Liberal section of Bolton's elite (as contrasted with Rochdale's) that, in spite even of this rebuff, the parliamentary application was not accompanied by any appeal to the public against the company. No meetings were held: all was to be accomplished by discreet negotiation. Not until February 1861 did the Bill's supporters begin to muster petitions. The result, on the Liberals' own admission, was 'much misunderstanding out of doors'.[64] Though the company was thoroughly unpopular in the town, important sections of the public were allowed to get the impression that it was the corporation that was refusing to negotiate. This 'dictatorial' image prompted the corporation, with its Bill only just lodged in Parliament, into an ignominious second offer of negotiations in lieu of legislation.

The company seems to have been more politically adept. From the start its defenders had campaigned in the town, appealing particularly to small consumers. They alleged that municipalisation would benefit only large consumers; that small ones would have to pay for municipal improvements as part of their gas bills, and that the application was an excuse for junketings by the corporation's parliamentary deputation at the ratepayers' expense. The company's response to the offered negotiations was to place the decision before a meeting of its own (mostly small) shareholders, who obediently endorsed the recommended rejection.

The result was that, by the time parliamentary proceedings opened, the corporation's rather modest petition was matched by a variety of counter-petitions — from ratepayers and consumers, and from wealthy (and mainly Conservative) individuals. In spite of the corporation's generous offers of compensation to gas shareholders, and many relevations of company inefficiency, the Bill emerged from the protracted Commons hearings in a sorry state. The corporation got power to purchase the gasworks, but only if three-fifths of the shareholders agreed, and it was prohibited from applying gas profits to rate relief. It was refused permission to build its own works.

Desperate to avoid further expense, the council again offered negotiations. Revealing its nervousness of the unpredictable parliamentary process and how far it might be prepared to go to avoid trouble, it asked whether 'the Company purpose opposing the Bill in the Lords and, if so, what they object to'.[65] The company reply was to petition against every clause. Worse still, the Lords changed the clause allowing purchase on a three-fifths shareholders' majority to one insisting on three-quarters. This proved the final straw. The council withdrew the now useless gas clauses. The modest improvement powers that remained received the royal assent in mid-July 1861. They had cost £5,000.

Relations with the company puttered irritably on throughout the '60s, becoming particularly bitter when the corporation discovered that the company was saluting the opening of Bolton's new park by building 'a black, ugly-looking pan, something like a fort' opposite the entrance.[66] A parks committee deputation to the directors elicited only the unhelpful suggestion that the corporation paint the gas-holder gold. The further discovery that the company planned to transfer its entire works to the park site brought the disappointing realisation that the council 'had no power to take hold of the Company as the case stood'.[67] Councillors expressed their sense of impotence by likening it to Tsar Nicholas.[68]

Party difference was not the only factor here, but it clearly still influenced relations between company and corporation. Certainly, when party was removed, as it was after the Conservatives captured the council in 1870,

matters proceeded smoothly to permanent solution. In the 1872 Improvement Act, albeit on financial terms very favourable to the company, the
council municipalised the undertaking. Typical of Bolton politics, it was done
with little reference to the public even in council elections.

Once again the elite's problems up to 1870 had originated from the top of
the economic ladder, and from a situation in which party difference had been
allied to institutional separation. Those further down the social scale had been
drawn in — by company propaganda — but participation was less active, did
not extend so far down the social scale and failed to bring the same exalted
expectations and policy advantages to lowly participants as in Rochdale. In
1861 6,150 of Bolton's 13,789 households were still unsupplied with gas.[69]
There are no figures for the post-municipalisation period. However, the
reason is partly that the spread of gas supply to small householders never
seems to have concerned the elite, either before or after 1872. Nor did such
matters as meter charges. Moreover, though gas prices were a perennial issue
from 1872 onwards, there seems to have been neither pressure nor desire to
reduce price differentials between large and small consumers.

The town hall

In spite of the burden of argument so far, there were issues after 1850 where
lowly members of the public had some influence. One was the town hall.
Admittedly the largely favourable opinions of Bolton's substantial ratepayers
were the main influence. The project emerged from dissatisfaction with
existing civic buildings — 'as bad as a gentleman's pigsty'[70] — and a desire
for something more prestigious. The 1864 Improvement Act, which granted
the relevant powers, went through, as we have seen, without public
discussion or even endorsement. The decision to build something more
ambitious than the £40,000 structure originally envisaged was taken (in
January 1865) only after the mayor had called a meeting of 'men of taste,
intelligence and wealth . . . the large ratepayers' to endorse 'the cost and style
of architecture'.[71] When a tower was added the town hall committee was said
to have simply 'endorsed the opinion . . . [of] persons of social position and
influence . . .'.[72]

On the other hand, the decision to build was preceded by an open-air
meeting 'chiefly of the working classes' which endorsed the project after
much argument.[73] Moreover the council had prevaricated for some years
before deciding even to seek power (the issue was first raised in 1857), and for
some weeks in 1865 before deciding on a large building. Both delays were due
to councillors' perceptions of small ratepayers' sufferings at times of
economic slump, and of their hostility to large municipal projects. Plans

costing up to £110,000 were being drawn up in the council in December 1864, but a hostile ratepayers' petition led to the imposition of a £50,000 limit in January 1865. The council decided to exceed this only when convinced by a ninety-minute peroration from the finance chairman, J. R. Wolfenden, demonstrating that Bolton's financial position would permit the construction of a much larger building for no more than a sixpenny rate.[74] Even the revised plans envisaged spending only £70,000.[75] Admittedly expenditure then rocketed out of control. Yet councillors still seemed to derive comfort from evidence that 'public opinion was in favour . . . and . . . principally . . . the working classes'.[76]

Parks and park administration

One issue in which public opinion may have been influential in promoting, rather than just endorsing, action was the council's decision to extend the recreation ground. This had originally been established by philanthropic effort in 1857 and given to the corporation. The possibility of extension arose during the cotton famine as part of the council's consideration of what employment-producing projects to propose to the government commissioners under the 1863 Public Works Act. The idea came from the sanitary committee and its chairman, and dedicated advocate of parks, Fergus Ferguson. However, there was also much outside pressure. In August 1863, while considering the proposal, the council received a favourable petition from several churchmen and '100 tradesmen and work people'.[77] In September there were public meetings in Bradford and Derby wards — the main catchment areas for the recreation ground. These eventually promoted two further petitions collectively signed by 1,400 of the wards' 1,700 ratepayers. They also formed a recreation ground committee.

The September council meeting authorised the finance committee to negotiate for the purchase of the adjoining land. This body, under its hostile chairman, J. R. Wolfenden, decided that the price was too high, and instead recommended the purchase of sixty acres at Spa Fields, on the opposite side of town, for a full-blown park. The council assented and the project was included in the 1864 Improvement Act.

However, the recreation ground committee continued to press for the extension, still backed by Fergus Ferguson from within the council. After long discussions the corporation resumed negotiations with the landowners in May 1864. Despite continued opposition from Wolfenden, councillors heavily endorsed purchase and extension in June.

How much influence outside opinion had here is difficult to establish. Public opinion was constantly referred to by both sides. Favourable manifestations certainly strengthened the arguments of the scheme's champions in the council. The resurrection of extension plans can be ascribed partly to continued pressure, as some council speeches testify.[78] On the other hand, the extension scheme first arose partly from the corporation's desire to find work for idle hands during the cotton famine. Philanthropic motives were probably quite as prominent as political ones, extension being described as 'a boon to the working classes'.[79] Finally, the influence of lowly sections of the public was clearly conditional. Bolton's council needed more than mere numbers to persuade it. What made outside pressure acceptable was its quality. As the scheme's promoters constantly pointed out, 'when a memorial ... came before them signed ... by all the large ratepayers in Bradford ward ... representing ... two-thirds of the rateable property ... it was entitled to favourable consideration'.[80]

More certain influence resulted from working-class pressure in 1867 to get the new park open on Sunday mornings. Influence was still subject to perceptions of quality, but less markedly so. The force of intensely mobilised public opinion occurred at a time of rising party conflict at both parliamentary and municipal level, and drew a thoroughly political reaction from councillors.

For many working men Sunday was the only time they could use the park. It had been open on Sundays afternoons from the start. In July 1867 the mayor received a petition demanding a public meeting from 900 people. As councillors noted, these included 'many members of the council and influential ratepayers'.[81] The meeting was crowded. Having listened to speeches from both manufacturers and working class radicals, it unanimously endorsed Sunday morning opening.

The parks committee had rejected the idea once before. Its initial response now was again negative, particularly when reinforced by a counter-petition from local Sunday schools. However, the subject was then brought before the full council. After long and acrimonious debate, with much argument about the legitimacy of public pressure, the committee was overruled by thirty votes to seven.

In March 1869 the council narrowly decided to extend wicked Sabbath pleasures further by allowing the sale of refreshments in the park. This brought a hostile petition from 1,400 ministers and Church members, many of them Wesleyans and, so the Sabbatarians claimed, 'working men and women'.[82] In response the council reversed its decision in April by eighteen votes to fourteen. A comparison of the April with the March vote reveals significant changes among the anti-Sabbatarians: one changed sides completely, one left the room before the April vote and five did not appear for the latter division at all.

The May council meeting received a further petition from 5,000 (presumably favourably to Sunday refreshments) requesting a public meeting. Both sides now organised furiously to produce what the press saw as a thoroughly working-class occasion attended by 2,000. After much angry debate the refreshment lobby narrowly won.

The council met the following day — its public gallery crowded — to consider the parks committee's response. Some saw it as 'cowardly and unmanly'; in fact it was thoroughly political. Faced with counter-pressures, and a bare majority at the public meeting favourable to Sunday refreshment, the committee made no explicit recommendation and instead effectively left the decision to the tenant of the park pavilion. The chairman saw it as 'a question between the tenant and the town generally'. His opponents interpreted the decision, rightly as it turned out, as 'tacit consent to . . . opening on Sunday'. After much debate the council endorsed its committee's proceedings by twenty votes to thirteen.[83] An analysis of this division shows a loss of Sabbatarian support compared with April — into the refreshment lobby, into abstention or into simple absence.

It was possible, then, for lowly participants to influence council policies occasionally. However, their impact was clearly limited — compared with their counterparts in Rochdale and with wealthier groups in Bolton. The relative unwillingness of party politicians to exploit popular grievances (the Conservatives made little attempt to do so over expenditure on the new town hall), the shortage of usable popular entry points to the political process, Bolton's weaker tradition of popular mobilisation and the elite's detached attitude to outside opinion all combined to limit the influence of those with little or no property.

Municipal expenditure

From the mid-1870s, however, there was a marked increase in popular political efficacy. Rising party conflict (taking place since 1867 and probably contributing to prevarication over park refreshment) coincided with rising small-ratepayer anxiety at the steady increase in municipal expenditure. Party competition enabled ratepayers to gain access to the political process via council elections. Their opportunities were also expanded by the 1875 Borough Funds Act. The result was sustained constraint on corporation policies.

Throughout the late '60s and early '70s municipal expenditure had been rising steadily: parks, new water and gas works, intercepting sewers, street improvements and a wedding cake of a town hall were all under way, with expenditure far exceeding estimates. At this stage, however, the municipal elite was relatively unconstrained. It was a period of prosperity and rising ratable values. Some projects had been financed under the favourable terms of the Public Works Act, whilst others were serviced (like so many things in Rochdale) by gas and water profits. Thus rates remained stable.

Conditions, particularly economic conditions, changed from the mid-1870s. Recession hit local industry, ratable value rose more slowly and municipal utility profits fell. The sinking fund, which had been suspended by the 1872 Improvement Act, was reinstated in January 1875 and now required payment of one-eightieth of the town's total debt every year.[84] From 1872 this began to produce substantial rate rises (borough rates rose 5*d* in the pound between 1872 and 1877, district rates by around 1*s*). The newly incorporated areas of Rumworth and Halliwell were particularly hard hit through having to pay for the sanitary neglect of their recently demised local boards. Finally, in 1874 and 1875, a series of financial scandals rocked the Conservative administration.

All this helped produce a ratepayers' reaction in the form of angry public meetings and ratepayers' associations. The Liberal *Bolton Weekly Journal* hopefully walked the streets in January 1878 and delightedly discovered

more discontent than we have known for years. Hardly a shopkeeper could be met, or a middle class man in any line, who was not bursting with a grievance . . . Rightly or wrongly, the Conservative Party are . . . the objects [of] . . . expletives that cannot be repeated.[85]

The Liberals began to exploit the situation, campaigning vigorously on an economy ticket in the 1875 and 1876 council elections and making four gains in the first of the two contests.

These real or apparent manifestations of popular irritation affected council policy. Councillors who had been warning for some years about 'what the ratepayers would think' were now joined by former expansionists, particularly as Conservatives hurried to steal Liberal electoral clothes. Protests at district rates in recently incorporated districts also produced results. After one angry ratepayers' meeting, payment for sanitary improvements in Rumworth was extended over twenty-five rather than (as previously) fifteen years, thus reducing the district rate for 1875 from 2*s* 7*d* to 2*s*.[86] In 1877 Halliwell's rate was reduced 1*s* in the pound by similar methods.[87] Finally, borough and district rates began to decline from August 1878. This was partly due to the introduction of a new form of sinking fund, but it was also because spending committees were economising — cutting back on proposed and current expenditure, refusing salary increases to their officials and allowing the finance committee greater supervision over their activities.

In view of the foregoing it is surprising that the council should have decided to apply for a new improvement Bill in 1880 — to extend the gas and water works, build a hospital, continue street improvements and expand borough boundaries. In fact it became an occasion for the administration of a more direct ratepayers' veto via the provisions of the Borough Funds Act. The council had already run into trouble in 1875 when a major attempt at borough expansion had been delayed for a year after rejection at a ratepayers' meeting. Now, in October 1880, and with active Liberal encouragement, a similar meeting rejected the application by eighty-two votes to eighteen. The council demanded a poll, only to find its Bill rejected again by 9,283 to 5,388. This was no triumph for large proprietors, since there were hostile majorities among both single and plural voters.[88]

As was to be the case in Salford some months later, the council marginally circumvented the rebuke by applying to borrow £300,000 for street improvements via a provisional order from the Local Government Board under the 1878 Public Health Act. For this, no public meeting was necessary. Nevertheless a change in the institutional system had, in the context of increased party conflict, given aroused ratepaying opinion an opportunity for political influence. The result had been an effective and extensive veto.

Notes

1 See, for example, *BC*, 20 April 1844, p. 3.
2 See Thomas Thomasson and C. J. Darbyshire, *BC*, 8 September 1838, p. 2.
3 *BC*, 20 July 1839, p. 2.
4 *BC*, 3 November 1838, p. 3.
5 E. G. Harwood, *BC*, 28 December 1878, p. 7.
6 See petition, *BC*, 22 January 1842, p. 7.
7 *BC*, 24 November 1838, p. 2.
8 *BC*, 10 September 1842, p. 2.
9 *BC*, 22 January 1842, p. 7.
10 *BC*, 30 October 1852, p. 7.
11 Workhouse Committee report, *BC*, 15 February 1840, p. 3.
12 E.g. *BC*, 10 March 1855, p. 3.
13 J. Entwistle, *BC*, 8 April 1848, p. 7.
14 See *BC*, 23 October 1847, p. 6.
15 *BC*, 26 June 1847, p. 5.
16 See comments quoted *BC*, 28 September 1861, p. 4.
17 W. Stott, *BC*, 25 February 1854, p. 4.
18 Mr Stork, secretary, Bolton Poor Law Association, *BC*, 21 February 1852, p. 3.
19 Comments at opening ceremony, *BC*, 28 September 1861, p. 3.
20 J. S. Birley, *BC*, 5 June 1847, p. 5.
21 *BC*, 11 September 1858, p. 4.
22 *Ibid*.
23 Quoted *BC*, 30 June 1853, p. 4.
24 Richard Stockdale, *BC*, 18 September 1847, p. 4.

25 *BC*, 22 May 1880, quoting from John Ashworth, *Recollections of Cobden*.
26 *BC*, 3 February 1838, p. 3.
27 See, for example, *BFP*, 1 May 1841, p. 3.
28 *BC*, 24 March 1832, p. 2.
29 *BC*, 10 November 1838, p. 2.
30 *BC*, 22 May 1880, quoting Ashworth, *op. cit.*
31 Quoted *BC*, 27 April 1839, p. 2.
32 Robert Heywood, *BFP*, 18 January 1840, p. 3.
33 *BC*, 17 April 1841, p. 3.
34 Parliamentary deputation report, *BFP*, 27 May 1843, p. 4.
35 Letter, *BFP*, 10 June 1843, p. 3.
36 *BFP*, 28 October 1843, p. 2.
37 *BC*, 28 October 1843, p. 4.
38 See Thomas Thomasson, *BFP*, 17 October 1846, p. 3.
39 Thomas Thomasson, *BFP*, 19 October 1844, p. 3.
40 Thomas Myerscough, *BFP*, 19 September 1846, p. 3.
41 *BFP*, 7 October 1846, p. 1.
42 T. R. Bridson, *BFP*, 21 November 1846, p. 3.
43 *BC*, 8 September 1849, p. 5.
44 *BC*, 22 September 1849, p. 5.
45 Quoted *BC*, 18 August 1849, p. 8.
46 Mayor, *BC*, 18 August 1849, p. 8.
47 See debate, *BC*, 20 October 1849, pp. 6-7.
48 *BC*, 9 March 1850, p. 5.
49 R. Dutton, *BC*, 16 February 1850, p. 7.
50 Debate, *BC*, 11 May 1850, p. 7.
51 See *BC*, 9 January 1869, pp. 5 and 7
52 R. Stockdale, *BC*, 14 September 1861, p. 4.
53 *BC*, 24 July 1858, p. 5.
54 Sanitary Committee letter to Home Secretary, *BC*, 18 July 1868, p. 7.
55 R. Lomax, *BC*, 7 August 1869, p. 7.
56 Fergus Ferguson, *BC*, 27 November 1858, p. 5.
57 *BC*, 17 May 1856, p. 3.
58 *BC*, 27 November 1858, p. 5.
59 See debate, *BC*, 15 June 1867, p. 7.
60 See report of medical inspector to local government board, *BC*, 11 May 1872, p. 7.
61 E. Cannon, *BC*, 18 August 1877, p. 7.
62 *BC*, 15 March 1879, p. 7.
63 R. Smalley, *BC*, 10 November 1860, p. 3.
64 J. Barlow, *BC*, 2 February 1861, p. 7.
65 Quoted *BC*, 15 June 1861, p. 7.
66 G. Nelson, *BC*, 5 May 1866, p. 7.
67 G. Nelson, *BC*, 15 September 1866, p. 7.
68 G. Nelson, *BC*, 5 May 1866, p. 7.
69 *BC*, 27 April 1861, p. 3.
70 Quoted 18 April 1863, p. 7.
71 R. Stockdale, *BC*, 12 November 1864, p. 7.
72 *BC*, 13 January 1866, p. 5.

73 *BC*, 29 October 1864, p. 3.
74 *BC*, 25 March 1865, p. 8.
75 *BC*, 19 August 1865, p. 7.
76 E. Barlow, *BC*, 20 January 1866, p. 3.
77 *BC*, 15 August 1863, p. 7.
78 See debate, *BC*, 18 June 1864, p. 5.
79 H. M. Richardson, *ibid*.
80 J. W. Latham, 19 September 1863, p. 7.
81 *BC*, 6 July 1867, pp. 7-8.
82 Fergus Ferguson, *BC*, 17 April 1869, p. 7.
83 *BC*, 15 May 1869, p. 3.
84 See *BC*, 16 May 1874, pp. 5 and 7.
85 *BWJ*, 12 January 1878, p. 3.
86 *BC*, 14 August 1875, p. 7.
87 *BC*, 8 December 1877, p. 5.
88 *BC*, 23 October 1880, pp. 5-7, and 6 November 1880, p. 7.

11

Salford politics

For reasons of space our treatment of Salford cannot have the depth accorded Rochdale and Bolton. It is possible only to summarise the character of the four variable factors and briefly illustrate their impact on the exercise of power. Our survey can best be divided at 1844 (when the town became incorporated) and, less certainly, at 1867 (when extension of the parliamentary franchise changed the municipal political calculus).

Up to 1844 party competition, the institutional system, leadership attitudes and popular mobilisation combined so as to ensure at least some effective participation in the political process for most social groups. Competition between Liberal and Tory sections of the elite was bitter and all-embracing. It was related to Salford's very open institutional system. This was multi-institutional, with civic power shared irritably between the boroughreeve and constables, the police commissioners and the town meeting; Poor Law functions being hazily divided between overseers, churchwardens, the vestry and (if the vestry appointed one) select vestry. The whole system was subject to heavy doses of popular election, nomination or ratification. The police commissioners were elected by the ratepayers in four polling districts, whilst the boroughreeve, constables, overseers and churchwarden were nominated by town, or vestry, meeting. Town meetings were also used as points of final policy decision. They could be called by either the boroughreeve or the churchwarden and overseers: if one authority refused to call a meeting when requested, the other could be tried. As in Bolton, and even more in Rochdale, rules about participation were dimly defined and almost unenforceable, particularly because of the ambiguous position of compounded ratepayers — those whose rates were paid by their landlord. Consequently public meetings were hard to control and 'often assumed the character of a bear garden'.[1] Other, less democratic bodies increased the chaos by playing a part in the process: the antique court leet, appointed by the lord of the manor (the Earl of Sefton), elected the boroughreeve and constables, whilst the county magistrates appointed the overseers.

Intense party competition in an open system encouraged populist leadership attitudes. Tories as well as Liberals recognised a tradition whereby 'public meetings [were] usually the test of everything'[2] and tended to use them even when not legally required to do so. In fighting to gain control of the offices of boroughreeve and constables from the Tory-dominated court leet, for example, the Liberals used town meetings for nomination purposes even though there was no legal necessity, and both sides sought vestry ratification of the overseers' nomination even though outgoing overseers had the right to nominate their successors. Leadership attitudes and the needs of political conflict themselves thus reinforced the openness of the institutional system.

Finally, popular mobilisation ran at a high level before 1844. Chartists and other radicals were well organised, and intervened extensively in local politics. Though normally allied with the Liberals, they were prepared to switch support to whichever of the major contestants offered most. Local leaders' assumptions about public meetings seem to have been shared by many inhabitants, and such occasions were invariably crowded and enthusiastic.

The resulting overall situation had important consequences. Local politics were difficult to control, impossible to dominate reliably and often subject to paralysis. Though the Liberals controlled most local government institutions for most of the period, they could never insure themselves against surprise attacks by their opponents, particularly when those attacks were supported by lowlier groups. To achieve success, both main contestants had to appeal downwards and give at least some concessions in return for support. Partly as a result, though local government was never run so as to disadvantage the elite and the class from which it was drawn, shopkeepers and working men influenced the process and could gain some advantages.

We can illustrate these arguments by looking briefly at elections and policy-making. Liberal electoral control was tightest over the police commissioners. Yet even early in the period their alliance with the radicals impelled them to include several of the latter among the 'Reform' lists of candidates. Even then they were never entirely safe from guerrilla attack. In 1838 a group of Tories suddenly appeared in the election room of one polling district and, having failed there, moved to the next district and 'decided the election'.[3] Though normally allied to the main contestants, the radicals sometimes sprang surprises off their own bat. In 1842 'Chartists mustered unexpectedly strongly in three ... districts and, in two ... obtained a temporary majority'.[4] It was supposed temporary because of election irregularities, and because many compounders had voted. But the police commissioners never invalidated the results, perhaps because the Liberals had themselves used compounders so often in the past.

More important surprises occurred in elections for executive office. At a town meeting in 1838, for example, Tories and Chartists combined to try 'to exclude from the management of municipal affairs all [those] friendly to moderate reform'. Failing to carry their list of overseers, they successfully demanded a poll under the Stourges Bourne Act to elect the churchwarden and select vestry. As a result, a Tory became churchwarden and Chartists captured the select vestry. The *Manchester Guardian* sadly ascribed it all 'to the indifferrence of the Liberal Party many of whom persisted in believing that the poll was illegal' and 'to the extra-ordinary activity of the Tories who canvassed as for an election and . . . paid the rates of [many] poorer voters'.[5]

The system's more oligarchic institutions could also cause trouble. In 1840 the Liberals carried their list of overseers through a vestry meeting against separate lists of Tories and Chartists. When the nomination came to be confirmed by the county magistrates the four Conservative justices caucused separately and appointed the Tory list. Since their seven Liberal colleagues appointed the Reformers' list, this left Salford with two contending sets of overseers for the ensuing year.[6] Similar difficulties occurred in 1843 when the court leet rejected the police commissioners' list (the commission had just taken over nomination from the town meeting) for boroughreeve and constables.

The vulnerability of leadership in this open system sometimes contributed to significant alterations in policy. In March 1837 Liberal support led to the election of three Chartist overseers sworn to oppose the introduction of the Poor Law 'by every means in their power'.[7] The Liberals' nomination of the Chartists partly reflected their own dislike of the Law. However, it also stemmed from the leftward bias and sensitivity to mass emotions imposed upon them by their need for radical support in an open and unpredictable situation.

Liberal dismay at the results produced more moderate overseers in 1838, but the Chartists, as we have seen, captured the select vestry. Immediately the vestrymen began 'to ride the high horse'. Declaring their 'want of confidence' in the overseers, and claiming 'not merely the legislative but also the executive power of the township',[8] they intervened in workhouse administration, harassed the overseers and generally used the select vestry as a platform for anti-Poor Law agitation. Eventually, after failing to force the overseers to call a town meeting, they called one themselves. It authorised them 'to oppose the Poor Law by every legal means', absolving them from any costs incurred.[9] They concluded an active year by commencing legal proceedings against the overseers.

The problems of local leadership, and the opportunities (this time more negative) available to lower-class groups before 1844, are also indicated by the aftermath of the court leet's substitution of Tory for Liberal candidates for boroughreeve and constables in October 1843. Controversy had arisen over permission granted by the Liberal surveyors of highways to the Manchester & Bolton Railway Company to build a viaduct along New Bailey Street. In April 1844, encouraged by both Tories and radicals, the infuriated shop-keepers and property owners of the district petitioned the new boroughreeve for a public meeting. He willingly complied and, after one of Salford's characteristically riotous assemblies, was authorised to oppose the railway company's Bill in Parliament.[10]

Tory boroughreeve and Liberal police commissioners also clashed when the latter applied to Parliament for an improvement Bill. After receiving a petition organised by Tories and radicals, the boroughreeve again called a public meeting. 'Mainly composed of working men', it condemned the Bill and instituted a hostile petition.[11] Thus Parliament was again presented with the bizarre spectacle of two parts of the same group of local authorities making completely opposite demands. The Bill survived but, as a result of the agitation legitimised by Salford's 'very extraordinary Boroughreeve', some amendments were made and around £500 of the town's money spent.

This chaotically open situation was ended abruptly by incorporation in 1844. In fact the characteristics we have been analysing as variables (particularly party competition and attitudes to outside opinion) began to change during the progress of incorporation itself and, in so doing, greatly improved local leaders' prospects of unhindered success. The issue is worth analysing for two reasons. It reveals that a really determined and united elite, pulling all the deferential strings to which it had access, could achieve success even in an open system like Salford's. However, it also shows the care with which that leadership had to operate under such a system.

The central motive for seeking incorporation was the impending loss of police powers to the county magistrates under the 1840 Police Act. Incorporation was the only way of avoiding this.[12] Another motive was probably the desire to escape from the paralysis, unpredictability and limited control of the old system. Whatever the truth of the matter, the process by which incorporation was sought represented a careful avoidance of all the difficult characteristics the system encouraged. As a result, of the incorporation proceedings in the three towns, Salford's was the most exclusively elite-centred and most private. This was possible because the Liberal instigators successfully prevented party division on the issue, and (connectedly) avoided all forms of mass consultation.

The moves towards incorporation first surfaced at a special meeting of the police commissioners in March 1841. Though the initiative was Liberal, and the commissioners were Liberal-dominated, there was great emphasis on the achievement of unanimity 'by inviting the general co-operation of gentlemen from every part of the borough and every shade of political feeling'. The aim was to avoid the problems experienced in Manchester and (as we have seen) Bolton, where party division had led to paralysis and 'endless litigation' over the legality of the new corporation.

The police commissioners called 'a meeting of the chief ratepayers' to deliberate and then call a public meeting.[13] The chief ratepayers met immediately. Here the emphasis was again on unity, and leading Conservative notables were persuaded to join in the enthusiastic endorsement of incorporation. The meeting elected a prestigious committee of around seventy — drawn from the wealthiest Tories and Liberals along with a few of the most respectable radicals — to enquire into the effects.[14] In August it spawned an even more impressive sub-committee of chief officers of the three townships within the parliamentary borough — Salford, Pendleton and Broughton.[15]

This body operated in total secrecy. There was no significant news of its deliberations from August 1841 until it produced its final report to the committee in December 1842. Even then the press was given only the report, which contained a carefully argued case for incorporating all three townships. No account was offered of the sub-committee's deliberations, or the committee's discussions and final decision.[16]

Nor was the town meeting promised by the police commissioners ever held. Instead, in January 1843, the committee chose to put its case to the public by petition-gathering. The campaign was accompanied by the distribution of 600 copies of the report, plus 3,000 more so that 'the working classes might have the information'. In addition to its prestigious mentors the petition was headed by the names (where they were different) of all Salford's office-holders in recent years. Petitioning was a far more controllable form of consultation than a public meeting. William Lockett, one of the central Liberal figures, revealed much about recent experience and current motivation in explaining that 'he had no objection to public meetings when they could be conducted in an orderly manner, but . . . public meetings of late years had been a disgrace to them'.[17]

Such secrecy and uncompromising elitism had minor disadvantages. It drove even moderate radicals into opposition. However, by the time they discovered how far things had gone there was little they could do, particularly since their potential allies in the Conservative section of the elite had been nobbled by the other side. In mid-January 1843, with the incorporators' campaign already well advanced, nine radical commissioners petitioned their body for a public meeting. Discussion was prevented on a technicality, so they turned to the overseers, who obliged. The belated town meeting dutifully condemned incorporation and set going its own petition. But it was too late. By early March the incorporators' petition had gathered a majority of both ratable value and ratepayers. After the statutory government enquiry, incorporation was granted in April 1844.

The incorporators failed in one important respect. The incorporation committee had included the chief officers of Pendleton and Broughton. Nevertheless township meetings in these wealthy districts, appalled at the likely expense of being joined with Salford's insanitary thousands, rejected incorporation and were ultimately excluded. Though temporary, this was to have crucial results for the exercise of power in the new borough.

In the twenty years or so after 1844 the trends that emerged during the incorporation process became more pronounced. Party competition declined rapidly, dying away altogether after 1850. There was a strong drive towards 'electoral arrangement' such that only forty-eight of the 264 council seats up for election between 1850 and 1867 were actually contested, none on a party basis. Constituency politics complemented the municipal peace. Joseph Brotherton, Salford's radical MP, was unopposed after 1841, and was succeeded by the cross-party Palmerstonian Liberal W. N. Massey.

The disappearance of party conflict was related to the probably deliberate contraction of opportunities offered by the institutional system. The decline of party made local elections less available for the expression of popular preference about policy and persons. The only contests in these years — between temperance and anti-temperance protagonists — were marginal to the main thrust of municipal activity. Incorporation also restricted the electorate to direct ratepayers, eliminating the compounders until 1859. Party peace and the elite's dislike of the pre-1844 system ensured that there was little incentive to get even legitimate ratepayers on to the electoral rolls. Along with weighted voting in the guardians' elections, the result was a system more heavily biased towards property than before. Meanwhile other pre-1844 institutions were abolished or became redundant, taking with them opportunities for lower-class participation. The boroughreeve, constables and select vestry disappeared. The churchwarden lost all, and the overseers most, of their poor relief functions to the guardians. Unlike Rochdale, but like Bolton, town and vestry meetings became less frequent, and their nominating, debating and decision-making functions became redundant or were dispersed to the council, guardians and outgoing overseers. Moreover the right to call public meetings now rested solely with the council. The radicals rightly perceived these developments as 'a narrowing of the former constituency to a dangerous extent'.[18]

Political mobilisation at the lower social levels also declined, mainly because of the demise of Chartism but also through lack of encouragement by Salford's no longer competitive elite. Even among electors there was more apathy, as newspapers constantly testified.

In this situation, and in the light of traumatic pre-incorporation experience, leadership attitudes became more hierarchical. The public's opinion was rarely sought. For councillors the representational, rather than the delegational, role was normative, one candidate enticing his electors thus: 'I pledge myself to nothing, bind myself to no party, nor expect, if elected, to be called upon to answer for my conduct.'[19]

These changes had important consequences for the wielding of power. Policy-making became less consultative. The important 1862 Improvement Act, for example, was not discussed at any town meeting, nor was it raised in the 1862 and 1863 council elections. Not surprisingly, even councillors occasionally worried about 'how little the general public . . . was permitted to know'[20] about major measures in these years.

Politics also became more controllable and predictable. There were fewer possibilities for electoral guerrilla attack. Policy-making was conducted through generally accepted channels, and was thus largely immune from intervention by the lower orders. When the elite took their interests into account (in sanitation, for example) it did so for philanthropic rather than political reasons. In many respects, municipal leaders' ability to achieve desired ends increased in this period. The 1862 Act, though subject to considerable opposition and important amendment, emerged unscathed in most of its broad outlines.

Politics did not close up completely. In spite of the unity of the elite, anti-incorporation radicals made significant electoral gains in the late-1840s. In 1853 the Ratepayers' Retrenchment Association captured control of nomination and election to the council and guardians in the Salford district from what was alleged to be a self-perpetuating council clique.[21] The association retained control until 1861, becoming, in its own estimation at least, a vehicle for the transmission of grievances from electors to elected.[22] Nevertheless its success also underlines the oligarchic point, since it led to a period of uncontested elections and electoral apathy.

However, policy-making was still not easy. The 1862 Improvement Act, for example, was opposed by Manchester Corporation, the Butchers' Association, the Cottage Owners, various charity trustees, railway companies, the Licensed Victuallers' Association, the Bridgewater trustees and Lord

Egerton. Manchester got the water supply clauses removed, whilst the charities accounted for those affecting them. Over 400 amendments were made, including important changes in the building and slaughterhouse provisions.

Yet, as the above suggests, political influence was restricted: to other local governmental institutions; to those outside the political circle but still mainly at the highest socio-economic levels; and more generally to those mobilised and able to use the entry points left after 1844. These comprised discreet private approaches to key councillors, and intervention at the point where, as we have seen, corporations were always vulnerable and thus conciliatory.

In Salford, included among those so mobilised, as the 1862 Act shows, were small proprietors. This group was more continuously organised than in Bolton, being held together partly by stronger resentment against the council's large and 'extravagant' group of wealthy proprietors — 'gentlemen who care not one farthing for us'.[23] Small proprietors were an important force behind the Ratepayers' Retrenchment Association of the 1850s. More specific consciousness also spawned several long-continuing occupational groups, including not just the licensed victuallers (well organised in most towns) but also the Butchers' Guardian Association and various associations of cottage owners and builders. As we have seen, both these latter groups managed to influence clauses in the 1862 Act. This was due largely to the corporate elite's desire to buy off parliamentary opposition, touchingly advertised in an obviously inspired letter to the press before the Bill's committee stage: 'if there are defects in the Bill, I can say from a knowledge . . . of those to whom [its] conduct . . . is committed that all reasonable requests will be conceded.'[24]

The final, most important and longest-standing source of difficulty after incorporation was unique to Salford. This was the conflict between the districts of Salford, Pendleton and Broughton. It is interesting since it shows how the institutionalisation of district consciousness could divide the governing elite and hamper policy-making long after the social basis of the original institutional arrangements had passed away.

When incorporated with Salford in 1853 the two 'out-townships' had both been richer but far less populous than the central township. They had refused amalgamation in 1844, and joined Salford only when threatened with government by county magistrate.[25] Both had, and continued to have, as many links with Manchester as with Salford. Their inhabitants (particularly Broughton's) harboured dark suspicions of Salford's teeming and scruffy thousands, with their acute and municipally expensive problems. However, though Higher Broughton remained the leafy suburban retreat of many of Salford and Manchester's wealthy citizens, Pendleton and Lower Broughton were rapidly urbanising, and became indistinguishable from the rest of the borough. Yet, because separateness had been institutionalised in 1853, corporate politics remained adversely frozen in the original mould until full amalgamation in 1892.

Until then the borough had a federal government. Pendleton and Broughton were granted a combined representation equal to half the council's total membership. Within the council, power was divided between a general legislature (the monthly meetings of the council) and three separate district legislatures. Each level elected its own specialist committees, and appointed its own professional servants, and there were separate borough and district rates. Councillors even met in three separate town halls and, between the council's monthly meetings, often had 'no more to do with each other's affairs than any man on earth has ... with ... the man in the moon'.[26] Council meetings often 'degenerated into the registration of the acts of the outlying districts'.[27]

The result was a long-term situation in which vetoes were easily applied, conflict and paralysis were frequent and positive action was difficult. Not everyone found it inconvenient. For some out-district politicians, paralysis was a happy state: it was cheap. Yet for many councillors federalism was a constant source of unwelcome obstacles.

There were times, firstly, when even the most parochial councillor wanted collective action but found it vetoed by other parochials. In 1867 the Irwell oozed disgustingly over Lower Broughton. Despite regular floods thereafter, and great pressure from Broughtonians on and off the council, no effective preventative action was taken for twenty years. One reason was the opposition of Pendleton, whose representatives absolutely refused 'to be taxed to the tune of £120,000' because 'they were entirely out of reach of the floods'.[28]

Secondly, district administrations were themselves sometimes at the mercy of local interests. In 1869 it was discovered that Pendleton's sanitary committee 'had not carried out the bye-laws [but] had made arrangements just to suit ... owners and others'.[29] The appeasement was not entirely willing, to judge by one councillor's sheepish apology: 'whilst the general council might be able to act independently of local prejudice ... Pendleton representatives had had ... threats issued to them if they took certain courses'.[30]

Thirdly, and not surprisingly, many general committee chairmen found life very difficult. At first, federal functions were largely restricted to finance (a concurrent power shared with the districts) and policing. Power moved steadily towards the centre, with general committees taking on functions relating to river conservancy, building surveillance, tramways and public health. Nevertheless local autonomy constantly inhibited federal action. Even at the end, for example, responsibility for the necessarily borough-wide function of public health was still divided concurrently between a general public health committee and several district scavenging and nuisance committees. This led to much frustration: in 1889 a committee, enquiring into the possibility of erecting artisans' dwellings, testified to long and bitter experience in reporting that, without full amalgamation, 'your committee, as a general committee, would be utterly powerless'.[31]

Finally, as already implied, federalism was a constant source of confusion, incoherence and corporate indignity. On at least two occasions — the 1862 Consolidation Bill and the 1869 Pendleton Road Trust Bill — Parliament was presented with the entertaining spectacle of a local Bill being supported by the corporation and opposed by one of its constituent districts and district committees. One problem here was water supply. Pendleton received water direct from Manchester. To the irritation of Salford and Broughton, and with active encouragement from the neighbouring corporation, it insisted on a series of separate arrangements, ending up in 1862 with Pendleton paying for and managing its water on a totally autonomous basis.

The late 1860s and 1870s saw further changes in the configuration of influence and the factors we have been isolating as importantly responsible for that configuration. Some changes occurred in the opportunities offered by the institutional system. The education board's establishment in 1870 increased the institutions and offices needing to be filled, thus making politics harder to control. The 1867 Franchise Reform Act, though having little direct impact on the municipal electorate, made municipal voters' favours worth bidding for in quest of constituency fortune. Finally, the 1872 Borough Funds Act, as elsewhere, opened important opportunities to all levels of ratepayer for at least negative influence — opportunities enhanced in Salford by the corporation's frequent need to seek improvement powers.[32]

Parliamentary franchise expansion revived party conflict in local affairs. Most council elections were now contested, producing the need to appease those whose votes were required. Municipal policies were regularly debated and pledges made about present and future actions. Yet party never ran as deep as in Rochdale: the main motive for local intervention was always parliamentary, and party division scarcely affected council debates. Pledges to the electorate were strictly individual and never programmatic. Parties therefore could never have a mandate for action. Thus opportunities for the electorate to influence policy were more limited than they otherwise might have been.

Nevertheless the impact upon individual councillors was considerable. Candidates increasingly made promises about action (support for baths, washhouses, parks, flood prevention, etc.) and/or inaction (keeping the rates down). External pressure came to be seen as legitimate, and there was increasing nervousness about the reactions of 'people outside'.[33] Such 'people' increasingly, and specifically, came to include 'the working classes' for the first time since 1844. Though economic dependency was certainly exploited to attract working-class votes, appeasement and promises of tangible benefit were also necessary, to judge by the behaviour of council candidates.

Finally, the 1870s also saw some broadening of political mobilisation. Small proprietorial organisation intensified, producing in particular the Salford Property Owners' Protection Association. Spawned by the council's increasing interest in sanitary regulations, this organisation of slum landlords became increasingly successful in gaining pledges of support from council candidates,[34] and in getting its officers elected to the council (both president and vice-president were there by 1875). It also actively approached councillors about relevant aspects of council policy.

Political activity spread beyond small property. In the late 1870s, 'the ratepayers' became increasingly exercised about expenditure. Finally, though mainly after 1880 and never on the scale evident in Rochdale, there were some more signs of renewed working-class political interest and participation.

Related to all these changes was a broadening of the influences on council policy. Policy-making still remained easier than before 1844 — the council managed to steer four improvement Bills through Parliament between 1867 and 1875. Moreover those with massive property (railway and canal companies, ground landlords, factory owners, etc.) were still the most important influence — their wishes being anticipated in framing and avoiding policy decisions, and appeased during the process of parliamentary ratification. Smoke regulation — or, rather, the effective absence of it — provides a good example. Yet their demands were not automatically acceded to, and conflicts among the greatly propertied sometimes simply induced paralysis rather than the decisive action desired by some. Perhaps the best example is the long and tortured efforts to prevent the Irwell flooding Lower Broughton.

Furthermore the gradient of influence became less steep. The influence of small proprietors, already evident in the '50s and '60s, increased in the '70s. This was particularly true of the Property Owners' Association. It considerably influenced the details of building regulations. Indeed, its approaches to the council on this issue before the Common committee stage of the 1875 Improvement Bill were so successful that it felt able to withdraw opposition, congratulating itself on the fact the 'through the efforts of your committee, several objectionable clauses were expunged from the first draft, other clauses were amended and some new ones introduced'.[35]

In fact, though detailed changes were made, the Act considerably toughened Salford's already fairly stringent sanitary and building regulations. Nevertheless they were often not enforced, as the death rate and appalling problems even in newly built working-class areas abundantly testified at the end of the '70s.[36] This was widely and plausibly ascribed to the association's influence.[37] Admittedly there were other factors at work, most notably the classic nineteenth-century urban problem of marrying regulation with the need to ensure the continued provision of cheap houses for poor people on expensive land. Nevertheless, within this parameter, the association was important.

There is also more ambiguous evidence of working-class influence in the 1870s. The working classes were still politically marginal (far more so than in Rochdale), and philanthropic motives were still as important as political ones in explaining attempts to alleviate their problems. Furthermore many slum dwellers were not politically salient at all, if only because of the residence requirements for municipal voting. Yet, given respectable help, working-class people could apply vetoes and gain some advantages. In 1867, much against its better judgement, the Salford section of the council was forced to refuse permission for a private slaughterhouse in a densely populated working-class district after hostile petitions from doctors, butchers, local employers and 144 residents.[38] In the 1870s plans for an isolation hospital were delayed, and the projected site was constantly changed as first one place and then another objected. Again working-class fears — of contamination and removal from the community — contributed to the agitation.

Meanwhile the council's concern with baths, washhouses, parks and the like are examples of more positive, if indirect, working-class influence. Philanthropy certainly played its part here. Nevertheless, councillors' desire to advertise electorally, in working-class wards, their attachment to projects 'for the working classes' suggest that currying popularity was another motivation.

Finally, as elsewhere, the 1872 Borough Funds Act offered ratepayers at all levels important opportunities for negative influence. It increased the corporation's need to neutralise opposition to the 1875 Improvement Bill, for example. As a result the Bill went through a ratepayers' meeting easily enough. In 1880, however, the council decided to apply for another ambitious Bill. The powers included extending borrowing by £600,000 at a time when economic slump was producing 'a feeling abroad that we are getting on too fast'.[39] The mayor convened the necessary ratepayers' meeting at 12 noon on a weekday, presumably to ensure a safely miniscule attendance. However, those present angrily insisted on meeting two days later at 8 p.m. After long discussion, and much jeering of councillors, the second, crowded meeting overwhelming rejected the Bill.

The veto was partial, since, in November 1881, the corporation obtained some of what it wanted by applying for a provisional order from the Local Government Board, thus obviating the necessity for a public meeting.[40] Nevertheless ratepaying opinion had achieved a considerable, and desired, effect. *The Salford Weekly News* remarked that 'the old inhabitants remember nothing like it'.[41] In fact institutional change and popular mobilisation had combined to produce a partial return to the situation before 1844.

Notes

1 *MG*, 6 February 1836, p. 3.
2 Lot Gardiner, *MG*, 27 April 1844, p. 6.
3 *MG*, 24 October 1838, p. 3. The result was eventually invalidated.
4 *MG*, 26 October 1842, p. 3.
5 *MG*, 4 April 1840, p. 2.
6 *ibid*.
7 J. W. Hodgetts, *MG*, 29 March 1837, p. 3.
8 R. J. Richardson, *MG*, 12 May 1838, p. 3.
9 *MG*, 20 June 1838, p. 3.
10 *MG*, 4 May 1844, p. 6.
11 *MG*, 27 April 1844, p. 6.
12 See police commissioners' report, *MG*, 20 June 1840, p. 3.
13 Quoted *MG*, 6 March 1841, p. 3.
14 *MG*, 13 March 1841, p. 3.
15 *MG*, 28 August 1841, p. 1.
16 *MG*, 21 December 1842, p. 1.
17 William Lockett, *MG*, 21 January 1843, p. 6.
18 R. J. Richardson, *MG*, 19 October 1844, p. 6.
19 Jon. Milner, *SWN*, 25 October 1862, p. 2.
20 C. E. Cawley, on improvement Bill, *SWN*, 4 October 1862, p. 3.
21 See H. D. Pochin, *SWN*, 19 January 1861, p. 3.
22 See Pochin, *ibid*.
23 'H', *SWN*, 31 October 1863, p. 3.
24 'One Concerned', *SWN*, 22 March 1861, p. 4.
25 *MG*, 23 April 1853, p. 9.
26 *SWN*, 4 April 1874, p. 3.
27 W. J. McKerrow, *SWN*, 2 November 1872, p. 2.
28 J. Walker, *SWN*, 1 October 1870, p. 3.
29 Mayor, *SWN*, 9 January 1869, p. 3.
30 S. Johnson, *ibid*.
31 Quoted *SR*, 2 November 1889, p. 7.
32 Bills were sought in 1868, 1870, 1871, 1875 and 1880.
33 See, for example, council debates, *SWN*, 4 February 1871, p. 3, and *SWN*, 5 October 1878, p. 3.
34 See *SC*, 31 October 1875, p. 3.
35 *SC*, 15 May 1875, p. 2. For clauses see *SC*, 19 and 26 September 1874.

36 See reports beginning *SWN*, 6 January 1877, p. 3.
37 For example, *SWN*, 4 August 1877.
38 See *SWN*, 23 February to 4 May 1867.
39 *SC*, 1 January 1880, p. 4.
40 See significant comments of Alderman Bowes, *SWN*, 5 November 1881.
41 *SWN*, 8 January 1881, pp. 2-3.

12
Conclusion

The foregoing pages have shown that municipal politics were far more complicated than a simple analysis of the political resources of the elites in the three towns might suggest; more complicated also than the theory that legitimised their rule. A gradient of power, broadly coinciding with the economic structure, there undoubtedly was. Social and economic substance certainly helped municipal elites to maintain themselves in office, and to achieve their policy ends. Furthermore, those among the class from whom they were drawn could, in general, achieve more of their aims, and serve more of their interests, than other groups further down the social scale. They could do so with less effort and in more of the various possible political circumstances.

On the other hand, the power of municipal elites was often limited and of unpredictable quality. It was limited by pressures flowing from the very economic and occupational circumstances which gave them such political advantage. Connectedly, it was limited by the complexity of municipal business and by the consequently rising influence of municipal servants. It was also limited by pressures from the world outside — both within and, even more, beyond municipal boundaries. The most acute and capricious limits came from Parliament. These operated not just by direct constraint but also by conditioning relations between the elite and those groups who felt themselves affected by policy decisions — any policy decisions large enough to require a parliamentary application. Here the sheer unpredictability and expense of the improvement process imposed conciliatory behaviour upon local authorities — sometimes of an almost desperate kind.

Meanwhile other groups further down the social scale — shopkeepers, publicans, slum landlords and even working men — could influence the political process. The circumstances allowing them to do so were more critical and narrowly constricted than for those higher up. But they did occur and could enable even working men to exert significant influence.

Even where those successfully applying pressure were drawn from the same economic level as the largest group among the municipal elite, the end result was often a state of paralysis. Even for them, and even when they wanted more, power was often simply the power of veto.

Nor does a simple elitist model of nineteenth-century urban politics properly embrace all those factors determining the configuration of power. The economic and social resources of the political elite, though crucial, were only one of several factors determining success or otherwise in the complex process of urban politics. Others included the possession of expertise, the degree of sectional conflict, the level of institutional proliferation, elite attitudes and group mobilisation. These helped to ensure that, though the important municipal role of men of substance remained a constant factor in the three towns, the configuration of power varied. Within important limits, it varied over time and accordinig to place.

In fact neither an elitist nor a pluralist model adequately describes municipal politics in Rochdale, Bolton and Salford. The process was not pluralist if the term is understood to mean a situation in which policy initiative and policy outcome were the result of a bargaining process embracing every interest affected, and in which the municipal elite was simply one of several competing power centres. This model certainly throws some light upon what was happening for some of the time, but in the last resort it is a caricature. So too is the elitist model — at least if it is taken to imply a process in which policy-making was easy for the group 'in charge', was predictable or could be undertaken without reference to those who felt themselves affected.

The elitist model then is no more than partly enlightening. Neither is the associated idea of the nineteenth-century industrial town as a paternalistic hierarchy based upon all-embracing deference and dependency. Though urban politics and society were hierarchical (and far more so than their twentieth-century counterparts), they included elements largely absent from the rural version. The urban hierarchy contained competing and conflicting layers — at least some of whom could successfully demand degrees of conciliation from whose above. In the last resort the municipal politics of these towns were distinctively urban. As a result they were also 'political'.

Index